PLACE, POWER, SITUATION, AND SPECTACLE

A Geography of Film

Edited by Stuart C. Aitken and Leo E. Zonn

Rowman & Littlefield Publishers, Inc.

ROWMAN & LITTLEFIELD PUBLISHERS, INC.

Published in the United States of America
by Rowman & Littlefield Publishers, Inc.
4720 Boston Way, Lanham, Maryland 20706

3 Henrietta Street
London WC2E 8LU, England

British Cataloging in Publication Information Available

Library of Congress Cataloging-in-Publication Data

Place, power, situation, and spectacle : a geography of film / edited
by Stuart C. Aitken and Leo E. Zonn.
    p.   cm.
Filmography: p.
Includes bibliographical references and index.
1. Motion pictures—Aesthetics.   2. Place (Philosophy)   3. Motion
picture locations.   I. Aitken, Stuart C.   II. Zonn, Leo.
PN1995.P58   1994   791.43′01—dc20   93-48855   CIP

ISBN 0-8476-7825-3 (cloth: alk. paper)
ISBN 0-8476-7826-1 (pbk: alk. paper)

Printed in the United States of America

For our mothers and fathers
. . . it's not worth watching unless it's real life

Contents

Part Three.   Taking Time with Places

Preface

Study of the interrelations between film and the politics of social and cultural representation offers a provocative research setting for geographers, and yet the subject is virtually ignored by the discipline. Such neglect has occurred despite the fact that space and place, subjects long within the geographic purview, are inextricably integrated with social-cultural and political dynamics and thus have become indispensable to cinematic communication. This volume of essays is not an attempt to stage any theoretical continuity for what is essentially an embryonic research area. Other sources offer much more coherent theoretical underpinnings than we are prepared to offer. For example, at about the same time that these essays were collected and sent to the publisher, Fredric Jameson's *The Geopolitical Aesthetic: Cinema and Space in the World System* (Bloomington: Indiana University Press, 1992) was published. Jameson's concerns are similar to those voiced by some of the authors in this volume. He extends Lynch's concept of cognitive mapping as a means of bringing together several disconnected moments in world cinema. Jameson views cognitive mapping as something that we all indulge in at a purely aesthetic level: "The social totality can be sensed, as it were, from the outside, like a skin at which the Other somehow looks, but which we ourselves will never see" (p. 114). The notion of a geopolitical aesthetic bolsters Jameson's earlier theoretical work on the political unconscious and suggests a need to unpack cinematic representations in order to find adequate allegories for our social existence. Cognitive mapping establishes the missing psychology in Jameson's notion of the political unconscious. The films that Jameson analyzes are narrative figurations (allegories) and examples of the way contemporary narrative "conflates ontology with geography and endlessly processes images of the unmappable system" (p. 4). It is unfortunate that none of the authors in the current volume had access to Jameson's book at their time of writing but, nonetheless, there are clear and important connections between some of the work here and Jameson's postmodern theorizing. At the very least, there is deep concern with establishing the intrinsic spatiality of representation and the hegemony of images as part of our political unconscious.

The importance of Jameson's theoretical position in *The Geopolitical Aesthetic* to geography, film analysis, and cultural studies notwithstanding, we do not want to impose a false unity (Jamesonian or otherwise) on what are essentially exploratory essays. Though sharing a general sympathy for the need to coalesce the categories of people, place, space, and society on the one hand, and reality and representation on the other, the essayists frequently disagree on how this can be accomplished and what the outcome may be. Many of the contributions fuse literary theory, film criticism, and poetics with more traditional approaches of interpretation and analysis from politics, history, and geography. Many utilize contemporary theoretical frameworks appropriate to film study on the one hand, while incorporating elements of the inevitable socio-cultural and political discourses which guide our understanding of the world on the other. But in their different ways each essayist is reassured of the importance of cinematic representation to understanding our *place* in the world, and that geographers can provide important contributions to film theory and criticism. It is toward this lacuna of research that this volume is directed.

Stuart C. Aitken and Leo E. Zonn
December 1993

Part One
Geographic and Cinematic Theory:
Framing Spaces and Sequencing Spectacles

1

Re-Presenting the Place Pastiche

Stuart C. Aitken and Leo E. Zonn

From a deeply focused aerial shot of a bleak desert landscape a lonely figure emerges walking with some purpose. He is wearing a red baseball cap and a polyester suit. We walk with this man—the camera uncomfortably close—and we sense his quiet desperation. His face reveals no expression or hint of emotion but his eyes make us uneasy. They are washed and wild like the landscape through which he travels. Much later, and once he is rescued from near death by his brother, we learn that the man, Travis, is on a quest that is motivated by a crumpled photograph in his pocket. The photograph depicts an empty lot in the town where he had hoped to fulfill the failed destiny of his parents by building a house for himself and his family. The town, Paris, Texas, provides an eponym for a Wim Wenders film (1984) that won the prestigious Golden Palm Award at the Cannes Film Festival (Studlar 1985, p. 359). The story revolves around Travis's search for self and family in a wasteland of American myths: the desert as the last frontier, the freedom of the automobile and the wandering male, and the sanctuary of the nuclear family.[1] Throughout, Wenders resurrects these myths and shows their destructive potential as his protagonist attempts to recover his life.

Paris, Texas has received considerable critical acclaim and academic attention not only in terms of its representation of contemporary American culture, but also with the way it grounds that culture in place and landscape images (cf. Kauffmann 1984; Lennett 1985; Wallis 1986; Denzin 1991). Wenders presents Travis's travels as a phenomenological experience that intensifies our notion of places as settings for the activities that embody self and society—desert sunsets dramatically backlight fading neon motels; canyon-rim homes in Los Angeles are juxtaposed with billboards and junkyards; freeways litter the landscape. Denby (1984, p. 52) observes that in Wenders's film "the landscape is an instant myth—it is a myth that has passed through the media and become self-conscious":

> . . . the West: huge open spaces, scraggly, inadequate little buildings under vast skies; the comic surrealism of plastic and neon out in the great Nowhere.

Paris, Texas, is a real place toward which Travis journeys but never arrives. But it is simultaneously the embodiment of an existential search for the past, a forward-looking frontier spirit, and a critique of the values that secure the nuclear family. After being reconnected with his son in Los Angeles, Travis crosses the desert again, this time in search of his wife whom he finds in a brothel in Houston. In the penultimate scene, Travis confronts his wife in the fantasy parlor where she works. They are separated by a one-way mirror through which clients can see the women, but the women can only hear the clients on a telephone. At one point, when she realizes she is speaking with Travis, she asks to see him. She must dim the light on her side of the mirror while he shines a lamp on his own face. The context of the brothel is diminished as Travis discloses him*self.* This image-event not only undermines the setting of the brothel's "peep show" but also establishes the cinematic environment as a metaphor for these two people's lives. As he tells why he left her, the faces of both Travis and his wife merge as one on the mirror. We realize that these two people are separated by layers of their own illusions that prevent them from connecting and sustaining their sought-after loving, familial relationship. Their illusions represent the dehumanizing myth of an American dream that physically separates Travis and his wife while allowing them only a fleeting glimpse of each other before they are, once again, caught up with images of themselves. The next day Travis reunites his son with his wife and drives into the Houston night toward the desert, framed by the luminous lights of the city and civilization. In *Paris, Texas,* places resonate palpably with the main characters and provide a cogent site for the deconstruction of the way contemporary Western society represents itself. What we are left with is a postmodern representation of "the flattest possible characters in the flattest possible landscape rendered in the flattest possible diction. The presumption seems to be that America is a vast fibrous desert in which a few laconic weeds nevertheless manage to sprout in the cracks" (Newman 1987, p. 58).

This book is concerned with a geography of film wherein people, spaces, and places are embodied in the cinematic vision. It is concerned with fiction and documentary film representations of our contemporary world. Study of the interrelations between film and the politics of social and cultural representation, and the use of film as a means toward understanding our *place* in the world, remains provocative but largely unexplored in geography. One of the main reasons for this neglect is the geographer's traditional emphasis on the material conditions of social life wherein representation is subsidiary to "physical reality." Such neglect has occurred despite the fact that space and place, subjects long within the geographic purview, are inextricably integrated with social-cultural and political dynamics, and thus are indispensable to cinematic communication. The way spaces are used and places are portrayed in film reflects prevailing cultural norms, ethical mores, societal structures, and ideologies. Concomitantly, the impact of a film on an audience can mold social, cultural, and environmental experiences. Clearly, a research direction focused on the production and consumption of space and place in cinema deserves serious geographic attention. If we, as geographers, agree with many of the commentators on the postmodern condition who see little difference between our political culture and our celluloid culture, between *real*-life and *reel*-life, then cinematic representation needs to be a key part of geographic investigation.

It is not our intention in this first chapter to presume to speak for the authors of the essays in this collection, nor is it our intention to summarize their work or encapsulate it within our text. This volume is not an attempt to stage any theoretical coherence or continuity for this embryonic research area. We introduce work of the essayists in this volume when it is pertinent to our arguments but, for the most part, we do not wish to impose a false unity on what are essentially exploratory essays. Though sharing a general sympathy for the need to coalesce the categories of people, place, space, and society on the one hand, and reality and representation on the other, the essayists frequently disagree on how this can be accomplished and what the outcome may be. Many of the contributions fuse literary theory, film criticism, and poetics with more traditional approaches of interpretation and analysis from politics, history, and geography. But in their different ways each essayist is reassured of the importance of cinematic representation to understanding our *place* in the world, and that geographers can provide important contributions to film theory and criticism. It is toward this lacuna of research that the current volume is directed.

The balance of this chapter is taken up with several related discussions that present themselves sequentially from more general to more specific aspects of the representation of people, place, and society. First, we look at the importance of political discourse and intertextual coherence in the representation of the everyday. Next, we question how the disciplines of geography and film theory come to terms with distinctions between representations of everyday life and the material conditions of everyday life. Third, we consider narrative convention in terms of how characters are situated and how places are created in film. Finally, we establish a thesis on spectators as voyeurs and their need for spectacle in order to reify the everyday.

Representation and Images: The Politics and Places of Everyday Living

To represent is to portray clearly before the mind, to give back to society an image of itself, or to act a part or a role. Representation is, of course, one of the oldest functions of art and theater. Among other things, representation reinforces a set of societal structures that help individuals to make sense of surroundings that are otherwise chaotic and random, and to define and locate themselves with respect to those surroundings. Of late, representation has taken on a broader set of meanings as the concept has been embraced by more and more academic disciplines. Cognitive psychologists, for example, now refer to the way individuals perceive the world as "frames of representation" (Bobrow and Collins 1975; Minsky 1975; Schuurmans and Vandierendonck 1985). Within a broader framework, Foucault (1970, 1972) has shown how at any given moment representations are grounded in an "episteme" (a knowledge set) that affects personal life as well as political, economic, and artistic life. Not surprisingly, then, much discussion in the social sciences, arts, and humanities has turned lately to the ways that everyday experience—the practice of living and the places that ground that practice—is *re*-presented to and with us. Put another way, it is now commonly felt that everyday experience is not immediately "present," but is *re*-presented simultaneously through the contradictory images that constitute our postmodern world and through the everyday pretensions of our gender, class, and racial identities. Geographers have begun to examine representations of, and the meanings attached to, places and the environment in terms of their relationship to power and contestation. Places and what we practice in them, then, are formed as much by our images as by our identities. In these sites we come in contact with the *re*-presentations of our lives and our works: in the omnipresent camera at banks and fast-food restaurants; in shopping malls; in gentrified neighborhoods; at computer terminals; in the evening televised news; in family videos and photograph albums; in narrative and documentary films. In these images are grounded the figures of the contemporary men, women, and children and the places they inhabit. The power of representations to intervene in the ongoing transformations of everyday life should not be underestimated.

The very heart of geography—the search for our sense of place and self in the world—is constituted by the practice of looking and is, in effect, a study of images. Ours is a visual, video, cinematic culture. It is a collage, a pastiche dominated by the mixed-media/video-audio text. Film and television have transformed society in the contemporary West, and perhaps in all other societies that have been touched by the camera. Commentators on this contemporary culture and society note a convergence between what is *real* in the everyday and how we *image* the everyday. Baudrillard (1987, 1988) argues that contemporary society knows itself only through the reflections that flow from the camera's eye and that this knowledge is unreflexive. Denzin (1991, p. viii) offers a similar reading of postmodern society and the cinematic selves that inhabit this structure:

> The postmodern self has become a sign of itself, a double dramaturgical reflection anchored in media representations on the one side, and everyday life on the other.

Denzin then points out some of the implications of *re*-presentations becoming stand-ins for actual lived experience. First, reality becomes a staged, social production. Second, the real is judged against its staged, cinematic counterpoint. Third, the metaphor of the dramaturgical (theater as life) society becomes the transactional reality.

Postmodern society, according to Denzin, Baudrillard, and others, is structured and reproduced by "life as image." Much of their understanding comes from Barthes (1987), who was one of the first theorists to decipher society's "images" and to reveal the importance of understanding the everyday cultural landscape through means other than language (Duncan and Duncan 1992). Whether or not we accept this position, it is clear that we have departed from a somewhat naive understanding of cinematic images as things that merely capture, mimic, or mirror people and places. Instead, as is clearly articulated by Jeff Hopkins in Chapter 3, these images are signifying events that are not passively observed but are actively reconstructed as they are viewed. Hopkins is careful to establish some of the ways that film images are used to create an "impression of reality" through a rapid succession of iconic signs. The primary element of his argument is a clear definition of cinematic "landscapes" and "places" whereby he establishes the nature of a geography grounded in representation. He points out also that approaching film as a semiotic landscape is not that far removed from some long-standing geographic concerns with the material landscape. The cinematic place as described by Hopkins comprises several types of time, space, and geography that coalesce to produce a *heterotopic* landscape. As viewers, we can "suspend our disbelief" and embrace the "dubious" meanings constructed within this landscape. For example, Denis Wood, in his essay on *The Outsiders* (1983), illustrates how filmmaker Francis Ford Coppola creates a heterotopic landscape wherein community is lost because everyone is trapped "outside" by allegiance to signs of membership to specific groups that are "substantially less than the human whole." Martyn Bowden in his semiotic analysis of *Chariots of Fire* (1981) and *The Loneliness of the Long-Distance Runner* (1962), provides another concrete example of the heterotopic landscape that Hopkins describes. Bowden shows how image-events in these two films are replete with semiotic codes that relate to the British class struggle. He also establishes the subtle intertextual relations of these films to the works of Britain's great subversive poet, William Blake.

Although films are not referential to some reality beyond themselves, they are clearly intertextual in that they embody other cultural texts and, as a consequence, they produce and communicate meaning. This meaning will be different to people of different places, cultures, classes, and historical moments. Unraveling this intertextuality is a problem of some complexity. The problem becomes more abstruse if we concede that most cultures and societies today have been touched in some form by film and television. The spectator's ability to "read" a film depends, additionally, on a familiarity with intertextual frames: a knowledge of film language at its present point of development and an understanding of appropriate narrative conventions. A discussion of the intertextual and multivocal representation of the "real" requires a consideration of the narrative conventions that a filmmaker may embrace in order to reveal their version of reality, and to recognize the complex social, political, and ideological forces that might affect those conventions. Before we discuss some of these narrative conventions as they relate to the production of place images, it seems appropriate to outline the ways in which some geographers and film theorists have approached the intertextuality and multivocality of how the real is represented.

Getting to *The Real* in Geography and Film

An introduction to contemporary theory in human geography would be obliged to describe a somewhat eclectic focus. Some would say that the writings of Doreen Massey, Michael Dear, David Harvey, and Ed Soja provide a coherent base for contemporary (postmodern) theorizing in geography. Others would suggest that we should bypass theory altogether by way of a direct appeal to the experience of places or a specifically geographic understanding of the world. Regardless, most would agree that human geography is grounded on the shifting intersections between society and space on the one hand, and people and place on the other. There is, of course, considerable discussion of the traditional categories that mold the comprehension of our place in the world and about how we *re*-present people, place, and space. The problem of grasping these shifting categories may be best summed up by Entrikin (1991, p. 5), who argues that from the decentered vantage point of theory, space becomes a set of generic relations and thereby loses much of its significance for human action. From the centered viewpoint of the subject, on the other hand, place derives meaning from its relation to an individual's goals and concerns. Entrikin's suggestion that place is best viewed from points "in between" provides one focus for the practice of academic geography. What follows is a brief discussion of some of the ways that geographers have tackled the "betweenness of place" through the study of popular media. This is followed by a brief discussion of how film theorists have struggled with the representation of geographic "reality."

Geographic Studies and Media Reality

Of late, there has been a growing interest among geographers in the portrayal of cultural landscapes through the mass media. Two collections of essays are particularly noteworthy precursors to the current volume. *Geography, the Media, and Popular Culture,* edited by Burgess and Gold (1985), was an early attempt to link the relatively unconnected body of literature in geography and media studies. The book establishes two schools of thought emanating from Europe and America, respectively. The European school focuses on the relations of media to other cultural and political forms and is dominated by structuralism and semiotics, while the American school is concerned with the effects of media on individual attitudes and behaviors and is dominated by social and cognitive psychology. More recently, Burgess (1990) has suggested that media research is tainted by the reductionist tendencies of a behavioral paradigm that emanates primarily from the United States. This criticism seems a little naive, particularly given the importance of feminism, deconstruction and postmodernism to media studies in the United States (cf. Penley 1988; Silverman 1988; Erens 1990; Denzin 1991). Credit should also be attributed to behavioral and perceptual geography for providing the discipline with its first set of coherent theories on images and person-environment relations (see Aitken 1991b, 1992). Regardless, reductionist aspects of a behavioral paradigm in media studies have ebbed in both Europe and America in favor of critical and cultural studies as researchers try to come to terms with the complex ideological functions of media texts through investigation of the production and consumption of meaning. In the essays in *Place Images in Media*, edited by Zonn (1990), the predisposition is toward the production of meaning in terms of the portrayers and creators of place images. The intent of this latter collection is to provide an understanding of the processes through which information is conveyed by various media, with a specific focus on representations of place.

Neither of these two volumes of work by geographers is collectively concerned with the specific links between geography and cinematic representation. Some individual studies by geographers have broached this topic. Early work by Zonn (1984, 1985), for example, focuses on Australian landscapes portrayed in the motion pictures of that country. His work draws on psychological theory to center the relations between the audience and the Australian landscape through the filter of the portrayed media image. Gold (1984, 1985) demonstrates how future urban landscapes portrayed in films such as Fritz Lang's *Metropolis* (1926) and David Butler's *Just Imagine* (1930) reflect contemporaneous social and political structures. It is only recently, however, that geographers have begun to pay attention to film as textual representations and the power of film to shape contemporary culture. In *The Condition of Postmodernity*, Harvey (1989) takes issue with the representation of culture in Ridley Scott's *Blade Runner* (1982) and Wim Wenders's *Wings of Desire* (1988). He sees both movies as parables in which postmodern conflicts are set in a context of flexible accumulation and time-space compression. The conflicts are between people living in different time scales and spatial resolutions. Harvey (1989, p. 322) feels that although both films are "Brilliant portrayals . . . of the conditions of postmodernity, and in particular of the conflictual and confusing experience of space and time, neither has the power to overturn established ways of seeing or transcend the conflictual conditions of the moment." He attributes this to contradictions inherent in the cinematic form itself, which relies on "reducing the complex stories of daily life to a sequence of images upon a depthless screen." Harvey's feeling that the mimetic qualities of cinema, although revealing, do little more than mirror the conditions of lived experience is not shared by all geographers working with film. Aitken's (1991a) essay on Bill Forsyth suggests that many of the films of this Scottish director are suffused with a broader narrative that subtly transcends and subverts some dominant discourses on Scottish culture. These discourses relate to a mythicized past of brave but unsuccessful heroes, or they portray the Scots as parochial, insular, poor, thrifty, humble, puritanical folk. The former discourse is bolstered by Hollywood films from *Rob Roy: The Highland Rogue* (1953) to *The Highlander* (1986, also *The Highlander 2: The Quickening*, 1992, and the eponymous Fox Network television series), while the latter is exemplified by a series of films from the Ealing Studios in London (*Whisky Galore* 1949; *Geordie* 1955; *Rockets Galore* 1958). These representations create a contemporary Scotland of diminished capacity in which political power and cultural greatness are historicized and thereby made inaccessible. Aitken (1991a) incorporates a detailed analysis of film structure and rhythm in Forsyth's Scottish films (*That Sinking Feeling* 1979; *Gregory's Girl* 1980; *Local Hero* 1982; *Comfort and Joy* 1984) to make the point that a complex montage that uses appositions, contradictions, and disparities at the level of the characters, the lines of dialogue, the environment, and the incidents that make up the immediate narrative can speak to a broader narrative that subverts dominant discourses. More recently, Aitken and Zonn (1993) have turned ideas concerning the relationship between immediate and broader narratives toward an investigation of Peter Weir's portrayal of masculinity and femininity in *Gallipoli* (1981) and *Picnic at Hanging Rock* (1975). They use transactional and psychoanalytic perspectives to interrogate the gender images in both these movies, linking them to several concepts that find currency in ecofeminism. Suggested in Weir's films is a broader narrative that speaks to a postmodern sexual order and its representations in social theory and contemporary cinema. Aitken and Zonn (1993) also highlight a dominant male ethos that is a pervasive part of Australian national identity. This use of popular cinema to reify national identity is taken up by Zonn and Aitken in Chapter 7. Focus is upon a much more insidious use of gender-biased national images in a children's film, *Storm Boy* (1976), which was supported by the Australian Film Commission and the South Australian Film Corporation.

Geographers have also considered the establishment of the broader narratives that may be found in documentary films. Natter and Jones (1993) focus on director Michael Moore's use of montage and rhythm in the documentary *Roger & Me* (1990) which is, ostensibly, about Moore's failed attempt to confront the president of General Motors, Roger Smith, but it is also about the social and economic consequences of General Motors closing plants in Flint, Michigan. Moore's broader narrative uncovers the local consequences of corporate greed. Natter and Jones liken Moore's work to that of Bertolt Brecht in that his aim is not only to entertain, but also to instruct through various techniques at the level of the immediate narrative (montage, popular music, defamiliarization, and alienation) for promoting new ways of thinking in opposition to capitalism (the broader narrative). They also raise issues about "objectivity" in the documentary tradition of filmmaking in that Moore is intent upon bringing his own perspective to the materials he portrays in *Roger & Me.* In Chapter 10, Wolfgang Natter elaborates on his discussion of the documentary objectivity in *Roger & Me* with an analysis of the narrative conventions used by Walter Ruttman in *Berlin, Symphony of a City* (1927). We will return to a discussion of realism in a moment but it is important to note that the "reality effect" of the documentary is, as with fiction film, the outcome of a set of successfully performed narrative conventions that are socially and culturally mediated (Natter and Jones 1993). Another geographer, Jenkins (1990), shows how an account of this mediation is enhanced with an understanding of the many "levels of explanation" that may be uncovered in documentary film production. He provides an impressive study of how the production of a documentary film influences place portrayal. His subject is David Kennard's 50-minute film entitled *Eating* (1984), which focuses on the diet and agriculture of contrasting areas in China. Jenkins details the biases of Western films on China and then tries to unravel the extremely complex set of practices, people, and events that comprise the film production process. Jenkins's perspective is in terms of the production of meaning, but he is clearly concerned with the biases of Western cinematic portrayals of the Third World. The nature of such biases, including a preoccupation with the efficacy of the nation-state, is pursued by Gerald Macdonald in Chapter 2.

Film Studies and Geographic Reality

Curiously, there is a certain resonance between contemporary theory in geography and in film studies, as epitomized by theorists such as Christian Metz, Stephen Heath, Sol Worth, Raymond Bellour, Norman

Denzin, Roland Barthes, Jean-Louis Baudry, and Thierry Kuntsel in that there is a certain iconoclasm against established categories. The major concerns for these theorists center around the production of meaning in a film text, the ways a text constructs a viewing subject, and the ways in which the very mechanism of cinematic production affect the representation and the *real*. Some of the discussion in film theory that relates to the practice of geography takes issue with the mimetic aspect of film, that is, its ability to create a fictional model of the world. This is about constructing a reality within the *mis-en-scène* of fictional cinema or the *authentic setting* of documentary films through the incorporation of a set of narrative conventions. We will say more about these narrative conventions in a moment, but first we need to contest the notion of realism in film. If film constitutes rather than represents reality, then we must re-think the fiction versus documentary cinema distinction that is traditionally based on an intended level of realism. We must also consider carefully who makes decisions about what is and what is not represented, how it is represented, the degree of "objectivity" associated with that representation, and the contexts of its reception.

In the 1930s and 1940s, the French poetic realism of Louis Lumière suggested that the space of film *is* the space of reality, and that film's ambition and triumph is to "reproduce life" (Sadoul 1972). Thus, the camera "captures reality" and delivers "nature caught in the act." Post-World War II neorealist filmmakers in Italy and Germany preferred natural light, outdoor contexts, and nonprofessional actors in everyday situations and narratives that corresponded specifically to events they portrayed. At the same time, Soviet filmmakers such as Sergei Eisenstein (1949) were breaking new ground with *Kino-Pravda* (Film Truth) and the use of montage editing (see Chapter 9 by Arthur Krim). Although John Gold and Stephen Ward (Chapter 11) establish the force of British documentary realism of the 1950s and 1960s as filmmakers attempted to establish the "ordinariness" of living in British New Towns, it was the neorealism of the English "kitchen-sink" dramas that captured socialist and humanistic thinking around ordinary people in everyday places (see Higson 1984).

Realism in American filmmaking at this time took a slightly different form. Although documentary filmmakers such as Paul Strand and Leo Hurwitz were influenced by Sergei Eisenstein and *Kino-Pravda*, they were much more concerned with documenting a "true" relationship with the events they were portraying than they were with Eisenstein's concern for "creating a cinematic effect." This kind of American realism reached its zenith with Andy Warhol's work. His first two films, *Sleep* (1965, a man sleeping for six hours) and *Empire* (1967, the Empire State Building just standing there), were so basic and mundane that they attracted little artistic or commercial attention (Colacello 1990, p. 29). Such blatant disregard for film technique and cinematic convention led commentators such as Arnheim (1969) to suggest that if film attempted to reproduce real life mechanically, then it did not constitute an art form.

A contemporary "realist" viewpoint in film finds its most convincing advocate in Kracauer (1960). In short, this perspective positions the viewer of films as more than a spectator in that he or she misses the *real* and is attracted to film because it gives the illusion of vicariously partaking of life in all its fullness. Accordingly, prudent filmmakers must represent events and characters in all their phenomenological being so that the spectator can assume the posture of participant. Film disguises the absent *real* with a simulated and constructed reality and makes good the viewer's lack, restoring him or her to parts of an imaginary wholeness (cf. Lacan 1978; Aitken and Zonn 1993). In addition, and most importantly, all film is inherently and unavoidably subjective and, as such, there arises the potential for the misuse of the concept of "objectivity" when it is applied to the making of "documentaries" because these forms of expression attempt to decenter the filmmakers (and an ideological position) in favor of subject matter that is fixed in the social and physical world. This thinking in film resonates strongly with the "crisis of representation" that now pervades most of the social sciences, including geography (cf. Clifford 1986; Clifford and Marcus 1986; Barnes and Duncan 1992). We can evoke a "crisis of representation" based on the simple perspective that nothing in the world is fixed and immutable. We ground things now, on moving foundations. There is no longer any place of overview from which to map human ways of life (Clifford 1986, p. 22). At the same time that it has a photographic relation to reality, film is a discourse, sometimes a personal vision, but in any case never more than a version of the reality of which it purports to be the representation (Hedges 1991, p. 35). Put simply, it has become clear that every version (images, representations, films) of an *other* is also, and perhaps more so, the construction of a *self* and the making of a text. American films about "exotic" locations usually say more about capitalism and Hollywood than they do about the cultural poetics within which they are filmed.

A challenge of pressing significance, then, is the conceptualization of film communication in terms of the societal structures that guide, and are guided by, both filmmaker and audience in a complex, dynamic, and symbiotic interdependency. There are signs of a greater interest in establishing the links between film and the specific geographical and historical contexts in which they are produced and consumed. This need has been recognized by media researchers, who have increasingly focused on the political significance of film and how it subverts or sustains dominant ideologies and cultural forms (cf. Short 1981; Rattigan 1991). Gerald Macdonald (Chapter 2) examines the collage of global cultural politics by focusing on the tension created between Third Cinema (the cinema of radical politics) and the Third World condition. An understanding of the production and consumption of film must include an analysis of the interdependence of places and meanings in today's global society that does not privilege film-as-commodity. The aim of Third Cinema, then, is to oppose the profit motive of Hollywood-based First Cinema on the one hand, and the elitism of art-oriented Second Cinema on the other. For Macdonald, a geography of or from film goes beyond the study of artistic and technical production to the social and political ramifications of its consumption. He asserts that Latin American filmmakers such as Fernando Solanos and Octavio Getino were among the first to understand and articulate the limited contexts of film discourse and narrative convention derived from global capitalism.

We return, then, to the ability of a film to produce and sustain meaning that, in both documentary and fiction film, is not derived from the film's degree of "realism" but on the successful construction of a set of narrative conventions. More importantly, it is through the disregard or deconstruction of narrative convention that dominant discourses may be contested. We turn now to a more explicit consideration of the relationship between narrative convention and the creation of places in the space of film.

Space and Place Creation in Film

It is precise that "events take place."
—Michael Snow (in Heath 1981, p. 24)

The ability of a film to sustain meaning is its greatest measure of success. The production of meaning that is understood by an audience constitutes the basic essence of cinematic communication, of course, but the actual processes of communication are quite complex in nature and function. At one level, the *space* created by film is simply the frame within which a subject is located, and twenty-four of these frames pass before our eyes every second. This space enables the subject of the film to unfold in a variety of ways that may be controlled by the filmmaker. More than neutral space, however, these shots demand to be read as real *places* with their own sense of geography and history. As such, they authenticate the fiction of narrative cinema and the "reality" of documentary cinema. This brings us to a question that today is posed with insistence, practically and critically, in filmmaking and film theory concerning the way in which cinematic space can construct places such that they "hold" the action of the film. As Larry Ford (Chapter 6) suggests, places did not particularly matter in the early motion pictures because they were usually perceived as mere backdrops to live action. Filmmakers soon realized that for action to be authenticated and for audiences to suspend their disbelief, the place and space of film could be used to great effect, and so they began using and extending the narrative conventions of literature to create places and spaces that could "hold" the action. Ford discusses the use of shadow to represent malevolent city streets and alleys in early 1920s and 1930s American Film Noir. The city becomes a place with human affectations: evil, sinister, alienating. He suggests that the portrayal of a sinister city was lost with the introduction of color and it is not until the more recent films like *Blade Runner* (1982, 1992) and *Batman* (1989) that the Film Noir genre has been successfully colorized. There are important narrative conventions in the use of color, and when a filmmaker such as Woody Allen in *Annie Hall* (1977) disregards them to effect a contrast between New York and Los Angeles, the results are quite provocative.

Although color and shading are an important part of narrative convention, most attention has been directed to "spatial and temporal articulations," and to "kinds of space" and their narrative determinations or disruptions (Burch 1973; Heath 1981). As Jackobson articulated many years ago: "Film works with various and varied fragments of objects which differ in magnitude, and also with fragments of time and space likewise varied; it changes the proportions of these fragments and juxtaposes them in terms of contiguity, or similarity and contrast" (1933, p. 46). Christina Kennedy (Chapter 8) gives a fine example of how a director juxtaposes film images and characters to create a narrative of spectacular and mythic proportions. David Lean's *Lawrence of Arabia* (1962) is a complex portrayal of a schizophrenic character in schizophrenic time and place. Lean highlights Lawrence's changing relations with the people around him and with the Arabic and British cultures in which he is enmeshed by portraying the desert in different ways. Thus, rolling dunes, expansive vistas, and desert sunsets highlight the development of Lawrence's heroism along with his grand plans for Arabia; alkaline-baked flats and monotonous rock-strewn landscapes underscore the deterioration of Lawrence's hold on himself and the Arab revolt.

The descriptive and narrative rhythm of film works continually to transform place once more into space as landscapes are decentered to accommodate action and spectacle. It seems, then, that there is in film a significant tension between the place in film and the space of film. There is, however, a way in which this tension is transcended by the animation of landscape as part of the narration or description. Herein lies an important geography of film. Place becomes spectacle, a signifier of the film's subject, a metaphor for the state of mind of the protagonist. The use of cinematic space in this way can be powerful. Places can be represented so as to cut against descriptive meaning and narrative flow, or they can be constructed within cinematic space to be used over and over again in a variety of circumstances. Using the space of film to create place is important because, as suggested by Michael Snow's words that began this section, cinematic image-events are bound by the authenticity of place. According to Heath (1981, p. 24), action in film is tightly dependent on the construction and "holding of place." Early film space is predisposed simply to the static image, a set of background scenes linked to a story. To link background scenes is to focus the spectator's attention on the actors and their dialogue. It is only when the background scene becomes the foreground/actor—a *mis-en-scène*, a dynamic place of action, a continuous space that draws in the spectator as a participant, a positioning and positioned movement—that cinematic narrative convention becomes important. Characters move in the space of a framed place and then exit, giving rise to the need for reframing with a camera movement or moving to another shot. The transitions thus affected pose acutely the problem of the filmic construction of space, of achieving a coherency of place and positioning the spectator as the unified and unifying subject of its vision. The vision of the image is its narrative clarity and that clarity is dependent on the negation of space for place, the constant centering of the flow of images, the events taking place, and the narrative movement (Heath 1981, pp. 38–39). The fixed space is problematic in that it does not create place. Cinematic space must be dynamic in the interests of the unity of the action and the place, and the spectator's view. That unity is conceived from the narrative conventions of literature that cinema has exploited and extended.

The rhythm and dynamic of film narrative—its aesthetic and communicative potential and its role in film perception—was an important focus of the Soviet film theorist-filmmakers of the 1920s and 1930s (cf. Jackobson 1933; Eisenstein 1943, 1949). Some of these theorists suggested that heightened acuity and spectator involvement in film is most often associated with the filmic violation of literature's narrative conventions through visual montage and other techniques. Eisenstein (1949) suggests that the "collision of ideas" that make up the cinematic image-event can be thought of as a special violation of narrative convention. Worth (1981, p. 51) reinterprets Eisenstein's "collision" as "conflict" and suggests a dialectic whereby an image-event represents a composite of "ideas," and from one image-event colliding with another there emerges a third image-event. Film images may comprise either ordinary or extraordinary events. A good filmmaker exploits the dialectic transformation that occurs with a satisfactory juxtaposition of ordinary and extraordinary image-events (Aitken 1991a). In short, they create spectacle.

The Voyeur and the Nature of Spectacle

> Narrative never exhausts the image . . . Narrative can never contain the whole film which permanently exceeds its fictions. (Stephen Heath 1975, p. 10)

There are no discontinuities in the time and space of real life. Not so in film. Why, then, is the juggling of space and time possible in film without causing distress in the viewer? There are two possible answers to this question. First, the composition and rhythm of a film and the adherence to some known narrative convention give the effect that some event is actually happening. Second, it establishes an "image." The creation of an image within some kind of narrative suggests that scenes diverse in time and space are not arbitrary. If film images gave a strong spatial impression rather than a place image that authenticates the fiction, then montage and other narrative conventions would probably be impossible. It is its partial unreality and our willingness to suspend disbelief that makes film such a powerful medium. A tension exists, however, between image and rhythm in the sense that although narrative struggles to fix the meaning of an image, there is always *more* than the narrative can hold in place. In this sense, Harvey (1989, p. 321) is right when he says that film reduces "the complex stories of daily life to a sequence of images on a depthless screen." Nonetheless, this suggestion misses the position of the spectator as an active participant who understands narrative convention and who is willing to suspend disbelief so as to be taken beyond the immediate narrative of a film. While image-events are predominantly organized in the interests of assuring narrative significance, they also develop as something fascinating in themselves, a source of visual pleasure, a spectacle. A tension is established, then, not only between space and place, but simultaneously between narrative and spectacle.

> Narrative—in part, the sense of something lacking, installing a desire to explore, to find out what is missing, to move into a new scene, and the possibility of achieving what is desired, thus motivated by a voyeuristic curiosity. And spectacle—the spectator confronted by an image which is so fascinating that it seems complete; no longer the sense of something lacking; voyeurism blocked in a moment of fetishism. (Higson 1984, p. 3)

There is also an important feminist geography here (cf. Aitken and Zonn 1993; Zonn and Aitken, Chapter 7). Mulvey (1975) argues that voyeurism and fetishism, as forms of visual pleasure, are part of the classic Hollywood film narrative whereby "the spectator looks, the camera looks, the male character looks, and the female character *is looked at*" (Saco 1992, p. 28). Put another way, in these films women are never represented as *self*, but rather as *other*, the dark continent, the love inspired in the hero, or the values from which the protagonist is trying to escape. Voyeurism involves a process whereby the "male gaze" seeks to exercise power over its subject by marking "her" as the "bearer of guilt" (Mulvey 1975, p. 11). Fetishism, on the other hand, involves the adoption of the female image as a spectacle so complete that it disavows the male castration complex. Rather than wanting to punish the female *other*, the fetishist raises it as an object of desire to the level of spectacle. Fetishism, thus, leads to the reification of the female image, as typified in the cult of the female movie star (Mulvey 1975, pp. 13–14). Mulvey's militant stance against the conventional voyeurism and fetishism of the male spectator's relation to women in Hollywood films offered the first feminist consideration of the relations among spectators, filmmakers, and narrative conventions within the confines of a patriarchal ideology (Penley 1988, p. 6). Flitterman (1985) has extended Mulvey's thesis to when the male character is made the object of desire (cf. Saco 1992, p. 29). Within this context, the genre of the "buddy-movie"—such as *Gallipoli* and *The Outsiders* (see Chapter 5)—is perceived by feminist writers as espousing an active homosexual eroticism that removes the need of woman represented as the *other* (e.g., Silverman 1988). The buddy-movie genre, they suggest, removes the perceived problem of women portrayed in contemporary narrative cinema having little relevance beyond their representation as sexual objects. These feminist critics suggest that preoccupation is with various kinds of male regression—physical, psychological, and historical—which connect nostalgia for the past and for childhood with male fears of the body (Modleski 1991).

Although there is much merit in feminist psychoanalytic theory, we feel that a viewer's participation in a film is dynamic and continually changing as the text evolves, and with the work of narrative convention. Such a perspective comes from transactional theory, and its value is that it leaves open the question of the production of sexual difference in film rather than assuming in advance the sexuality of the character or viewer. In short, feminist psychoanalyses of film narratives do not go far enough because their construction of the spectator, like Baudrillard's "life as image," is solely in terms of the process of interpellation. We argue with Saco (1992, p. 30) that the possibility of intervention by the spectator must remain open, and that we need a theoretical dialogue that can account for the ways in which spectators and filmmakers may consciously resist dominant narratives.

But films are still representations of the *real* and, as such, when place is an integral part of the narrative, it is often used metaphorically as a "geography of the mind." This metaphorical work is a surrogate text for life that is often discursive in form and disjunctive in impact. Put another way, places hold action within cinematic space so as to legitimize the representation as a state of mind. We mean this in the same sense as Jameson (1984, p. 90) when he describes "cognitive mapping" as a basis for understanding situational representations (images) as part of a "vaster and properly unrepresentable totality." Cinematic space, then, may be viewed as a cognitive mapping that serves to reaffirm the *self* by partially apprehending the *real.* This ideal institutes a particular mode of looking as observation, a praxis for the geography of film, a belief that we can *see the real* in cinematic representation. Place portrayal becomes a "sign of reality"—the implication is that it speaks a geography, a history, a memory, a meaning.

Earlier in this chapter we questioned the distinction (for geography) between representations of reality and the material conditions of reality. If that same question had been posed at the start of cinema's history, the answer would have become apparent with little problem. In short, the answer would have resounded Louis Lumière's emphasis that the space of film *is* the space of reality, and that film's ambition and triumph is to "reproduce life" (Sadoul 1972). Later, this suggestion was discredited because it meant that the camera "captured reality" and delivered "nature caught in the act." Perhaps, today, the notion that the *reel* is also the *real* would be more credible because, in another important sense, reality—the match of film and world—is a matter of representation, and representation is in turn a matter of discourse, and discourse is, in part, the organization of images and the construction of narrative conventions. The camera does not mirror reality but creates it, endowing it with meaning, discourse, and ideology. And this endowment can and should be contested.

If we agree with this position, then it would seem that both geographers and film theorists should be converging on similar concerns. These are concerns that revolve around presenting and *re*-presenting the dynamic contexts of lived experience. Geographers see this as being grounded primarily in the places we inhabit, whereas film theorists see a grounding in cinematic space. Our belief is that lived experience is a coalescence of *re*-presentations anchored in media images on the one side and our places and practices on the other. Clearly, much remains to be said about the portrayal of people and places through film and how cinematic representation can bolster or subvert the discourses that frame contemporary geographies.

Notes

1. The story was inspired by Sam Shepard's "Motel Chronicles" (1982). Shepard also wrote the screenplay for the film.

References

Aitken, S. C. 1991a. A transactional geography of the image-event: The films of Scottish director Bill Forsyth. *Transactions, Institute of British Geographers* (New Series) 16 (1): 105–18.

Aitken, S. C. 1991b. Theory development in contemporary behavioral and perceptual geography I: Personality, attitudinal, and spatial choice theories. *Progress in Human Geography* 15 (1): 53–67.

Aitken, S. C. 1992. Theory development in contemporary behavioral and perceptual geography II: The influence of ecological, environmental learning, societal/structural, transactional and transformational theories. *Progress in Human Geography* 16 (4): 552–61.

Aitken, S. C., and L. E. Zonn, 1993. Weir(d) sex: Representation of gender-environment relations in Peter Weir's *Picnic at Hanging Rock* and *Gallipoli*. *Environment and Planning D: Society and Space* 11: 191–212.

Arnheim, R. 1969. *Film as Art*. London: Faber.

Barnes, T. J., and J. S. Duncan, editors. 1992. *Writing Worlds: Discourse, Text and Metaphor in the Representation of Landscape*. London and New York: Routledge.

Barthes, R. 1987 (original 1971). *Image, Music, Text*, translated by S. Heath. New York: Hill and Wang.

Baudrillard, J. 1987. *Cool Memories*. Paris: Éditions Galilée.

Baudrillard, J. 1988. *America*. London: Verso.

Bobrow D., and A. Collins. 1975. *Representation and Understanding: Studies of Cognitive Science*. New York: Academic Press.

Burch, N. 1973. *Theory of Film Practice*. London: Secker and Warburg (first published in French as *Praxis du cinéma*. Paris: Gallimard, 1969).

Burgess, J. 1990. The production and consumption of environmental meaning in the mass media: a research agenda for the 1990s. *Transactions, Institute of British Geographers* 15: 139–61.

Burgess, J., and J. R. Gold, editors. 1985. *Geography, the Media, and Popular Culture*. New York: St. Martin's Press.

Clifford, J. 1986. Introduction: Partial Truths. In J. Clifford and G.E. Marcus, editors, *Writing Culture: The Poetics and Politics of Ethnography*, pp. 1–26. Berkeley: University of California Press.

Clifford, J., and G.E. Marcus, editors. 1986. *Writing Culture: The Poetics and Politics of Ethnography*. Berkeley: University of California Press.

Colacello, B. 1990. *Holy Terror: Andy Warhol Close Up*. New York: HarperCollins.

Denby, D. 1984. Review of *Paris, Texas*. *New York Times*. November 19, p. 52.

Denzin, N. 1991. *Images of Postmodern Society: Social Theory and Contemporary Society*. Newbury Park, Calif.: Sage Publications.

Duncan, J. S., and N. G. Duncan. 1992. Ideology and Bliss: Roland Barthes and the Secret Histories of Landscape. In T. J. Barnes and J.S. Duncan, editors, *Writing Worlds: Discourse, Text and Metaphor in the Representation of Landscape*, pp. 18–37. London and New York: Routledge.

Eisenstein, S. 1943. *The Film Sense*. London: Faber.

Eisenstein, S. 1949. *Film Form*. New York: Harcourt.

Entrikin, J. N. 1991. *The Betweenness of Place: Towards a Geography of Postmodernity*. Baltimore: John Hopkins University Press.

Erens, P., editor. 1990. *Issues in Feminist Film Criticism*. Bloomington and Indianapolis: Indiana University Press.

Flitterman, S. 1985. Thighs and whiskers: The fascination of "Magnum, P.I." *Screen* 26(2): 42–58.

Foucault, M. 1970. *The Order of Things: An Archaeology of the Human Sciences*. A translation of *Les Mots et Les Choses*. New York: Vintage Books.

Foucault, M. 1972. *The Archaeology of Knowledge and the Discourse on Language.* Translated by Rupert Swyer. New York: Tavistock Publishing.

Galan, F. W. 1983. Cinema and semiosis. *Semiotica* 44: 21–53.

Gold, J. R. 1984. The City of the Future and the Future of the City. In R. King, editor, *Geographical Futures.* Sheffield: Geographical Association.

Gold, J. R. 1985. From "Metropolis" to "The City": Film Visions of the Future City. In J. Burgess and J.R. Gold editors, *Geography, the Media, and Popular Culture*, pp. 123–43. New York: St. Martin's Press.

Harvey, D. 1989. *The Condition of Postmodernity.* Cambridge: Basil Blackwell.

Heath, S. 1975. Film and system: Terms of analysis. *Screen* 16(1): 10.

Heath, S. 1981. *Questions of Cinema.* Bloomington and Indianapolis: Indiana University Press.

Hedges, I. 1991. *Breaking the Frame: Film Language and the Experience of Limits.* Bloomington and Indianapolis: Indiana University Press.

Higson, A. 1984. Space, Place, Spectacle: Landscape and townscape in the "Kitchen Sink" film. *Screen: Incorporating Screen Education* 25 (July/October): 2–21.

Jackobson, R. 1933. Upadek Filmu. *Listy pro umeni a kritiku* 1: 45–49. Quoted in F. W. Galan, 1983, Cinema and semiosis. *Semiotica.* 44: 21–53.

Jameson, F. 1984. Postmodernism, or the cultural logic of late capitalism. *New Left Review* 146: 53–92.

Jenkins, A. 1990. A View of Contemporary China: A Production Study of a Documentary Film. In L. Zonn, editor, *Place Images in Media: Portrayal, Experience, and Meaning*, pp. 207–29. Savage, Md.: Rowman and Littlefield.

Kauffmann, S. 1984. Invasion of the culture snatcher; Review of *Paris, Texas. New Republic* 3 (December): 26–27.

Kracauer S., 1960. *Theory of Film.* London: Oxford University Press.

Lacan, J. 1978. *The Four Fundamental Concepts of Psycho-analysis.* Translated by Alan Sheridan. New York: Norton.

Lennett, R. 1985. Review of *Paris, Texas. Cinéaste* 14: 60.

Minsky, M. 1975. A Framework for Representing Knowledge. In P. Winston, editor, *The Psychology of Computer Vision*, pp. 211–77. New York: McGraw-Hill.

Modleski, T. 1991. *Feminism Without Women: Culture and Criticism in a "Postfeminist" Age.* New York: Routledge.

Mulvey, L. 1975. Visual pleasure and narrative cinema. *Screen* 16(3): 6–18.

Natter, W., and J. P. Jones. 1993. Pets or meat: Class, ideology, and space in *Roger & Me. Antipode* 25(2): 140–58.

Newman, C. 1987. Review on the state of the American Novel. *New York Times*, July 17. Quoted in D. Harvey, 1989, *The Condition of Postmodernity*, p. 58. Cambridge: Basil Blackwell.

Penley, C., editor. 1988. *Feminism and Film Theory.* New York: Routledge.

Rattigan, N. 1991. *Images of Australia: 100 Films of the New Australian Cinema.* Dallas: Southern Methodist University Press.

Saco, D. 1992. Masculinity as Signs: Poststructuralist Feminist Approaches to the Study of Gender. In S. Craig, editor, *Men, Masculinity, and the Media,* pp. 23–39. Newbury Park, Calif.: Sage Publications.

Sadoul, G. 1972. *French Film.* New York: Falcon Press.

Schuurmans, E., and A. Vandierendonck. 1985. Recall as communication: Effects of anticipation. *Psychological Research* 47: 119–24.

Shepard, S. 1982. *Motel Chronicles.* New York: Bantam Books.

Short, K. R., editor, 1981. *Feature Films in History.* London: Croom Helm.

Silverman, K. 1988. *The Acoustic Mirror: The Female Voice in Psychoanalysis and Cinema.* Bloomington and Indianapolis: Indiana University Press.

Snow, M. 1981. Quoted in S. Heath, *Questions of Cinema,* p. 24. Bloomington and Indianapolis: Indiana University Press.

Studlar, G. 1985. Review of *Paris, Texas.* In F. N. Magill, editor, *Magill's Cinema Annual, 1985: A Survey of 1984 Films,* pp. 359–64. Englewood Cliffs, N.J.: Salem Press.

Wallis, A. D. 1986. Structure and Meaning in the Cinematic Environment. In J. Wineman, R. Barnese, and C. Zimring, editors, *The Cost of Not Knowing,* pp. 123–33. Madison, Wis.: Omnipress.

Worth, S. 1981. The Development of a Semiotic of Film. *Studying Visual Communication.* Philadelphia: University of Pennsylvania Press.

Zonn, L. 1984. Landscape depiction and perception: A transactional approach. *Landscape Journal* 3: 144–50.

Zonn, L. 1985. Images of place: A geography of media. *Proceedings of the Royal Geographical Society of South Australia* 84: 34–45.

Zonn, L., editor. 1990. *Place Images in Media: Portrayal, Experience, and Meaning.* Savage, Md.: Rowman and Littlefield.

Filmography

Annie Hall. 1977. United Artists/Jack-Rollins-Charles H. Joffe. Director, Allen, W.

Batman. 1989. Warner Bros. Director, Burton, T.

Berlin, Symphony of a City. 1927. Independent. Director, Ruttmann, W.

Blade Runner. 1982 (re-released Director's cut, 1992). Warner Bros. Director, Scott, R.

Chariots of Fire. 1981. Enigma Productions. Director, Hudson, H.

Comfort and Joy. 1984. Kings Roads Productions. Director, Forsyth, W.

Eating. 1984. Ambrose Video Publishing Inc. Director, Kennard, D.

Empire. 1967. Independent. Director, Warhol, A.

Gallipoli. 1981. Associated R&R Films. Director, Weir, P.

Geordie. 1955. Ealing Studios. Director, Macleod, A.

Gregory's Girl. 1980. Samuel Goldwyn Productions. Director, Forsyth, W.

The Highlander. 1986. Thorn EMI. Director, Mulcahy, R.

The Highlander 2: The Quickening. 1982. Thorn EMI. Director, Mulcahy, R.

Just Imagine. 1930. Twentieth Century Fox. Director, Butler, D.

Lawrence of Arabia. 1962. Columbia Studios. Director, Lean, D.

Local Hero. 1982. An Enigma Production for Goldcrest. Director, Forsyth, W.

The Loneliness of the Long-Distance Runner. 1962. Woodfall Films. Director, Richardson, T.

Metropolis. 1926. Ufo. Director, Lang, F.

The Outsiders. 1983. Warner Bros. Director, Coppola, F.

Paris, Texas. 1984. Orion. Director, Wenders, W.

Picnic at Hanging Rock. 1975. Picnic Productions. Director, Weir, P.

Rob Roy: The Highland Rogue 1953. Walt Disney Productions. Director, Disney, W.

Rockets Galore. 1958. Ealing Studios. Director, Macleod, A.

Roger & Me. 1990. Independent. Director, Moore, M.

Sleep. 1965. Independent. Director, Warhol, A.

Storm Boy. 1976. South Australian Film Corporation. Director, Safran, H.

That Sinking Feeling. 1979. British National Film School. Director, Forsyth, W.

Whisky Galore. 1949. Ealing Studios. Director, Macleod, A.

Wings of Desire. 1988. Orion. Director, Wenders, W.

2

Third Cinema and the Third World

Gerald M. Macdonald

This chapter confronts the problem of the relationship between Third Cinema and the Third World. It is a problem of some complexity, and unraveling it suggests one avenue by which geographic thinking can inform film analysis, and vice versa. It is fundamental to my conception of this problem that all cinema is produced and consumed in a highly interconnected global industry of capital, personnel, and ideas, and that film discourse, everything written or said about film, is an integral part of this production-consumption matrix. As such, geographic analysis must derive from the underlying economic, cultural, and aesthetic processes of this communication and entertainment medium.

To the extent that film production and consumption are composed of physical activities, they must be located in space and can therefore be identified, defined, and analyzed as processes. We can, for instance, look at the spatial concentration of capital, personnel, and technology by studying its stability or movement, the locational decision-making process, the impact of capital movement on various peoples, and any number of other related issues. We can, in effect, treat cinema the same way we treat automobiles and soybeans. In this way, geography can make significant contributions to the field of film analysis, which all too often treats the film message as though it were completely autonomous from the material world of film production.

Cinema also involves the production of meaning and, as such, is far less amenable to geographic analysis. Where, for instance, do we locate cinematic meaning—in the place the film is made, in the mind of the scriptwriter or director, or in the mind of the audience? Certainly all of these perspectives are currently and profitably used to expand our understanding of film's role in society. It is possible to think of Hollywood as the geographic center of a high-technology, highly capital intensive escapist brand of profit-driven cinematic entertainment that has a disproportional impact on world cinema, to subscribe to an auteurist approach to film analysis in which the role of the director is privileged in the filmmaking process, or to appreciate the contributions of semiotic theory to understanding how audiences decode film language. It is also possible to hold these beliefs simultaneously because while physical objects—electricians, film stock, cameras—are bound by physical laws, meanings are not.

Thought of in this way, cinema is quite unlike automobiles and soybeans, because while a geography of film can be written solely from the perspective of film production, the film message can only be understood in the interactions between the moments of production and those of consumption. I contend that to the extent that geography has influenced the film discourse of nongeographers, it is a production-biased geography, and a simplistic one at that. A more dynamic and powerful geography of film must include an analysis of the interconnectivity of places and meanings in today's world.

In the following pages I will appropriate a theoretically already well developed division of the global film industry into First, Second, and Third Cinema. This division has developed over the past century in waves of reaction to and against the metropole-centered film industries of the colonial powers, or what is now called First Cinema, the cinema of corporate profits. Second Cinema, the so-called "art cinema," is the cinema of the post-World War II European city exemplified by the neorealist genre. Finally, Third Cinema is the radical/subversive cinema that developed in Third World countries with the intent to radicalize directly and call to action members of the audience.

These cinematic categories are not, however, historically, geographically, or conceptually discrete. While often associated with a particular time or place, all cinematic practices coexist in ever changing relationships to one another in today's world. Indeed, by focusing on the purpose—profit, art, subversion—rather than the points of production/consumption, First, Second, and Third Cinema, respectively, defy attempts to be placed in simple categories. We need look no further than the media and film work of Madonna to appreciate the power (and profitability) of the intersection of art and subversive message.

The central critique of my analysis is that the primary regions that are expressed in film discourse are those of the nation-state, that the nation-state provides a limited and inadequate framework for developing a geography of the global film industry, and that the primacy of the nation-state reflects a point-of-production bias that is central to a First Cinema, profit-driven activity. Second Cinema, which developed in the aftermath of World War II in reaction to specific material circumstances, including the dominance of capital-intensive First Cinema, emphasizes film-as-art and is concerned with the universal application (and appreciation) of aesthetic principles. This universalizing has had the dual effect of globalizing the impact of Second Cinema while despecifying its origin and meaning, thus legitimizing the depoliticization of cinema. Third Cinema is the cinema of radical politics. Its primary aim is to subvert the institutions of the dominant society through direct influence on the viewing audience. In this capacity it is the cinematic equivalent of Hoffman's *Steal This Book* (1971). It is also a self-reflexive cinema that attempts to reform cinematic practice along egalitarian, nonhierarchical lines. In this dual role it opposes both the profit-motivated status quo of First Cinema and the elitism of Second Cinema.

While global cinema can be thus divided, it is not so easy to assign individual films to each division. Many filmmakers are influenced by a variety of factors, and many films have a variety of messages. All too often, some kinds of messages, particularly racism, sexism, and homophobia, are the unintentional result of ignorance on the part of the filmmakers. Even more problematic are the issues surrounding audience or critic readings of films. The products of First and Third Cinemas are often read as Second Cinema, and interestingly, the products of First and Second Cinemas are sometimes used in revolutionary contexts.[1] What I propose in these pages is not, therefore, a new regionalization of the global film industry, but rather a geographically specific analysis of the interconnectivity of this industry.

I conclude with a reading of Kidlat Tahimik's *Mababangong Bangungot* (1975, *Perfumed Nightmare*), and use this film as a model for understanding the relationships among places and filmmaking in today's global film industry. Indeed, without understanding these relationships, we cannot begin to appreciate the dynamic geography of film on a global scale.

First Cinema: The Cinema of Profit

First Cinema is generally thought of as the cinema typified by Hollywood. It is, before all else, the cinema of corporate profit. It requires massive capital investments in technology, production facilities, and personnel. Capital investment on this scale requires mass consumption on a comparable scale in order to return the desired profit. The "Hollywood film" has solved this problem through a remarkably coherent set of economic, technical, and aesthetic practices. What is not often considered is that one of these practices is film analysis itself. We should not be surprised to find that the First World-created world order of independent, territorially discrete, sovereign nation-states is paralleled by our thinking in terms of discrete national cinemas.[2] This conception of world cinema as the sum of its national parts not only seriously limits our understanding of the processes of meaning construction in the film medium, but also misleads us to the extent that our fixation on national boundaries implies a primacy for national culture in film discourse.

Interestingly, geography has had virtually no effect on film scholarship except as the underlying, and unexamined, assumption of the primacy of national cinema. Occasionally, films produced in particular regions such as Africa, Asia, the Middle East, and the Third World are studied together, and in the very largest industries, such as India's, films are grouped by language, which is de facto regionalization (Armes 1987; Downing 1987; Lent 1990; Diawara 1992).

The task for geography is to confront simultaneously world film and world-film analysis as different aspects of the First Cinema phenomenon. A useful tool for this analysis is the national film study, which is a kind of industrial and aesthetic history and filmography of a particular nation. In developed countries with productive, well-established film industries, or First Cinema, national studies comprise a tiny fraction of film scholarship. In Third World countries, however, the national film study is often the seminal work in the field, and the first major work to be considered seriously in Western circles. A national film study often symbolizes in the Western mindset the coming-of-age of a Third World society's cinematic industry. What the propensity toward national film analysis suggests is a point-of-production bias that is better suited to understanding film as a physical entity than as a medium of communication. It is no accident that this bias privileges film-as-commodity, since this is the foundation of the First Cinema.

I am not suggesting that national boundaries are entirely insignificant. Capital availability, tax laws and production incentives, customs regulations, censorship laws, and cultural formations do affect the film industry. However, virtually no one (outside of the First Cinema filmmakers themselves) who is interested in film is solely interested in the unique set of logistical problems of profitably uniting capital, technology, and personnel in space and time to produce many thousands of feet of printed film stock.

From a geographical perspective, the ironic conclusion that must be drawn from examining national film industries is that the nation is largely irrelevant to the film industry.[3] This is certainly true in the early years, prior to World War II, when films were by and large controlled by outside capital. And in the later years, as local capital began to take over local production, technology and ideas about filmmaking were still imported. What is even more important is that in most countries, U.S. and Western imports still dominate domestic viewing. This is profoundly important because film viewers come to expect the kinds of films that are produced in the West, in terms of both technical quality and subject matter. Filmmakers take considerable financial and career risks in deviating from these viewers' expectations.

It is also useful to examine national film consumption. This is helpful and does expand our understanding of global cinema, but it often creates the same problem for analysis as does production-biased regionalization. If world production is slanted toward the West, then so too is world consumption. The same national studies that describe the problems of national film production also describe the problems with developing and maintaining a national film audience. The Indonesian film industry provides some valuable insights in this respect.

Heider (1991) has argued that Indonesian films reflect Indonesian culture. Indeed, his study *Indonesian Cinema* is subtitled *National Culture on Screen*. Although Heider argues his point thoroughly and convincingly, his perspective is always that of Indonesian-produced films. If we look at Indonesian-consumed films, a vastly different picture emerges, one that Heider discusses briefly but with little interest. The average Indonesian does not watch film. If he does (the film-going audience is overwhelmingly teen-age boys), he is likely to be watching an American, Indian, or Chinese film (Heider 1991).

Conversations I had with Indonesian filmmakers in Jakarta in 1988 confirm this situation. Indonesian filmmakers typically target five urban markets—Jakarta, Bandung, and Yogyakarta on Java, Denpasar on Bali, and Medan on Sumatra. If a movie succeeds in these markets, it will likely turn a profit for its producers. With Indonesia's population approaching 200 million, the vast majority of it rural, these five cities represent an insignificant market share for Indonesian film.[4] Thus we might understandably ask, is Indonesian cinema about typically Indonesian situations as Heider suggests, or is it about American heroes like Arnold Schwarzenegger and Sylvester Stallone?

The ultimate conclusion to be drawn is that nation-states are incomplete regions for the purposes of analyzing cinema. Neither from a production nor a consumption standpoint do political boundaries sufficiently divide, group, or structure world cinema. If global cinema is more than the sum of all the national cinemas, then the task confronting us is to develop a set of regions more meaningful and more powerful in explaining the phenomenon as a communications medium. Accordingly, we need to look at the production and consumption of film meaning as well as the production of the film itself.

Second Cinema: Art Cinema

If in the first half of the twentieth century a single, capital-intensive film industry quickly penetrated into colonial markets and cultures, the industry began to diversify in purpose and style in the immediate aftermath of World War II. The changes in film practice paralleled the changed material conditions throughout much of Europe. The ravaged cities of the former metropoles resembled the urban centers of the colonial world. Vast populations of refugees, hard economic times, and dependence on foreign investment and political domination were characteristic of London, Paris, and Rome as well as Calcutta, Jakarta, and Dakar. These social conditions provided the potent setting in which a new genre of filmmaking, neorealism, was created.

Neorealism is significant because the aesthetic principles at its core were well suited to the material and social needs of emerging ex-colonial states and because it represented the first true alternative to First Cinema. Filmed with natural light, often outdoors, and plotted to use non-professional actors in everyday situations, these films evoked a realism that is well adapted to carry a message of social commentary and criticism. The fact that these techniques do not require expensive sets, lighting equipment, actors, or scriptwriters made neorealism a very attractive filmmaking technique in underdeveloped countries.

Neorealism also provided an aesthetically valid alternative to First Cinema. These films not only were made on a low budget, but were praised for exactly those qualities made necessary by postwar conditions. Out of this critical praise came a reevaluation of cinema as art, or at least some cinema as art. All prior cinema was then reinterpreted in this light and the fundamental division between art and entertainment thoroughly permeated the film criticism. Not surprisingly, because the Western conception of art requires artists as autonomous, creative, inspired beings, so too Second Cinema requires the personification of a guiding vision generally in the person of the film director.

An excellent example of this relationship between First and Second

Cinema was recognized at the 1992 Oscar awards. Satyajit Ray received the life achievement award from the American Academy of Motion Picture Sciences. Ray's work not only epitomizes Second Cinema in the global context, but parallels the First Cinema–Second Cinema divide within India where his independent 1955 Bengali language *Pather Panchali* (Song of the Road) marked a critical break from the studio-dominated Hindi language film industry. It is also indicative that his films are better received and better known (subtitled) outside of India than inside. His work established the oppositional, nonstudio, and non-Hindi-speaking cinema of India. Ray is also a well-respected critic of cinema in India. His writings have helped to establish the way we understand this cinema at the same time that his films have created the cinema (Ray 1976).

Ray's Oscar is the perfect symbol of the state of global cinema. First Cinema recognizes the contributions of Second Cinema, while not the films themselves, as a means of appropriating the patina of a higher calling, of an artistic vision. Thus, First and Second Cinemas exist in an uneasy symbiosis. Commercial cinema creates the material conditions for huge financial success on a global scale, while Second Cinema directs critical thinking away from the industry itself and toward the filmic language.

This neorealist generation of Third World filmmakers has had a tremendous impact on the national cinemas of the world. Director/producer/scriptwriters, like Ray, applied the techniques learned in Europe to the problems of the newly emerged states of the Third World. Their early works now comprise the "canon" of cinema in these countries; their political efforts helped establish national support for an indigenous film industry; their writings influenced subsequent generations of filmmakers. Indeed, for these very reasons, neorealism remains a powerful aesthetic force in world cinema today.

Rodrigo D., a 1990 feature film from Colombian filmmaker Victor Gaviria, is an excellent example of the continuing influence of neorealism. It is widely hailed as an updated neorealist treatment of the spiritual, and to some extent material, destitution of middle-class youth in Colombia today. Indeed, its American distributor declares its kinship with the neorealist classics *Los Olvidados* (The Damned) by Luis Buñuel (1950) and *The Bicycle Thief* by Vittorio De Sica (1949), and in a recent review West and West (1992) refer to it variously as a punk version of *Los Olvidados* and as a continuation of the neorealist project.

The film is set in the suburban hills above Medellin, where drug-inspired violence and lawlessness create a dystopic backdrop of gang warfare and assassination squads. Rodrigo, the main character and one of a group of amoral street kids, wants only to be a punk rock drummer. Punk music provides the background score throughout, as we view the various gang members idling about, stealing motorcycles or cars, or engaging in small-time drug deals. The film ends with Rodrigo's jump from a downtown skyscraper intercut with scenes of several gang members murdering another member of the gang.

There is little question that, indeed, *Rodrigo D.* is neorealist in subject, conception, and filming. The comparison to *Los Olvidados* is obvious on the level of subject matter. Both deal with gangs of violent youth facing the oppressive, even fascist, authority of the state as a consequence of the breakdown in social order and parental control. Perhaps the more direct cinematic antecedent is De Sica's *Umberto D.* (1952) rather than Buñuel's *Los Olvidados*. While *Umberto D.* and *Roberto D.* are quite different as humans—Umberto a kindly, aged pensioner living in Rome—the situation they face is quite similar. Rodrigo wants only to start a punk band, Umberto to live out his remaining years peacefully at his apartment with his small dog. Neither is able to achieve his desires because of the situation within which each finds himself. In the end, Umberto, holding tightly to his dog, places himself in the path of an on-coming train but steps back at the last instant. He is able neither to give up his beloved dog nor to take it with him in his death. For Rodrigo, there is no dog, and he jumps.

The point here is that if *Rodrigo D.* is so clearly premised on earlier neorealist films, then how much is truly Colombian, and how much is art? This is not to say that there is nothing significantly Colombian about the film, nor that it does not stand on its own as a piece of cinema, merely that to fully appreciate its contribution a film-goer needs to be aware of these other influences. If we ultimately decide that *Rodrigo D.* is part of a self-reflexive world cinema, then we must seriously modify our concepts of national cinema as well as develop more sophisticated means of examining cinema.

Third Cinema: The Cinema of Subversion

Not surprisingly, Third Cinema arose in the context of cinema in the Third World, and understanding it requires some background in the history and the problem of cinema in the Third World. Cinema was introduced to the world very soon after its invention through the 1896 traveling exhibition by the Lumière Brothers (Sadoul 1972). This introduction for the Third World meant, of course, cinema brought to the colonial administrative center from the metropole for the entertainment of the European colonizers. The earliest productions made in the colonies were limited in number and tended to be ethnographic studies of the colonized. If the urban population was large enough to make an indigenous film industry profitable, then capital investments were made from the colonizing country, but even where domestic film production was fairly strong prior to World War I—China, Brazil, India—the domestic market was dominated by foreign imports (Armes 1987). These conditions continued through the first four decades of the century. Few (and in the case of many countries, none) of these earliest films exist today. This is the result both of the deterioration in film stock and of a lack of interest in preserving these products. In many countries, the oldest extant films date from the late 1940s or early 1950s.

World War II brought a filmmaking hiatus to much of the colonized world, and the few films that were produced tended to be war propaganda. Following the war, the great wave of independence that swept the colonized globe also brought with it the first stirring of a "national" cinema. Colonial filmmakers of this era were, like other literary and political elites, drawn from the ranks of the privileged classes. They had received European language educations, frequently in Europe, and returned home with their European values, particularly nationalism.

Just as political leaders struggled with the questions of constructing a nation-state that would represent the indigenous peoples of a territory defined by European conquest and domination, so, too, filmmakers struggled with the questions of defining an aesthetic practice that would give voice to the creative aspirations of the indigenous peoples. In both the political context and the artistic, the medium of expression, the nation-state and film respectively, was foreign (Georgakas and Rubenstein 1983). It is in this period that neorealism had its greatest impact.

By the 1960s, radical political movements throughout the world were not only beginning to be expressed in film, but also were beginning to have an impact on cinematic practice. Consciously rejecting narrative plot structure and aesthetic visual languages, these films sought direct political engagement with the audience. Indeed, this rejection of Western film made Third World filmmakers and critics among the first to understand and articulate the limiting context of film discourses that derived chiefly from Western imperialism, both economic and cultural. These radical political movements in much of the Third World were soon followed by a period of political repression from which many countries are only now emerging. Many of the filmmakers who came of age

during these years fled into exile, while others accepted to varying degrees government-imposed censorship. During this period, national
capital, usually with state support and protection, began to expand cinematic facilities, create university programs in film production and study,
and otherwise lay the foundation for an expanded industry. Therefore,
for what is today the Third World, the earliest films were by any measure
"foreign." The technology was introduced from the metropole; the vast
majority of films shown were imported from Europe and the United
States; the subjects filmed and the structure of the narrative were Western in conception. These conditions prevailed even in countries where
film production was established for the local market.

The Third Cinema critique of film practice provides the basis for a
conceptual reformulation of a global geography of cinema. Third Cinema grew out of a radicalized cinema in Latin America in the 1960s.
Among its early proponents were filmmakers and critics Julio Garcia
Espinoza of Cuba and Fernando Solanas and Octavio Getino of Argentina. Espinoza's crucial manifesto, "For an Imperfect Cinema" (1983),
had as galvanizing an effect on the film community as had the earlier
neorealist filmmakers. He argued that the technical perfection of Western cinema was, by virtue of the necessarily imposed technical isolation
of the audience from the filmmaking process, almost always reactionary.
In other words, perfect cinema legitimizes the status and power distinctions of which it is a product. Central to Espinoza's thinking and to the
practice of Third Cinema is the revolutionary transformation of art from
elitist to universal practice: "Art has always been a universal necessity;
what it has not been is an option for all under equal conditions" (Espinoza 1983, p. 30).

Solanas and Getino echo the primacy of the relationship between art
and the revolutionizing practice in their manifesto, "Toward a Third
Cinema" (1983). To them the reproduction of the distinction between
filmmaker and audience is the reproduction of bourgeois society in the
ex-colonial context. For them social revolution does not begin with the
taking of political power but "at the moment when the masses sense
the need for change." It is in this space that revolutionary film practice
emerges.

Third Cinema, unlike other manifestations of cinematic practice, explicitly recognizes that all cinema emanates from global capitalism and
serves bourgeois ideological needs. Only by understanding both the
constraints of this system and its effects can a new cinema emerge. Also
significant is that the space in which this new cinema operates is both
extremely local and universal. It is the intention of this cinema to trans-

form society. It achieves its goal by engaging the audience in immediate social, political, and aesthetic concerns. In so doing, Third Cinema raises at least the potential for universal statements about the conditions and causes of human misery and oppression. In Solanas and Getino's words, "*Truth, then, amounts to subversion*" (italics Solanas and Getino 1983, p. 19).

It is little wonder that the goals and practices of Third Cinema, once articulated in the Latin American context, quickly spread worldwide, first to other Third World countries but soon to the oppressed regions and peoples of the First World as well. With the diffusion of Third Cinema practice also came the diffusion of the characterization of the First and Second Cinemas. Today, filmmakers the world over create cinema in a sharply defined context of purpose—profit, art, subversion. It is the intersection of this global purpose with the realities of global geography that to a large extent determines the way we read world cinema.

Third Cinema: Geography and Practice

In the following pages, I analyze the Philippine film *Mababangong Bangungot* (*Perfumed Nightmare*), which was written, directed, filmed, produced, and edited by Kidlat Tahimik. I will address the issue of the spatial relationships between places in the world today on two levels, that of production of the film as Third Cinema and as the film message about the contemporary world.

Tahimik's film is an idiosyncratic journey toward a revolutionary consciousness both in its existence as a film and through its narrative of the conflict produced within the main character, Kidlat himself, as he becomes disenchanted with the dream of Western technology. [Because of the inherent confusion between the main character and the filmmaker, I will use Kidlat to refer to the character and Tahimik, the filmmaker.] Its importance lies in the inseparability of these two. For here indeed, the medium is the message, and in what is perhaps just as significant, the message is the medium.

The film's story line is a first-person account of a young jeepney driver's (Kidlat's) obsession with all things American, particularly rocket ships. His dream is to visit America and meet his hero—Dr. Wernher von Braun, the man who invented bridges to the moon. One day an American appears in his village and offers to employ Kidlat in his business in Paris and eventually to take him to America. In Paris, Kidlat becomes disillusioned with modern technology, and on the day before he is to travel to America, he comes to a full revolutionary consciousness and blows away [literally] the appearance of the superiority of Western over traditional ways.

Tahimik's own life represents a similar trajectory. Born in the Philippines in 1942, he describes his youth as "sleeping in the cocoon of his Americanized dreams" (Deocampo 1985, p. 18). He attended the University of the Philippines and, on his parents' wishes, received his master's degree from the Wharton School of Business at the University of Pennsylvania. Disenchanted, he left for Paris where he began work on *Perfumed Nightmare.* The film was completed in bits and pieces over a two-year period. Its total cost was a minuscule $10,000 when a typical Philippine film cost over $100,000, and it immediately began to attract international attention and win Tahimik critical acclaim upon its release in 1977.

The making of a film about a young Filipino's revolutionizing experience in Paris is the revolutionizing experience of a young Filipino in Paris. The full extent of this dual identity permeates the film and constitutes an extraordinary exposition of geographical reality and metaphor, and is in many ways typical of Third Cinema.

The central question in *Perfumed Nightmare* is interconnectivity of places in the post-World War II world made possible by advancement in communication and transportation technologies. Growing up in an American-dominated postwar Philippine village, Kidlat becomes obsessed with rocketry by listening to Voice of America broadcasts about the Apollo moon landing. So taken is he that he forms his own chapter of the Wernher von Braun fan club, awakes every morning beneath a picture of Miss America, and writes letters to Voice of America requesting them to replay the first words spoken on the moon.

Kidlat also drives a jeepney (World War II vehicles transformed into minibuses), a position that affords him a broad view of the activities of the entire village. We go with him on his rounds driving the statue of the patron saint of the village back and forth to the church. We travel with the richest person in the village as she transports a huge block of ice from her factory. And we travel with Kidlat as he picks up the American who will take him to Paris but who is too proud to sit in the jeepney with the other passengers and their chickens and pigs.

It is this role as a jeepney driver, a transportation technology virtually synonymous with the Philippines, and as a lover of advanced Western rocket technology that sets up the fundamental conflict in the movie. The idea is made explicit when Kidlat responds to the question "Why do you want to go to America so much?" with the answer "Because there I could be an astronaut, here I am only a jeepney driver."

It is unlikely Tahimik spent his youth glued to VOA. Certainly his arts training at the University of the Philippines and his later business degree from Wharton suggest that his parents were professionals, and in all likelihood his was a privileged urban youth. What is likely is that he spent much time in the movie theaters of Manila watching American imports.

The introduction of cinema to the Philippines coincided almost exactly with the arrival of the American colonial presence there; the first movie house was opened in Manila by two Swiss businessmen in 1897 (Lumbera 1986, p. 37). By 1912, American companies had begun producing films in Manila for the Philippine market. This marked the beginning of the American-import domination of the local market through availability, technical superiority to the local product, and control of key distribution networks (Armes 1987, p. 152). Philippine filmmakers, struggling to survive, began to copy Hollywood tactics and to create special markets such as movies based on serialized novels and popular comic strips (Reyes 1986, p. 220).

In the post-World War II years, the Philippine film industry saw something of an artistic florescence spurred by political events and their impact on the national consciousness, but by 1960, rampant commercialism and the overwhelming dominance of just three movie studios signaled a long period of artistic decline. It is this unfulfilled promise of a vibrant indigenous cinema that informed the consciousness of a young Tahimik. Surely, the polish and technical mastery of the Hollywood cinema was a key element in his "cocoon of Americanized dreams." Again, East and West, modern and traditional, meet in the film narrative and through the filmmaking process.

Kidlat's journey toward America is interrupted by a year-long stop in Paris where he works refilling bubble-gum machines in the business "empire" of his American patron. While there, he befriends a couple who run a small food stall in an outdoor market that is being pushed aside by the imminent opening of a huge supermarket in the neighborhood. Kidlat travels to Germany where he watches the last of the hand-built copper *swebelturm*—onion tower—being raised. He returns to France to find his friends finally driven out of business. The bankruptcy of the West is made explicit in the dedication ceremony for the new supermarket when the keynote speaker proudly proclaims, "*Liberté, égalité, fraternité, supermarché.*" Kidlat comes to understand that the modern technology that pushes aside the traditional is not inherently superior. He confronts his American patron and sees beneath the superficiality of his American dream, now his perfumed nightmare.

Certainly his bubble-gum apprenticeship is meant as a commentary on his Wharton years where his business education would have taught him principles of business devoid of social content. That is to say, a bubble-gum empire posing no possible social benefit is the quintessential modern business, employing grossly exploited laborers and making rich and powerful men of its owners. To escape the nightmare, Kidlat understands the superficiality of his experience with the West and particularly with the Western idea of progress. To escape the dream, Tahimik tore up his diploma—"It's part of my past. It's not relevant to me"—and made a film showing the superficiality of the Western world (Deocampo 1985, p. 18).

Technology

The interrelationship between modern and traditional technology is the basis by which Tahimik seeks to expose the dream as a nightmare. His rejection is not, however, of all things Western or modern, but a rejection of the ethically and socially detached organization and control of that technology. This is obvious in Kidlat's humorous adoration of Wernher von Braun. The dream of visiting the stars obscures the reality of the V bomb attacks on England and the nuclear missiles of the Cold War. The reality of Kidlat's world is as much the connection made by the rocket of mass destruction as the connections made by the transportation technologies associated with rocketry.

The jeepney is another central metaphor. Before leaving for Paris, Kidlat visits the Sarow Motors in Manila, which is the Philippines' largest indigenously owned automobile manufacturer. As Kidlat informs us, "despite the recession, last year production increased 40 percent to five jeepneys per week." Jeepneys are hand-made from parts from old World War II jeeps. No jeep ever goes to waste, every part is cannibalized and used over and over again. The finished jeepney is then brightly hand-painted, making each a truly unique product.

For Tahimik, his film is his product, hand-made at every step, and completely idiosyncratic. It is also, like the jeepney, made from Western hand-me-downs, in Tahimik's case, a twenty-year-old Bolex camera. Western technology per se is not at fault. Indeed, both jeepneys and cinema were introduced by the West. Rather, the problem is with the human and social control over technology. Bubble-gum empires and Hollywood escapist cinema are at best amoral abstractions. Jeepneys and Tahimik's film are objects of beauty in both their form as a product and their socially derived meaning from a culturally nonalienated production process. Thus, the confrontation resulting from the diffusion of Western technologies into traditional societies is not a simple matter. Certainly not one of good versus bad. Nor does Tahimik argue the rejection of Western technology, but rather the rejection of the kind of technological determinism implicit in the cultural imperialism of the West.

This quest to identify neither with the West nor with some romanticized pure precapitalist social order, but rather to seek a new way, is characteristic of Third Cinema. In this practice, traditional ways are not inherently superior to the hegemony of Western culture. Some traditions are to be rejected, some appropriated, invoked, or transformed. As the Moroccan Zaghloul Morsy explained, "Whether we try to refute it, liberate ourselves from it or assent to it . . . the West is here with us as a prime fact, and ignorance or imperfect knowledge of it has a nullifying effect on all serious reflection and genuinely artistic expression" (Willemen 1989, p. 19).

Tahimik's film is characteristic of this new relationship between the First World and the Third World. It is not merely his own awakening political consciousness, but a vehicle for the awakening of others. This is particularly important in the film industry of the Philippines because his is an aesthetic as well as political statement. Among film critics and analysts of the industry, little that can be said is good. It has been estimated that of the approximately 150 films per year produced in the Philippines, about four or five are of critical significance. The rest fall into the category of escapist, genre films, the best known being the *Bomba* or bold film, a soft-core sexploitation with little plot and even less technical merit. The reasons for this situation are many. High government taxes, strict censorship, highly paid actors and actresses, highly centralized distribution networks that have become a major force in film production in recent years, and an audience trained to expect Western-style movies have combined to drive up the cost of film production and inhibit experimentation and investments in quality (Francia 1987, pp. 212–18; de Castro III 1986, p. 188). Even the few Philippine directors of critical note such as Lino Brocka or Ishmael Bernal make concessions to the prevailing practices of the industry. They are practitioners of Second Cinema, the *auteurist* cinema of European and American art theaters. Their work, however technically refined, implicitly accepts Western aesthetic dogma.

It is in such a milieu that an experimental film movement has arisen in the Philippines in recent years. The seminal impact of Marcos's declaration of martial law in 1972, combined with a new generation of college-based film students and lightweight, fairly inexpensive equipment, has contributed to the avant-garde movement (Deocampo 1985). Tahimik is considered a principal contributor to this movement. As an outsider, he has great artistic freedom, but little access to a Philippine audience (Lent 1990). By making a movie critical of American dominance in the Philippines, he is making a direct attack on the Philippine movie industry.

Conclusion

The dual nature of Tahimik's world is thus the simultaneity of oppression–liberation. It is through the most oppressive feature of the postwar world, the threat of nuclear annihilation, that the oppressed begin the trajectory toward liberation. Indeed, it is the connections made by the rocket bridge that stimulates the mental connections to awaken us from the dream. Tahimik's world is not, however, a place where the traditional (good) needs to reject evil (the West) by rejecting all that is modern. In short, his world is not the script of a B-movie melodrama, but instead it is a world in which the Western development model is rejected or at least questioned when applied to other contexts. It is a world where contact between peoples does not imply the obliteration of one people or culture by another. It is a world in which there is more than one dynamic, more than one logic. It is also a world in which the total liberation of one place implies the liberation of all places. If the Philippines can never be totally free while connected metaphorically to the West by the rocket, then the wind that blows from the Philippines must blow away the rockets in the West. If jeepneys and bamboo houses are to survive and prosper in the Philippines, then onion towers and food stalls must flourish in Europe.

This is the world of the Third Cinema, which is a cinematic practice that seeks to be an active element in the development of a revolutionary consciousness. It is a practice caught "between the contradictions of technologised mass culture . . . and the need to develop a different kind of mass culture while being denied the financial, technological and institutional support to do so" (Willemen 1989, p. 13). Third Cinema rejects the simplistic retreat into reactionary utopianism, rejects the categorical rejection of the West, and impels us to accept a new understanding of the world. For the spaces and places of our liberation are connected by rocket and bridge and mass media to the places of any liberation.

Notes

1. See John R. Groch, "What is a Marx Brother?: Critical Practice, and the Nation of a Comic Auteur," *The Velvet Light Trap*, No. 26, Fall 1990, pp. 28–41, as an example of the First Cinema read as Second Cinema. The scene in Tomas Gutierrez Alea's "Memories of Underdevelopment," when pornographic film clips are used to show the oppression of women in bourgeois society is an example of how presentation can affect the reading.

2. A very large literature of national film studies exists. Virtually every country with any film industry has one or more books dedicated to the subject. Representative of the genre are Berry's *Chinese Cinema*, Chanan's *The Cuban Image*, Johnson and Stam's *Brazilian Cinema* and Shohat's *Israeli Cinema*.

3. Perhaps the best example of the conundrum of nationality with respect to cinematic writing is Slide's *The Cinema and Ireland* (1988). Because of the paucity of film production in Ireland, Slide was forced to examine a large number of intersections between Ireland and cinema. The resulting work includes chapters on Irish who migrated to the industry in Hollywood, the portrayal of the Irish in American cinema, the influence of Irish literature on cinema, and American films produced in Ireland in addition to the more standard treatment of films produced in Ireland by the Irish for an Irish domestic audience. Indeed, Slide's introduction is a virtual *apologia* for daring to broach such a topic, yet its eventual publication suggests how uncritically we accept the primacy of the nation-state in such matters of analysis.

4. Interview with Harun Suwardi, Film Committee of the Jakarta Arts Council, Jakarta. July 1, 1988.

References

Armes, R. 1987. *Third World Filmmaking and the West.* Berkeley: University of California Press.

Berry, C., editor. 1991. *Chinese Cinema.* London: BFI Publishing.

Chanan, M. 1985. *The Cuban Image: Cinema and Cultural Politics in Cuba.* Bloomington: Indiana University Press.

de Castro III, P. 1986. How Much Does It Cost to Produce a Dream Movie? In C. del Mundo, Jr., *Philippine Mass Media.* Manila: Communication Foundation of Asia.

Deocampo, N. 1985. *Short Film: Emergence of a New Philippine Cinema.* Manila: Communication Foundation of Asia.

Diawara, M. 1992. *African Cinema: Politics and Culture.* Bloomington: Indiana University Press.

Downing, J.D.H., editor. 1987. *Film and Politics in the Third World.* New York: Praeger.

Espinoza, J.G. 1983. For an Imperfect Cinema. In M. Chanan, editor, *Twenty-Five Years of the New Latin American Cinema*. London: British Film Institute and Channel Four.

Francia, L. 1987. Philippine Cinema: The Struggle Against Repression. In J.D.H. Downing, editor, *Film and Politics in the Third World*. New York: Praeger.

Georgakas D., and L. Rubenstein, editors. 1983. *The Cinéaste Interviews*. Chicago: Lake View Press.

Groch, John R. 1990. What is a Marx Brother?: Critical practice, industrial practice, and the notion of the comic auteur. *The Velvet Light Trap* 26: 28–41.

Heider, K.G. 1991. *Indonesian Cinema: National Culture on Screen*. Honolulu: University of Hawaii Press.

Hoffman, A. 1971. *Steal This Book*. New York: Buccaneer Books.

Johnson, R., and R. Stam. 1982. *Brazilian Cinema*. East Brunswick, N.J.: Associated University Presses.

Lent, J. 1990. *The Asian Film Industry*. Austin: University of Texas Press.

Lumbera, B. 1986. Problems in Philippine Film History. In C. del Mundo Jr., editor, *Phillipine Mass Media*. Manila: Communication Foundation of Asia.

Ray, S. 1976. *Our Films, Their Films*. New Delhi: Orient Longman, Ltd.

Reyes, E.A. 1986. 1984: Towards the Development of a Nationalist Cinema. In C. del Mundo Jr., editor, *Philippine Mass Media*. Manila.

Sadoul, G. 1972. *French Film*. New York: Falcon Press.

Shohat, E. 1989. *Israeli Cinema: East/West and the Politics of Representation*. Austin: University of Texas Press.

Slide, A. 1988. *The Cinema and Ireland*. Jefferson, N.C.

Solanas, F., and O. Getino. 1983. Toward a Third Cinema. In M. Chanan, editor, *Twenty-Five Years of the New Latin American Cinema*. London: British Film Institute and Channel Four.

Suwardi, H. 1988. Film Committee of the Jakarta Arts Council. Jakarta, July 1.

West, D., and J. West. 1992. Rodrigo D.: No Future. *Cinéaste* 18 (4): 47–49.

Willemen, P. 1989. The Third Cinema Question: Notes and Reflections. In J. Pines and P. Willemen, *Questions of Third Cinema*. London: BFI Publishing.

Filmography

The Bicycle Thief. 1949. Independent (Italy). Director, De Sica, V.

Los Olvidados (The Damned). 1950. Independent (Mexico). Director, Buñuel, L.

Mababangong Bangungot (*Perfumed Nightmare*). 1975. Independent (Philippines). Director, Tahimik, K.

Rodrigo D. 1990. Independent (Colombia). Director, Gaviria, V.

Umberto D. 1952. Independent (Italy). Director, De Sica, V.

3

A Mapping of Cinematic Places: Icons, Ideology, and the Power of (Mis)representation

Jeff Hopkins

If place construction lies at the core of human geography (Tuan 1991, p. 684), then the notion of a *cinematic place* is a fundamental concern for a geography of film. Understanding the formation and sociopolitical implications of such a place poses a particularly abstruse challenge because of the incorporeal nature of the film environment. Through the blending of people and technology both in front of and behind the screen, a two-dimensional photographic image of projected light and shadow becomes an illusionary, three dimensional, cinematic landscape. This landscape has its own geography, one that situates the spectator in a cinematic place where space and time are compressed and expanded and where societal ideals, mores, values, and roles may be sustained or subverted. The pleasure of film lies partially in its ability to create its own cinematic geography, but so too does its power. The cinematic landscape is not, consequently, a neutral place of entertainment or an objective documentation or mirror of the "real," but an ideologically charged cultural creation whereby meanings of place and society are made, legitimized, contested, and obscured. Intervening in the production and consumption of the cinematic landscape will enable us to question the power and ideology of representation, and the politics and problems of interpretation. More importantly, it will contribute toward the more expansive task of mapping the social, spatial, and political geography of film.

This chapter offers an introductory field trip into the abstract and sparsely mapped landscape of cinema by way of a semiotic approach to the question of representation in, and the interpretation of, film. Approaching film as a semiotic landscape—as a human-made, cultural construct of systematically related signs and sign systems—compliments

47

several long-standing geographical concerns of landscape assessment while providing theoretical insight about the production and consumption of the film image from a highly developed branch of film studies. After clarifying the concepts of "cinematic landscape," "cinematic place," and "semiotics," I discuss the way film images are used to create an "impression of reality" through the rapid succession of iconic signs. Attention is not focused on the meanings of place as portrayed in film, but on the semiotic processes that create the film image and encourage viewers to experience an ideologically charged cinematic place. The power of the film image to (mis)represent the material and social world lies, I argue, in its ability to blur the boundaries of space and time, reproduction and simulation, reality and fantasy, and to obscure the traces of its own ideologically based production.

Film as a Semiotic Landscape

Film studies, semiotics, and geography share a visual juncture that provides a provocative source of insight into the fabrication of culture and the (re)making of society's mores, norms, and values. The visual constitution and central role of "landscape" in geography, the fact that film is primarily a visual medium, and the concern of semiotics with the production and interpretation of culture in all its modalities, all combine to provide a potentially rich discourse on the (re)presentation of culture through film.

Attempts to describe, explain, and evaluate the making, medium, viewing, and implications of film have included a wide variety of perspectives, ranging from the aesthetic (Arnheim 1957), anthropologic (Collier 1967), linguistic (Bollag 1988), and psychological (Wolfenstein and Leites 1970), to more recent feminist (Kaplan 1983), Marxist (Zavarzadeh 1991), and psychoanalytic (Berland 1982) approaches. Semiotics has, in particular, become a particularly well developed branch of film studies over the past thirty years, making major contributions to our understanding of the structure or "language" of film, the constitution of the film image or sign, and the communicative processes of film (e.g., Wollen 1972; Metz 1974; Lotman 1976; Worth 1981; Winfried, 1990). Although such geographical concepts as "space," "place," and "setting" have been employed by film theorists (e.g., Lotman 1976; Boggs 1978; Schnathmeier 1987), and despite the interdisciplinary nature of film studies, there has been, with notable exceptions (e.g., Burgess and Gold 1985; Eyles and Peach 1990; Aitken 1991), surprisingly little work done by geographers. The breadth of potential research a geography of film poses is, as discussed in closing, immense. Let me begin, therefore, by situating the specific concerns of this chapter with icons, (mis)representation, and interpretation, into the much larger concepts of landscape, place, and semiotics.

Approaching film as a landscape is a logical point of entry into the geography of film. Landscapes, be they natural or cultural, physical or imaginary, are first and foremost visual constructs (Porteous 1990). Scape is a suffix meaning "representation" or "view of" (Sykes 1982, p. 935); land-scape is a representation of the land: the actual or imagined environment that surrounds us (Jakle 1987). Landscape is, in other words, a site of sight, a cultural image that represents and structures our surroundings (Cosgrove and Daniels 1988). A landscape may be represented through various media: flora and fauna in a park, paint on a canvas, printed words in a novel or poem, verbal statements in a conversation, the photographic image of a postcard. Landscape painting, literary landscapes, and landscape photographs are, for example, well-established areas of research in geography (e.g., Pocock 1981; Cosgrove 1984; Marsh 1985; Osborne 1988; Sandberg and Marsh 1988). Exploring the realm of cinema, perhaps the most popular and accessible mode of visual representation in contemporary society with the exception of television, is not a radical departure from more conventional landscape studies; it is a reasonable augmentation of our principal interest in the "scaping" of our world.

A landscape of film, or a *cinematic landscape,* might be defined in the broadest sense of the term as a filmic representation of an actual or imagined environment viewed by a spectator. Such a landscape is a particularly sophisticated and powerful form of representation because of its medium. Through a rapid succession of static photographs, an illusion of depth, volume, and motion is produced, which, when combined with sound (dialogue, music, sound effects) creates an environment where the boundaries between the real and the imaginary, fact and fiction, are blurred. Other media, such as literature, painting, or theater, may also blur our sensibilities, but film is peculiar because of the semblance of actuality attributable to the film image and the obscurity of its very production (Baudrillard 1987; Allen 1991). In other words, the sights/sites look "real" while the processes of their production remain enigmatic if not magical. As discussed below, this milieu of verisimilitude, where distinctions between the real and the imaginary become nebulous, situates the spectator in a cinematic place where the pleasure, the power, and the ideology of film are first manifest.

A *cinematic place* challenges the conventional notion of place because it is not tied to a specific location in physical space. *Place* is most commonly defined as a center of felt value (Tuan 1977, p. 4; cf. Billinge 1986, p. 346). *Center* implies a position in a spatial system, a location, but a center of value need not be physically accessible or fixed in absolute space (Adams 1992). A center is merely a focal point that may take many forms: a person, an artifact, an imaginary environment conveyed through a novel. As Tuan notes, place is a center of meaning constructed by experience; it must be felt (1975, p. 152). Film is a center of meaning insofar as it is a focal point for the construction of ideas, values, and shared experiences. Film is physically accessible only in the sense that one may enter a theater and select a seat, or switch on a videocassette recorder and collapse onto the living room couch, but these are merely points of departure into the cinematic place. Only a viewer's state of mind, a "willing suspension of disbelief" (Boggs 1978, p. 22), will permit experience of the cinematic place. Physical location is extraneous—a theater or living room anywhere will suffice—but the situation of the viewer remains fixed; the center of felt value remains grounded in the experience of film, in the viewer-media relationship. The cinematic place is not, therefore, limited to the world represented on the screen (a geography in film), but the meanings constructed through the experience of film (a geography of film). The meanings constituted through film do not simply reflect or report on space, place, and society, but actively participate in the production and consumption of the larger cultural systems of which they are a part.

Given its theoretical insight and analytical utility into the (re)production and interpretation of culture, semiotics—the study of signs, sign systems, signification, and communication—provides a means of mapping the cinematic landscape and thus intervening in the fabrication of the cinematic place. Viewed from a semiotic perspective, culture is a perpetual process of producing meanings of and from the continual succession of social practices and shared experiences (Fiske 1989). Because culture is both mediator and medium of social interaction, cultural creations such as film may be interpreted semiotically, that is, as a systematically related collection of signs or texts (Gottdiener 1982; Sebeok 1986). The fundamental underlying assumption is that humans constitute themselves and their world by and through signs and sign systems of their own making.

A "sign" is "everything that, on the grounds of previously established convention, can be taken as something standing for something else" (Eco 1976, p. 16). "Signification" is the social process whereby "something" (signifier) comes to stand for "something else" (signified), and by questioning this process, semiotics is made applicable to an immense range of objects, events, topics, and disciplines, including geography and film studies. The semiotic endeavor is, therefore, primarily herme-neutic; to develop and apply theory about the production of culture and the processes of interpretation (Denzin 1985; Jules-Rosett 1990). This task is closely allied to some long-standing concerns of geography: un-derstanding the meanings of landscapes; what places signify for people; and how landscapes and places may be interpreted (Smith 1988). Ap-proaching film as a semiotic landscape, as a socially constructed cultural image or sign system that represents and structures an environment, provides a way of questioning the very representation and interpretation of the cinematic place.

Iconic Illusions of the Cinematic Place

The cinematic landscape is a highly complex set of aural and visual sign systems created by the filmmaker, film medium, and film spectator. At-tention here is limited to the semiotic production of the visual signs of the film medium as viewed by the spectator rather than, say, the commu-nicative effects intended by the filmmaker or the possible visual or aural messages received by the film viewer. The screen image is the premier component of the cinematic landscape because it is the projected pho-tograph that provides the basic structure, the initial focal point, for the construction of ideas, values, and shared experiences by the audience. Places are, of course, more than simply visual constructs, but the sonic signs of the cinematic place go beyond the scope of this chapter. Like early film audiences who saw silent pictures, let us first acquaint our-selves with visual imagery before attempting "talkies."

Film is, according to Worth, "images in motion over time through space with sequence" (1981, p. 54; cf. Aitken 1991). By critiquing the film image as an iconic sign and revealing its illusion of motion over time through space, we can begin to subvert the power of film by better understanding how the spatialities and temporalities of the cinematic place are constructed. Once this is mapped, I will turn to the issues of power, ideology, and (mis)representation.

Spectators are willingly seduced into the cinematic place, at least partly, because of the authority ascribed to sight. Given the fact that 90 percent of human knowledge about the external world is attributed to visual perception (Dodwell 1966; cf. Gold 1980, p. 52), the power of the film image to "make believe" is considerable. For example, when the motion-picture camera was invented by Thomas Edison, it was greeted as the machine that would objectively apprehend *reality* as it really was (Worth 1981). Instead of representing the world through hand-drawn images or descriptive prose that might resemble or evoke a similarity to the *real* world, the photographic image was regarded as a true mapping of the world before the camera. Film captured the visible truth: seeing was believing.

What the film viewer witnesses is not, however, the *real* but what Metz calls "the impression of reality": the sense of experiencing an almost real spectacle (1974, p. 4). The production of the "almost real" or "cinematic reality" is one of the key problems in film theory, the intricate and varied explanations of which go far beyond the scope of this chapter. My concern here is limited to two notions that will provide some acumen for the cinematic place: the signification of the film sign (the photographic image that stands for something else) and the appearance of motion generated by a rapid succession of static, serial images. Iconic forms and the iconic illusion of motion combine to encourage the viewer's fabrication of an imaginary space and time, a "cinematic place," and this is where the power and ideological effects of film begin to unfold.

Using Charles Sanders Peirce's sign trichotomy of icon–index–symbol to describe how signs are created, interact, and operate within films, an explanation may be proposed whereby we come to terms with the "impression of reality," the "suspension of disbelief," and the temporalities and spatialities of the cinematic place (Peirce 1955). The trichotomy is not, contrary to popular practice, a static typology of mutually exclusive signs. Icons, indices, and symbols are not sign-types per se, but rather three kinds of signification: iconization, indexicalization, and symbolization (Eco 1985). Any one film sign or frame may be constituted by all three processes but to varying degrees that, as discussed below, lie at the heart of a film's ability to encourage "make believe" (Leskosky 1988).

SIGN TYPE	SIGNIFIED BY	PROCESS	EXAMPLES
ICON	Resemblance	Can see	Photos, statues
INDEX	Causal connection	Can synthesize	Smoke → fire
SYMBOL	Social convention	Must learn	Words, rituals

As summarized in the diagram, the relationship between the signifier and the signified determines the type of signification. The relationship may be one of resemblance, causal connection, or conventional association (Berger 1984). When the relationship is one of resemblance, as in the case of a photograph, the sign is an *icon*; the signifier (photograph) resembles the signified (persons, object, or phenomenon represented by the photograph). An *index* is a sign whereby the signifier is physically, causally, or symptomatically connected to the signified. Smoke is, for example, an index of fire because the former is caused by the latter. A *symbol* is the most abstract form of sign because it must be learned; no physical/visual resemblance or causal connection need exist between the signifier and the signified. The written word "city" and its verbal pronunciation are, for instance, socially constructed abstract symbols standing for a particular kind of human settlement in the urban hierarchy. A film sign—a photographic image that stands for something else—may be signified in all three ways but to varying degrees with varying results.

For example, let us imagine one frame in a documentary film depicting a wide-angle shot of a city's skyline. Is the film image an icon, an index, or a symbol? How strong might be the impression of an "almost real" film city, and how much effort might be required to "willingly suspend" one's disbelief that the film city is merely a projected image of light and shadow rather than an actual city? The film city is signified by all three semiotic processes. The projected image is an iconic sign because it convincingly represents or resembles what viewers visually experience, or might expect to experience, as a city in the everyday material world. The image is also an index because it has a causal connection to the material world. The skyline on the screen has been created by light reflecting off a "real" city and hitting raw film stock to produce a representation on the film of the city. The city image may also be read as a symbol of any one of a number of socially constructed conventions: adventure, mystery, progress, temptation, and so forth. Because it is a documentary film, a so-called "live-action" authentic record of actual events using real people and objects in an actual space and time (Singleton 1986), spectators are more apt to accept the film city as real, which will lessen the effort necessary to suspend their disbelief.

Let us now consider the other end of the cinematic reality continuum. Imagine one frame in an animated film, a cartoon, depicting the skyline of a city. Let us again ask if the film image is an icon, an index, or a symbol. How strong might be the impression of an "almost real" film city? How much effort might be required to "willingly suspend" one's disbelief that the film city is merely a projected image rather than an actual skyline? The animated image, like the documentary image, is also constituted by the three modes of signification, but to differing degrees and with varied effects. The cartoon city is an iconic sign because it is recognizable as a city; it resembles a skyline, albeit a photographic image of a hand-drawn representation of a city's skyline. There remains a causal connection to the real world, but the indexical relationship is less direct. The city image on the screen is also created by light reflecting off an object in front of the camera, striking raw film stock, and producing a representation on the film of the skyline, but the city in front of the camera was never "real," it was a hand-drawn representation. The symbolism of the cartoon city is, therefore, heightened because its signification is more abstract: the city image is a filmic representation of a hand-drawn representation of an imaginary skyline. The city image may still be read as a symbol of adventure or mystery, for example, but a viewer who has learned to read cartoons will also expect the unexpected. Because the film is a cartoon, an "animated" series of photographed drawings of fictitious events, people, objects, times, and spaces (Singleton 1986), the spectator is less likely to accept the film city as "real" and anticipate, indeed he or she may enjoy, distortions in what one might visually experience, or expect to experience, as a city in the everyday material world. The impression of reality is diminished while the effort necessary to willingly suspend disbelief is intensified.

Although all film images, whether in documentaries or in cartoons, have varying degrees of iconicity, indexicality, and symbolism that function to heighten or diminish the impression of reality and the suspension of disbelief, the process of iconization is, perhaps, the single most important aspect in the fabrication of the cinematic place because the film image is a visual representation. Visible resemblance to the real world, not causal connection or social convention, renders the film image immediately legible (Jayyusi 1988). For the viewer to successfully engage in the "transference of reality," to leave the real world and enter, if only partially, the imaginary cinematic place, the spectacle on screen must resemble at least vaguely the spectacle of everyday life (Mitry 1963, p. 183; cf. Metz 1974, p. 11). "The spectacles of real life have motion," says Metz (1974, p. 7), so the power of film to encourage transference lies primarily in its ability to project an iconic illusion of movement.

The illusion is produced through a combination of artistry, technology, and sensory-deception. Part of the artistic beauty of cinema lies in the ability of a director and editor to successfully assemble a series of shots or scenes into a "montage" to give the spectator an impression of continuous movement (Baudry 1974; Mamet 1991). The perceptual-cognitive processes that enable or compel spectators to construe movement when a series of static, photographic images (icons) are projected onto a screen, at twenty-four frames per second, is not fully understood (Anderson and Anderson 1978; Nichols and Lederman 1978; Laughlin, McManus, and D'Aquili 1990). Nevertheless, the rapid succession of iconic signs is, for all intents and purposes, interpreted as motion, and motion is used by both filmmaker and film viewer to signify film space and time, give continuity and unity to the film narrative, and structure the cinematic place (Fell 1975).

"Motion" pictures are signs with a high degree of iconicity because they convincingly resemble movement in the real world, but why should movement encourage an impression of reality and a state of disbelief unattainable in another visual medium, such as painting or still photography? Metz argues that motion increases the sense of objective reality in three ways (1974, pp. 7–9). First, because movement is part of the everyday experience of life, the appearance of objects and people moving through space and time on the screen promotes a sense of "live" action, a "real" event. Second, motion imparts a sense of corporeality, depth, and volume to the film image that still images cannot evoke; it makes a flat surface appear three dimensional. Finally, motion in cinema is experienced as motion in the real world. In other words, the visual experience of motion in cinema cannot be distinguished from the visual experience of motion in the real world: cinematic motion is not real but there is a real presence of motion in cinema.

Several techniques can be used to represent motion, all of which foster a sense of movement through space and time for the viewer (Leskosky 1988; Bordwell 1991). A live-action film, such as a documentary, photographs events in front of the camera (a "profilmic event"), which are then projected as a moving representation of the actual event. A cartoon, however, produces movement where none had existed in empirical reality. By photographing a series of individual drawings, each depicting a slightly different pose and/or perspective, and then projecting them as a rapid and unified collection of images, a visual sense of motion is produced, not re-produced. The position and movement of the camera can also create a sense of motion that represents space in different ways. "Low-angle," "pan," "tilt," and "tracking" shots, for example, define not only the space of the image but also the perceptual position or perspective of the spectator. The impression of motion can also be accelerated or slowed by running the film through the camera at speeds greater or lesser than the normal twenty-four frames per second. Time is, therefore, also affected by motion; indeed, motion is time. The speed of the camera movement and the duration and order of film images may, for example, reinforce, modify, or shift the sense of time. Whether produced by profilmic or animated events, camera movement, or special effects, motion plays a crucial role in defining the experience of film space and time.

The Pleasure of Geographic Omnipresence

TYPE	TIME	SPACE	GEOGRAPHY
Subjective	Experience of time (Temporality)	Experience of space (Spatiality)	Of film → Cinematic Place
Fictitious	Era, day, night	Setting, location	In film → Portrayal of Place
Objective	Clock time	Screen, seating	Of theater → Site of Spectator

Source: Inspired by Fell 1975, pp. 57–81.

If successful, the iconic images of form and motion promote a kind of spatial and temporal transference that encourages the fabrication of the cinematic place, a place that is, in postmodern parlance, *heterotopic*. As summarized in the diagram, there are several types of time, space, and geography operating within the film environment. There is the objective sense of time and space in the material environment of the movie theater. The film commences, plays, and ends in what might loosely be called objective "clock time," with the viewer physically seated a certain distance from the screen inside a tangible movie theater. When the lights dim and the projector commences, the viewer is likely to become less conscious of the screen edges, the curtains, the auditorium, and other spectators; the geography in the film unfolds. Through the use of iconic images, fictitious times, spaces, and places are portrayed on screen; the psychological distance between film and spectator wanes. The deprivation of clues to the passage of "real" time, combined with such filmic tropes as a flipping calendar signifying the passage of time or period costumes depicting a past era, will entice viewers to discard objective or clock time and synchronize their inner sense of time with that expressed on the screen. By virtue of being enclosed in a dark, windowless theater, viewers are also denied evidence of the physical space they occupy beyond their immediate person. The iconic images of other settings and the illusion of motion projected onto the screen encourage viewers to dismiss objective or immediate space and enlarge their subjective sense of space to include that space portrayed before them; the geography of film unfurls.

By juxtaposing signs signifying other times and spaces, therefore, film promotes expansions and compressions in the viewer's temporal and spatial sensibilities; boundaries of time and space may become permeable and blurred. The viewer is simultaneously inside and outside the film, construing both fantasy and reality, switching back and forth across distances, visiting various settings and times, experiencing what Fell has termed a kind of "geographic omnipresence" (1975, p. 63), without ever leaving his or her seat. This interface—a kind of contradictory, composite place of the real and the imagined, of other times and spaces—is heterotopic: a space "capable of juxtaposing in a single real place several sites that are in themselves incompatible" (Foucault 1986, p. 25; cf. Soja 1989, p. 17). For those willing to engage in the suspension of disbelief, a state of mind made so easy by the verisimilitude of the icons and illusion of motion, their temporalities and spatialities may collapse into one schizophrenic, albeit pleasurable, present where the boundaries of past, present, and future, of here and there, are distorted into one heterotopic "now" and "everywhere."

The cinematic place is a peculiar situation, straddling the real and the unreal. Viewers do not seriously believe they transcend physical space and objective time, whereby they "disconnect" with the real world, as Mitry suggests (1963, p. 183; cf. Metz 1974, p. 11), and completely reconnect with another. The transference of reality is intermittent at best. Spectators are spatial and temporal hypocrites engaged in a form of play that requires what Lotman calls "a two-fold experience"—simultaneously forgetting and not forgetting that the experience is imaginary in origin (1976, p. 17). This dual relationship can create a complex semiotic situation whereby distinctions between the real and the imaginary are difficult, if not impossible, to make. The time and space portrayed on the screen are indeed imaginary, but the temporal and spatial experience is genuine. Much of the power and the ideological effects of film are found, consequently, in the dubious meanings constructed through the experience of film, an experience that is first and foremost geographical.

The Power and Ideology of (Mis)representation

The power and ideological effects of the cinematic place are not simply found in the content or connotations of the film image and the narrative they help to create (e.g., stereotyped gender roles, the moral of the tale), but in the very fabrication of the iconic forms and illusion of motion that encourage the temporalities and spatialities of film. Space and time comprise the framework within which people order their experiences (Lynch 1972, p. 241) and the film experience is no different; space and time constitute the abstract canvas of the cinematic place. The "scenography," as Bordwell so eloquently terms film space (1991, p. 229), is not a passive backdrop but a powerful agent in structuring the film experience. Moreover, the signification of film time and space—the social and technical processes whereby light and shadow are taken as standing for another time and space (something else)—is, itself, ideologically charged. Perhaps the power of film to (re)produce society's norms, values, and mores lies in its ability to misrepresent that which it stands for in a subtle, almost invisible, manner. That power is first exercised in the signification of film space.

"Power" is, in very broad terms, an asymmetrical social relationship whereby one person, group, or institution has the ability to influence, if not determine, how other people, groups, or institutions act (Abercrombie et al. 1988a). If power is exercised in a way that excludes the participation of other people, groups, or institutions, then the relationship may be described as one of "domination." "Ideology" is a process that facilitates the pursuit of particular interests and sustains specific relations of domination. In semiotic terms, ideology is a " '*system of signification which facilitates the pursuit of particular interests*' and sustains specific '*relations of domination*' " (Thompson 1981, 1984; cf. Gregory 1986, p. 214). Signification is necessarily ideological because the process of making meanings intrinsically excludes other meanings, and the social conventions that enable the sharing of meanings are themselves ideologically framed. All signs are ideologically laden, therefore, because the process of signification is a form of ideological discourse (Eyles and Evans 1987). Signs are a vehicle for the exercise of power and domination that may be achieved and maintained through a number of ways: force, persuasion, consensus, or by an appeal to authority (Wrong 1979).

The power of filmmakers lies in their ability to dictate the fabrication of the film, to script and sculpt its presentation, and then project it to a captive audience who are unable to participate in the production of the images before them. The connotation or signified of the signs and the narrative they comprise is the most obvious manifestation of the way ideology operates through film (Thompson 1990, pp. 60–66). The meanings attributable to the film image, intentional or not, may legitimize existing ways of doing or thinking by depicting characters, gender roles, and social relations as "correct" and "natural," thereby excluding or perhaps denigrating other alternatives. The underlying social values and mores portrayed may, furthermore, be obscured by special effects and spectacles. Clearly filmmakers wheel immense power in the shaping of the cinematic place through the ordering and content (meaning) of the film signs they select, and in this sense, they may dominate spectators.

The power of the film medium lies in its capacity to hide the mechanics of its own production. A less obvious and far more subtle means of ideological expression is found in the fabrication of the actual image or signifier that stands for "something else." In other words, the light-and-shadow that signifies or constitutes the signified or connotation (meaning) of a film image is itself ideologically charged. Signifiers may be said to dominate the spectator in two ways. First, the production or signification of the film image is not a direct relationship between spectator and screen; there is always the presence of a hidden third factor: the camera (Metz 1975). Spectators cannot know what technical preparation went into the presentation of the projected image. The film medium empowers the filmmaker and disempowers the audience by concealing special effects, lighting, makeup, filtered lenses, and the staging of people, objects, and events in front of the camera (Barthes 1982). Second, because the production of the image is hidden, the relationship between the signifier and the signified can be faked and subsequently misinterpreted by an audience persuaded by the authority they ascribe to their own sight that what is presented on screen has a resemblance to the *real* world. The ability to convince through iconic resemblance and the illusion of motion, while masking the production of its own signifier, intensifies the ideological effects of the cinematic place by promoting objectification, reification, alienation, and dissimulation (Abercrombie et al. 1988b, 1988c). The so-called magic of the silver screen is a form of objectification whereby spectators render cultural creations that embody human creativity separate from their human creators (e.g., real people, not staged actors, leaping tall buildings). The images may be reified and alienated if viewed as natural or autonomous entities beyond human control (e.g., the popular actor as God-like figure). The dominant position of the film image relative to the spectator may also be concealed or dissimulated by presenting itself as something it is not.

What the film image is not is a reproduction of reality. Unlike the early film enthusiasts of the twentieth century, contemporary theorists now recognize that film does not reflect reality but images (Baudry 1974). Film images may resemble the "something" that they stand for, but they are not the "something." They merely have an iconic, indexical, and/or symbolic relationship with whatever they stand for. In every kind of visualization, be it a sketch, a painting, or a photograph, there is a degree of resemblance or iconicity, but some signs such as those in film, particularly documentaries, also have a high degree of indexicality. The masking of the signifiers' production and the authority ascribed to the iconic forms and illusion of motion may make the suspension of disbelief so effortless, and the impression of reality so closely reminiscent of the visual experience of the real world, that film images may be misconstrued as having a point-to-point conformity with objective reality: a direct, indexical relationship with the empirical world. Paradoxically, it is through such conformity with the real that the film sign gains its power to misrepresent reality. This conformity is, as Baudrillard observes, "the evil demon of images" (1987). When the distance between the signifier and signified diminishes to the point where the film sign does not stand for anything other than itself, when there is a breakdown in the signifying chain such that the image is self-referential, the meanings signified are not real but *hyperreal* (Baudrillard 1983). In other words, when the icons resemble perfectly something that never existed, then the images are not reproductions of the real, but "simulacra"— copies for which there are no originals.

In essence, therefore, the power of film may lie (quite literally) in its ability to misrepresent. This power is exercised by filmmakers to sustain an ideology of make-believe. This ideology is achieved through a medium capable of masking the production of its own signifiers. These signifiers dominate an audience whose willing suspension of disbelief and impression of reality are fabricated through their own iconization of film signs and the authority that viewers attribute to their own sense of sight. If successful, these combined semiotic processes may promote temporal and spatial sensations that constitute a heterotopic milieu wherein distinctions between the real and the imaginary, the reproduction and the simulation, may be difficult, if not impossible, to discern. To engage in the cinematic place is an act of "misrecognition" (Doane 1991, p. 19) founded upon misrepresentation. The power of the film spectator must lie, therefore, in the ability to experience film critically.

Coming Attractions: More Questions, More Maps

Studying film for its aesthetic beauty and its means of technical and artistic production is a worthy endeavor in and of itself, but not for the geographer. The social, political, and spatial implications of film must surely be our primary quest. If this is the case, then the only ideological effects of film that matter, that have any significance for studying the cultural politics of film, are those felt outside the theater. Perhaps the fundamental issues should revolve around the values, mores, social structures, and geography portrayed in film, and their impact, if any, on the real world. What happens, for instance, if and when the meanings attributed to images on the screen are transferred by an audience to the material and social world? Does the hyperreal—has the hyperreal— become a model for reality? If film images can influence clothing styles, musical tastes, toys, and our vocabulary, is it not naive to think they do not participate in the structuring of our values, our social relations, and perhaps our behavior in, and the construction of, the *real* world? Is there not a geography *from* film awaiting our exploration?

Apprehending the society–film relationship and its implications for the larger social, political, and geographical realms of which it is a part is, perhaps, the major goal of a geography of film. Like conventional film theorists, we are concerned with the construction and narrative of film and the portrayal on screen of spaces, places, people, power, mores, and values, but only as a means of understanding the geographical experiences of film and the possible ramifications for the geography beyond the theater. It is almost trite to argue, as I have, that films can lie, that the film image can distort empirical reality, that real life may imitate "reel" art; it is quite another matter to understand how these occur. This process is important if we are to understand how the geographical experience of film operates, if we are to begin our critical reading of film. Many more questions need to be asked and more maps need to be made.

In this preliminary mapping of the cinematic landscape, I have provided an explanation of the way an iconic film image may encourage spectators to experience an ideologically charged time and space, a center of felt value, that is constituted on an abstract canvas of light and shadow. I employed a semiotic approach as a means of understanding the fabrication of the film image and its role in creating a cinematic place. Interpreting film is a slippery endeavor made all the more daunting, as I have shown, when the complexities of (mis)representation in film are made explicit. In an age where the image is said to dominate, in a "society of spectacles," where media-environments are becoming more sophisticated, and fantasy increasingly permeates our social and material geographies, there is much to learn from a geography of film.

Acknowledgments

This paper was made possible through a postdoctoral fellowship at Mc-Master University sponsored by the Social Sciences and Humanities Research Council of Canada.

References

Abercrombie, N., S. Hill, and B. S. Turner. 1988a. Power. In *Dictionary of Sociology*, pp. 192–93. London: Penguin.

Abercrombie, N., S. Hill, and B. S. Turner. 1988b. Alienation. In *Dictionary of Sociology*, p. 8. London: Penguin.

Abercrombie, N., S. Hill, and B. S. Turner. 1988c. Reification. In *Dictionary of Sociology*, p. 205. London: Penguin.

Adams, P.C. 1992. Television as gathering place. *Annals of the Association of American Geographers* 82: 117–35.

Aitken, S.C. 1991. A transactional geography of the image-event: The films of Scottish director Bill Forsyth. *Transactions, Institute of British Geographers* 16: 105–18.

Allen, J. 1991. Self-Reflexivity in Documentary. In R. Burnett, editor, *Explorations in Film Theory*, pp. 103–20. Bloomington: Indiana University Press.

Anderson, J., and B. Anderson. 1978. Motion Perception in Motion Pictures. In T. de Lauretis and S. Heath, editors, *The Cinematic Apparatus*, pp. 76–95. London: Macmillan.

Arnheim, R. 1957. *Film as Art*. Berkeley: University of California Press.

Barthes, R. 1982. The Photographic Message. In S. Sontag, editor, *A Barthes Reader*, pp. 194–210. New York: Hill and Wang.

Baudrillard, J. 1983. *Simulations*. New York: Semiotext(e).

Baudrillard, J. 1987. *The Evil Demon of Images*. Sydney: University of Sydney Press.

Baudry, J. 1974. Ideological effects of the basic cinematographic apparatus. *Film Quarterly* 28: 39–47.

Berger, A. A. 1984. *Signs in Contemporary Culture*. New York: Longman.

Berland, D. I. 1982. Disney and Freud: Walt meets the id. *Journal of Popular Culture* 15: 93–104.

Billinge, M. 1986. Place. In R. J. Johnson, D. Gregory, and D. M. Smith, editors, *The Dictionary of Human Geography*, p. 346. Oxford: Basil Blackwell.

Boggs, J. 1978. *The Art of Watching Films*. Don Mills: Benjamin/Cummings.

Bollag, B. 1988. Words on the screen: The problem of the linguistic sign in the cinema. *Semiotica* 72: 71–90.

Bordwell, D. 1991. Camera Movement and Cinematic Space. In R. Burnett, editor, *Explorations in Film Theory*, pp. 229–246. Bloomington: Indiana University Press.

Burgess, J., and J. Gold. 1985. *Geography, the Media and Popular Culture.* New York: St. Martin's Press.

Collier, J. 1967. *Visual Anthropology.* New York: Holt, Reinhart, and Winston.

Cosgrove, D. E. 1984. *Social Formation and Symbolic Landscape.* London: Croom Helm.

Cosgrove, D., and S. Daniels. 1988. Introduction: Iconography and Landscape. In D. Cosgrove and S. Daniels, editors, *The Iconography of Landscape*, pp. 1–10. New York: Cambridge University Press.

Denzin, N. K. 1985. Towards an interpretation of semiotics and history. *Semiotica* 54: 335–50.

Doane, M. 1991. Misrecognition and Identity. In R. Burnett, editor, *Explorations in Film Theory*, pp. 15–25. Bloomington: Indiana University Press.

Dodwell, P. C. 1956. Studies of the Visual System. In B.M. Foss, editor, *New Horizons in Psychology*, 15–44. Harmondsworth: Penguin.

Eco, U. 1976. *A Theory of Semiotics.* Bloomington: Indiana University Press.

Eco, U. 1985. Producing Signs. In M. Blonsky, editor, *On Signs*, pp. 176–83. Baltimore: Johns Hopkins University Press.

Eyles, J., and M. Evans. 1987. Popular consciousness, moral ideology, and locality. *Environment and Planning D: Society and Space* 5: 39–71.

Eyles, J., and W. Peace. 1990. Signs and symbols in Hamilton: An iconology of Steeltown. *Geografiska Annaler* 72: 73–88.

Fell, J. L. 1975. *Film: An Introduction.* New York: Praeger.

Fiske, J. 1989. *Reading the Popular.* Boston: Unwin Hyman.

Foucault, M. 1986. Of other spaces. *Diacritics* 16: 22–27. Translated from French by Jay Miskowiec.

Gold, J. R. 1980. *An Introduction to Behavioural Geography.* New York: Oxford University Press.

Gottdiener, M. 1982. Disneyland: A utopian urban space. *Urban Life* 11: 139–62.

Gregory, D. 1986. Ideology. In R. J. Johnson, D. Gregory and D. M. Smith, editors, *The Dictionary of Human Geography*, pp. 214–15. Oxford: Basil Blackwell.

Jakle, J. A. 1987. *The Visual Elements of Landscape.* Amherst: University of Massachusetts Press.

Jayyusi, L. 1988. Toward a socio-logic of the film text. *Semiotica* 68: 271–96.

Jules-Rosette, B. 1990. Semiotics and cultural diversity: Entering the 1990s. *American Journal of Semiotics* 7: 5–26.

Kaplan, E. A. 1983. *Women and Film: Both Sides of the Camera.* London: Methuen.

Laughlin, C. D., J. McManus, and E. D'Aquili. 1990. *Brain, Symbol and Experience.* Boston: Shambhala.

Leskosky, R. 1988. The Illusion of Reality and the Reality of Illusion in Animated Film. In T. Prewitt, J. Deely, and K. Haworth, editors, *Semiotics 1988*, pp. 460–65. Lanham, Md.: University Press of America.

Lotman, J. 1976. *Semiotics of Cinema.* Ann Arbor: University of Michigan Press.

Lynch, K. 1972. *What Time Is This Place?* Cambridge: MIT Press.

Mamet, D. 1991. *On Directing Film.* New York: Penguin.

Marsh, J. 1985. Postcard landscapes: An exploration in method. *Canadian Geographer* 29: 265–67.

Metz, C. 1974. *Film Language: A Semiotics of the Cinema.* Chicago: University of Chicago Press.

Metz, C. 1975. The imaginary signifier. *Screen* 16: 14–76.

Mitry, J. 1963. *Esthétique et Psychologie du Cinéma*, vol.1, pp. 182–92. Paris: Editions Universitaires. Vol. 1, pp. 182–92.

Nichols, B., and Lederman, S. J. 1978. Flicker and Motion in Film. In T. de Lauretis and S. Heath, editors, *The Cinematic Apparatus*, pp. 96–105. London: Macmillan.

Osborne, B. S. 1988. Fact, symbol and message: Three approaches to literary landscape. *Canadian Geographer* 32: 267–69.

Peirce, C. S. 1955. *Philosophical Writings of Peirce*, edited by J. Buchler. New York: Dover.

Pocock, D., editor. 1981. *Humanistic Geography and Literature.* London: Croom Helm.

Porteous, J. D. 1990. *Landscapes of the Mind.* Toronto: University of Toronto Press.

Sandberg, L. A., and J. S. Marsh. 1988. Literary landscapes: Geography and literature. *Canadian Geographer* 32: 266–76.

Schnathmeier, S. 1987. The unity of place in Elia Kazan's film version of "A Streetcar Named Desire" by Tennessee Williams. *ARS Semiotica* 10: 83–93.

Sebeok, T. A., editor. 1986. *Encyclopedic Dictionary of Semiotics.* New York: Mouton de Gruyter.

Singleton, R. S. 1986. *Film Maker's Dictionary.* Beverly Hills: Lone Eagle.

Smith, D. 1988. Towards an Interpretative Human Geography. In J. Eyles and D. Smith, editors, *Qualitative Methods in Human Geography*, pp. 255–67. Oxford: Polity Press.

Soja, E. W. 1989. *Postmodern Geographies: The Reassertion of Space in Critical Social Theory.* London: Verso.

Sykes, J .B., editor. 1982. *The Concise Oxford Dictionary.* Oxford: Clarendon.

Thompson, J. B. 1981. *Critical Hermeneutics.* Cambridge: Cambridge University Press.

Thompson, J. B. 1984. *Studies in the Theory of Ideology.* Berkeley: University of California Press.

Thompson, J. B. 1990. *Ideology and Modern Culture.* Stanford: Stanford University Press.

Tuan, Y. 1975. Place: An experiential perspective. *The Geographical Review* 65: 151–65.

Tuan, Y. 1977. *Space and Place: The Perspective of Experience.* London: Edward Arnold.

Tuan, Y. 1991. Language and the making of place: a narrative-descriptive approach. *Annals of the Association of American Geographers* 81: 684–96.

Winfried, N. 1990. *Handbook of Semiotics.* Bloomington: Indiana University Press.

Wolfenstein, M., and N. Leites. 1970. *The Movies: A Psychological Study.* New York: Atheneum.

Wollen, P. 1972. *Signs and Meaning in the Cinema.* Bloomington: Indiana University Press.

Worth, S. 1981. *Studying Visual Communication.* Philadelphia: University of Pennsylvania Press.

Wrong, D. II. 1979. *Power: Its Form, Bases and Uses.* Oxford: Basil Blackwell.

Zavarzadeh, M. 1991. *Seeing Films Politically.* Albany: State University of New York.

Part Two
Making People and Places

4

Jerusalem, Dover Beach, and Kings Cross: Imagined Places as Metaphors of the British Class Struggle in *Chariots of Fire* and *The Loneliness of the Long-Distance Runner*

Martyn J. Bowden

The mind is its own place, and in itself
Can make a heav'n of hell, a hell of heav'n.

—John Milton
Paradise Lost, Book I

Alan Sillitoe's award-winning novella *The Loneliness of the Long-Distance Runner* (Sillitoe 1959) is a classic example of the neo-Marxist critique of sport (Guttmann 1978). A young offender is made to run cross-country at a borstal (prison for young offenders) and trained like a racehorse for a "Derby" between the best runners in Her Majesty's borstals. Leading the race in the final stretch, he pulls up just short of the winning post, refusing to play the game. In effect, in a long and deeply premeditated act, Sillitoe's runner, like the neo-Marxist critics, condemns organized sport as a perversion of the human spirit and rejects the Sports Establishment as an institution (Guttmann 1978). The film version of the novella, directed by Tony Richardson with screenplay by Sillitoe, is a classic of British realism (1962), more Marxist in interpretation (Guttmann 1978) than the short story. In both versions the working-class antihero, tempted by the Establishment with the perks of a career in running and a consequent middle-class life, trains hard for an important race. In the novella the race is against other borstals. In the movie it is against the best of a prominent English Public School (private prepschool for the upper classes). This change in the story offers the writers the chance to introduce the question of privilege and to emphasize the inequities of the class system. Only at the last minute does the runner realize that his running has been used as a means to effect his socialization and that unwittingly he has almost been inculcated into the militarism, nationalism, and imperialism of the Establishment, symbolized by the "types" in the "posh seats" exhorting him to breast the tape.

In this British film about runners a number of additional themes are introduced and these were adopted with reverence and developed extensively in the other British film about runners, the Academy Award-winning *Chariots of Fire* (1981). The main story of *Chariots* and of *Loneliness* is the battle between young manhood and the power elite. Elders of the English Establishment attempt to divert three runners from their life's purpose. One is tempted by privileges proffered to win a race (Colin Smith in *Loneliness*). Another is browbeaten by demands that he give up his professional coach and thereby prospectively lose a race (Harold Abrahams in *Chariots*). The third is bombarded with arguments by aristocrats as to why he should deny his principles and run in a race on the Sabbath (Eric Liddell in *Chariots*). All three resist the pressures applied by the Establishment, cross swords with the symbolic representatives of the King (Queen) of England, His (Her) Majesty's Government, and win, each in his own way. The code for this main story in *Chariots* is Kings Cross, London's functionalist/modernist railway station that is a massive symbol of the age of manufacturing and the symbolic gateway to the British Empire for Scots. Kings Cross also serves as metaphor for the skirmishes among the runners themselves.

The grand metaphor of both films is William Blake's Jerusalem in England. The great English poet-painter's visionary Jerusalem is an imagined ideal place that is the antithesis to Britain's "dark Satanic mills" of the Industrial Revolution (beginning in about 1750) and to the hellish cities epitomized by London (Kazin 1946, p. 1216; Schorer 1946, pp. 248–49; Williams 1985; pp. 148–49). The hymn called "Jerusalem" is played facetiously and to give poignancy to the scenes of living hell in "the unholy city" (Williams 1985, p. 149) appearing simultaneously on the screen in *Loneliness*. The code word "Jerusalem" is sung twice by the young prisoners. In *Chariots* the title itself conjures up the code word "Jerusalem" to British viewers, and the word is again sung twice, this time by an ecumenical congregation at the end of the movie. This confirms that the heroes beat the Establishment and built their holy cities.

The poet William Cowper (1731–1800) wrote "God made the country and man made the town" (Darby 1953), and this idea of the pervasiveness of God in the English countryside and of His absence from British industrial cities is made explicit in Blake's "Jerusalem" (1820). Close to God and with their bodies made sound by running and training in God's country, the runners think more clearly than when they are in cities, and they win their races. The satanic mills, products of the chariots of fire (machines) of the Industrial Revolution, are also the antithesis of the English pastoral embedded in Blake's "Jerusalem." In both movies the liberating effects of the English countryside and of the pastoral are extended to the beach as the place of innocence and escape, and particularly to "Dover Beach" (1867) of the poet Matthew Arnold (Trilling 1949). This most famous beach in English poetry becomes a visual code in *Chariots*. It is the obvious background to the soul-searching of Eric Liddell and to his momentous and inspirational decision. It is also a metaphor of the cycles of life and faith.

To Blake Jerusalem was, above all, a symbol of freedom, a place of individual regeneration standing in opposition to the endemic institutions and social tyranny of the Establishment in his time (1757–1827). All three major runners in their battles with the English Establishment epitomize Blake's position on freedom and institutions to the extent that each runner makes a Faustian compact with his own version of Mephistopheles to beat the institutions of the Establishment arrayed against him. But as in Blake's cosmology and in his "heavenly cartography" (Schorer 1946, p. 113) derived from Swedenborg, so in the runners' cosmic maps there is often little to choose between heaven and earth and hell. "Blake frequently wiped out the old spatial and temporal distinctions between heaven and earth, since God is in man here and now, and he abolished hell entirely" (Schorer 1946, p. 146). Furthermore, Blake's major criticism of his spiritual father, John Milton, in Blake's poem of that name prefaced by his most famous poem/hymn "Jerusalem," is that Milton in *Paradise Lost* (Hughes 1935) "had put himself on the side of the angels, the repressive forces, when in reality he was 'of the Devil's party without knowing it,' the party of the revolutionary prolific" (Schorer 1946, pp. 343–44). In *Chariots*, two of the devils are revolutionary thinkers and the visionaries of the future in athletics, and the repressive forces are the institutions: national, religious, and Olympic.

One objective of this chapter is to identify and demonstrate how a symbolic geography and cosmology, much of it derived from the poetry and writings of William Blake and Matthew Arnold and also from the Faust legend, is woven into the narrative of the two related films, *Chariots* and *Loneliness*. A second objective is to show how the pervasive class struggle in Britain, epitomized in the personal battles of the young with the power elite of the English Establishment is deeply embedded in the films' symbolism of imagined places (Jerusalem, Dover Beach, Kings Cross) and imagined environments (the pastoral, milltown) as metaphors.

Jerusalem: Heaven in England's Green and Pleasant Land

To Americans the derivation of the title of the film *Chariots of Fire* may remain a mystery even after several viewings. The phrase occurs as "chariot of fire" at the end of the last line of the third verse of the hymn sung in the memorial service for Harold Abrahams that ends the film. The English, by contrast, needed neither to hear the hymn nor to see the film to place the phrase. To them it is as familiar as "the rockets' red glare" or any other phrase in "The Star-Spangled Banner" is to an American. "Chariot of fire" comes from "a boldly idealistic song" that from the "1920s assumed almost the position of a secondary British National Anthem" (*Oxford Companion to Music* 1970, p. 537). It is sung as a morning hymn more frequently and with more gusto than any other hymn in the assembly halls of the state schools. It is short (four verses, two minutes), nationalistic, conveniently nondenominational, and probably the only song whose words are known by heart, by most, if not all, schoolchildren in England.

As a preface to the lengthy story-poem "Milton," the untitled poem beginning "And did those feet in ancient time, Walk upon England's mountains green?" was written by William Blake. As a Romantic critic of Utilitarianism, Blake fought alongside the new English working class "against exploitive and oppressive relationships intrinsic to industrial capitalism" (Thompson 1968, p. 915). His vision, expressed as a question in the untitled poem, is of "Jerusalem builded here, Among these dark Satanic mills?" His quest is expressed in the last verse: "I will not cease from Mental Fight, Nor shall my Sword sleep in my hand, Till we have built Jerusalem, In England's green and pleasant Land" (Blake in Kazin 1946, p. 412). Blake, whose lifetime is often cited as spanning the decisive period in the pattern of changes that we call the Industrial Revolution, was passionately committed to the tragedy of the period and, in the era of the making of the English working class, was the last great English poet who spoke to all classes (Bronowski 1944; Williams 1961). After Blake, writes Edward Thompson (1968, p. 915), "no mind was at home in both (high and popular) cultures, nor had the genius to interpret the two traditions (Romantics and Radical craftsmen) to each other."

The words of Blake's visionary poem were set to music by Hubert Parry in 1915–16 for the "Fight for Right" movement in the Queens Hall, London, on the encouragement of Robert Bridges, England's poet laureate who hailed from Lancashire with its cotton mills, coalfields, steel works, and chemical industries. As a hymn it later "made a great impression when sung at the meeting in the Royal Albert Hall, in March 1918, to celebrate the attaining of the final stage in the 'Votes for Women' campaign" (*Oxford Companion to Music* 1970, p. 537). Almost immediately it became known by the English everywhere as "Jerusalem" (even though Blake had already given that title to a long story-poem). As an "intense vision of a world other than the real industrial England . . . it has long been a Socialist hymn of millions of its working people" (Kazin 1946, p. 32). The words of the poem "without direct mention, recall to our minds the days of infant factory labour, child chimney-climbing sweeps, farm labourers at ten shillings a week and men transported for life for poaching a hare," reports the *Oxford Companion to Music* (1970, p. 537).

It was director Tony Richardson's inspiration in *Loneliness* to use the words and music of "Jerusalem" at critical junctures to emphasize that for many of the English working class the aspiration to "build Jerusalem among these dark Satanic mills" was still as unrealistic as it had been in Blake's lifetime. "Jerusalem" is there in the background as the runner's hardworking trade unionist father dies alone (of industrial cancer?) in a rudimentary bedroom in a gray and boxlike prefabricated house, ominously overtopped on all sides by towering mills. The music plays again as the prefab, one of thousands built to house those "bombed out" during World War II, is torn apart by "coppers" who invade the home without warrant and, in effect, make the home a prison. And it is "Jerusalem" that plays as the prisoners at the bottom of the disciplinary heap, the runner Colin Smith the lowest among them because he refused to win the cross-country cup for the governor, engage in the meaningless task of disassembling World War II gas masks in a cramped Nissen hut. Interestingly, Richardson freezes the prisoners in a still while on the soundtrack the music of "Jerusalem" rolls on, suggesting that they are locked hopelessly and eternally into their place in British society.

The speaking of the code word "Jerusalem" is given to someone unobtrusive who does not understand its meaning, in this case the prison chaplain who is so out of touch with the English working-class life of the prisoners that he does not know that the hymn is secular and rarely, if ever, sung in churches of any denomination: "Now, lads, I want you to join us in singing that fine old hymn you've heard so often in chapel, Jerusalem."[1] The words and music of "Jerusalem" come together as all the boys in the prison's assembly hall sing it with the gusto they learned in the schools. But the pictures that accompany the singing show Colin's erstwhile adversary, Stacey, being brought back in handcuffs in a police car, and then being beaten up in a prison cell underneath the assembly hall where the prisoners sing of building "Jerusalem in England's green and pleasant land." In each instance the ideal open pastoral space of the England envisioned in "Jerusalem" is contrasted with the tightly confined spaces in which the state and its minions have the working class trapped. Throughout the film the symbols reminiscent of the Industrial Revolution pervade and dominate the landscape: the towering factory chimneys, gloomy terrace housing and prefabs, dark and dank railway stations filled with soot, trains belching smoke and steam, quarries gouged into the hillsides, high brick walls with broken glass cemented on the top, barbed-wire and chain-link fences keeping people out. The only escape from the living hell of the dark satanic mills of Nottingham for the characters in the film is the brief trip to the beach at Skegness and to Ruxton Towers Borstal, facetiously called by the prisoners a "holiday camp."[2]

"Jerusalem" is a boldly idealistic vision of a better place and society with wrongs righted. For the cynical Colin Smith in the novella of *Loneliness* there is no Jerusalem. His action that ends the story is long premeditated and he uses his running time to think only of himself and of improving his skills as a thief (Sillitoe 1959, pp. 10–12). By contrast the Colin Smith of the movie is an embryonic Marxist ("share and share alike; all for one, one for all; united we stand, divided we fall") thinking about Jerusalem in England ("That's how most people live. I'm beginning to see that it should be altered"). The main wrong that needs to be righted in a future Jerusalem is that of the workers' "slaving [their] guts out so that the bosses can get all the profit. Seems all wrong to me." The solution is to give the workers the profits. This will happen if Colin has "anything to do with it." The problem is that he didn't "know where to start" until his flash of creativity in the last race.

The use of "Jerusalem" as an alternative national anthem of the young was extended to the upper classes by director Lindsay Anderson in *If . . .* (1969), which deals with violent revolt by privileged students within the "prison" of their English Public School (Kael 1979). This opens the way for the use of "Jerusalem" as a code in the stories of upper- and middle-class runners in *Chariots*. The code is introduced in the film's title phrase and in the singing of the hymn that ends the movie. For both runners in *Chariots* and the governor in *Loneliness* the idea of Jerusalem in Britain is bound up with the pervasive British version of *mens sana in corpore sano* (a sound mind in a sound body) introduced into the English Public Schools and to Oxford and Cambridge universities in the mid-nineteenth century. Good athletics were seen as the sine qua non of British power and Empire.[3] The best—Olympic winners—were heralded as kings and gods.

Aware of this weakness of the English and of the Establishment for Olympic winners, Harold Abrahams with his "arrows of desire" and his "chariot of fire" (Kazin 1946, p. 412) drove himself unmercifully. By winning the Olympic 100 meters, he removed all the obstructions blocking his entry into the "corridors of power" placed there by the Christian Establishment because of his Jewishness. His Jerusalem was, therefore, a selfish one: the keys to the kingdom ("England's green and pleasant Land") and a victor's crown in heaven. In *Loneliness* the governor's thinking on his own behalf and on Colin Smith's was somewhat similar. Both would move up the social and economic ladder if the governor's protégé "could represent his country at the Olympic Games . . . one of the best ideas that civilization ever had." And Colin could "have a great future ahead of [him] as an athlete," escaping from the satanic mills to a Jerusalem in the middle-class suburbs complete with "a great big Jaguar and a fancy tart answering . . . fan letters" (see also Sillitoe 1959, p. 34).

Eric Liddell's Jerusalem in *Chariots* is a new city of faith to be built in the shadow of the collieries and the steel mills of lowland Scotland, relying on the missionary activity and drawing power of Scotland's greatest athlete. Liddell is in the tradition of the "muscular-Christian" missionaries who came originally to the toughest working-class cities of England— Liverpool, Manchester, and East London—beginning in the 1860s. From their mission churches, these young athletic parsons out of Oxbridge revolutionized English sport, plugging Christ as they organized cricket, athletics, and soccer on church lands (Walvin 1975; Allison 1978; Mason 1980; Bowden 1993). It was these muscular Christian Jerusalems in working-class England—religion-based sporting communities led by young Public School and Oxbridge-educated athletes—that were models for the Glasgow Students' Evangelistic Union crusade that co-opted Liddell, an English (minor) public-schoolboy and Edinburgh University student, in the spring of 1923 (Magnusson 1981, pp. 32–34). The object of Liddell's muscular Christianity was "Scotland [who] pours out his Sons to labour at the Furnaces" (Blake in Kazin 1946, p. 463).[4]

In the year before the Olympics, Liddell runs and wins before crowds of cloth-capped workers on tracks dominated by the symbols of the Industrial Revolution: the pithead towers of the Scottish coalfields, coke ovens, grimy terrace houses.[5] In the driving rain he wins the race and the crowd stays on. Like Christ in the gospels, he talks in parables about ordinary things (Magnusson 1981, p. 34) such as winning a race, and asks "where does the power come from to see the race to its end?" The rains suddenly stop, the clouds clear, the sun comes out, and the heavenly answer is "the Countenance Divine" (Kazin 1946, p. 412) in Blake's "Jerusalem." In further answer to his question Liddell quotes Jesus: "Behold, the Kingdom of God is within you," and completes the parable: "If you commit yourself to the love of Christ, then that is how you run the straight race." Jerusalem is within the faithful wherever they are: Blake's "Jerusalem in every Man" (Bronowski 1944, p. 24).

There is another gloss on Liddell's Jerusalem. The filmmakers, in their research on the saintly Liddell, cannot help but have discovered that "at the peak of his athletics career, ministers wrote sermons about the goodness of his life, comparing him to Christ" and that "he came to live his life in a way which people, reminiscing over his incandescent memory, would over and over again call Christ-like" (Magnusson 1981, pp. 10, 33). And, indeed, there are suggestions in *Chariots* that Liddell is Christ at the Second Coming. He is the miracle worker changing driving rain to blazing sunshine. He is "set at God's right hand on high," his right hand clasped by the right hand of the already immortal Abrahams (God to Liddell's Christ) when raised on the shoulders of his fellow athletes after winning the Olympic 400 meters. A caption reveals that Liddell died in China in a Japanese internment camp. We need no more help from the filmmakers to "know" that Liddell was "crucified" by some Japanese Pontius Pilate known as a type from *The Bridge on the River Kwai* (1957).[6] If Liddell is Christ, then Jerusalem is where he lived, ran, and preached: the Scottish Lowlands, London 1923, Paris 1924, the Chinese missions at Tientsin and Siaochiang, and the camp at Weihsien (Magnusson 1981).

To Blake, and to the filmmakers and their runners, Jerusalem is a visionary place antithetical to the mills and cities of industrial and modern Britain. It is a place where humankind is free from the constraints of the institutions of Church and State, free from the repression of a class-ridden society, and free to worship and meet God without intermediaries.

The Effects of English Pastoral on the Runners

Deeply embedded in the idea of Blake's Jerusalem is the notion also that it is synonymous with pastoral Britain unspoilt by the Industrial Revolution and by its agents of landscape change, the steam and internal combustion engines: chariots of fire. When they go into the British countryside all three runners flourish. The working-class Colin Smith, whom his fellow cons immediately size up as a "miserable sort of a bloke," is smiling, carefree, and genuinely happy as he runs free in his early-morning training sessions through a carefully landscaped garden. His lonely figure plods over dewy pastures closely cropped by sheep and deer. A tall Scots pine or two and the occasional clump of beeches and elms dot the landscape. And then he is across the stream and into the trees. Borrowing from Leni Riefenstahl's marathon sequence in *Olympia* (1936), Richardson puts the camera in the runner's eyes and conveys a brilliant moving kaleidoscope of overarching branches and shimmering sunlight. Colin does a hop, step, and jump through puddles like a little kid, goes through the overarm bowling action of a cricketer (conjuring up images of that most pastoral scene, cricket on the English village green), and does a long backslide down a leafy bank. His flashbacks, as he lies there and as he runs subsequently, are all happy memories, particularly of his only other foray outside the dark satanic mills: to the open beaches and dunes of Skegness with his girlfriend, Audrey. Colin's times improve so much that the governor has Olympic aspirations for him and is confirmed in his simplistic belief that sound athletics make for reformed minds. And it is in that very same English landscape where Colin the thinker gets the inspiration to win by beating all comers to the winning post but refusing to cross the line. This solution to his problem produces the biggest smile of all. England's green and pleasant land works wonders on the city boy.

The influence of the pastoral is even more clearly specified in *Chariots*. Eric Liddell trained at the Powderhall track in Edinburgh. But the movie is at pains to show that with his curious running action "swinging his arms very high, bringing his knees well up, and throwing his head well back" (Magnusson 1981, p. 37), he is untrained and "runs like a wild animal" (Abrahams's characterization in *Chariots*). As such we see him run first on a field in the Highlands in his stockinged feet, street shirt, and long trousers with suspenders. Liddell is apparently dressed the same but with some sort of shoe when we see him, next running wild like a mountain goat or sheep ("the Holy Lamb of God on England's pleasant pastures seen?") on the steep and broken flanks of a mountain ("And did those feet . . . [run] . . . upon England's mountains green?"). And our final glimpses of his training are of his running unleashed with other animals (greyhounds?) on a vast and trackless beach left by the ebbtide.

The two members of the English elite train in two different versions of English pastoral. Lord Alexander Lindsay is a fictional adaptation from Lord David Burghley, England's gold-medal hurdler at the Amsterdam Olympics of 1928 and bronze medalist at Los Angeles in 1932 (Wallechinsky 1984, pp. 18, 56–57). Lindsay is heir-apparent to the estates of the Marquess of Exeter and the ultimate symbol of the gentleman athlete and amateur ("To me the whole thing's fun. I don't need it. Cast care aside and all that, what?"). His training hurdles are set up on an immaculately kept lawn that sweeps down from the front door of sumptuous Highbeck House (Weatherby 1981, p. 101) to an ornamental pond backed by flowering trees: an English pastoral idyll. Each of the hurdles has a glass of champagne set on it ("Well, Coote, I shed a drop I want to know. Touch but not spill, what?"). Clad in an expensive white dressing gown over his white athletics slip and shorts, the cigarette-smoking Lindsay has his servant, Mildred, bring him his spikes: the English lord training in his country estate.

Harold Abrahams, one-track-minded in his obsession to run them off their feet, is always seen training on a straight and narrow path. We see him first running the edges of a quadrangle in the College Dash, and then on a path across the greensward within the high walls of a Cambridge University quadrangle. Soon after, he runs down a tree-lined approach road to an English lordly estate, exhorted by well-dressed passengers in an open coupe. Abrahams is later seen on a carefully laid out, straight, grassy path between two long rows of tall elms. He runs with the hounds and their master dressed in black and white hunting attire: the quintessential sport of the landed aristocracy/gentry in their English countryside. Even the athletic meetings of Abrahams and the Cambridge quartet are held on a track bounded by grass and tall deciduous trees in open country, as is Abrahams's training with his coach, Mussabini. Nothing but the most carefully planned and planted English pastoral for the best-trained athlete in the land.[7]

The character and style of each of the major runners are determined by the type of pastoral environment in which each trains. And the training of all four runners in the English and Scottish countryside is critical to their victories.

The English Beach as Pastoral

One facet of the countryside that figures prominently in both movies is the beach. For the working class it has long been the place of temporary escape from the daily grind and drudgery of the life of milltown and coketown. Colin's financial windfall from his father's life insurance is immediately used ("easy come, easy go") to pay for an overnight trip to Nottingham's favorite seaside resort, Skegness. The effects on Colin of a dose of English pastoral are startling. He is pleasant, loving, open, and sincere as he reminisces and confides in Audrey. The Colin of Skegness is smart in dress and in ideas, serious and mature in looking to the future, and thoughtful about power, justice, and society.

Dover Beach and the Sea of Faith

The beach at Dover has a similar effect on Liddell in *Chariots*. Faced with a potentially life-shattering crisis, he thinks things through and makes the correct decision for him. With courage he decides not to run on the Sabbath in the Paris Olympics: a momentous decision that sends shockwaves throughout the Christian world.[8] The decision is placed at Dover because Matthew Arnold in "Dover Beach" likened the ebb and flow of faith to "the grating roar Of pebbles which the waves suck back, and fling At their return, up the high strand, Begin, and cease, and then again begin, With tremulous cadence slow, and bring The eternal note of sadness in." The poet was writing in despair that "the sea of faith . . . once . . . at the full" was now "retreating . . . down . . . the naked shingles of the world" (Trilling 1949, p. 166). The Christ-like Liddell, evangelical crusader, saintly missionary, was by his life and his action in sight of both Dover Beach and "the cliffs of England . . . Glimmering and vast, out in the tranquil bay" attempting to stem this ebbing tide of faith.

The Beach and the Ages of Man

Liddell and his young colleagues leaving from Dover, survivors and successors of the lost generation, were also aware, not without a touch of guilt, that they would soon be running on soil recently (1914–18) "Swept with confused alarms of struggle and flight, Where ignorant armies clash(ed) by night." Arnold's "darkling plain" of Dover Beach (Trilling 1949, pp. 166–67), moved with poetic license a few miles up the coast to Broadstairs, Kent, is the image that dominates recollections of *Chariots*. The film poster of Britain's young Olympic athletes running all together on the beach in 1924 is evoked by Lord Lindsay to initiate the narrative, and the same image closes the film. Small, dim figures loom out of the haze and sea mist. All are clad in white and become large as life in front of the camera. And then the fastest and the best of their generation pass by the camera into middle age. At their passing, a figure in black stands and the athletes disappear once again into the sea spray and distant haze. The image is a metaphor of the cycle of life: the quickly passing moment of glory of the athlete and the long goodbye of the aging athlete living on memories.

Far away from the cares of the everyday world, where the sea meets the land as the tide, the beach is a special form of English pastoral. To the British working classes it means an annual week of happiness; in two runners it stimulates clarity of thought; in poets and philosophers it suggests metaphors of the cycles of life and faith.

Chariots of Fire and Chariots of the Gods

Throughout both movies there is a double meaning to the phrase "chariot of fire." In one sense it is the unearthly drive, the fire in the belly of the two immortals. Lord Lindsay, in his panegyric that opens the film, speaks of the English Olympians as "those few young men with . . . wings on our heels," invoking the Roman god Mercury with wings on his sandals (and the Greek Hermes, the winged messenger) and reminding us that Abrahams "ran them (the opposition and the English Establishment) off their feet." When the "Countenance Divine" changes teeming rain to shining sun at East Wemyss, the rolling thunder in the heavens above reminds us who is behind Liddell. And when the thunder carries as sound-over to Abrahams playing with fire in his Cambridge room, we know who is behind Abrahams: "my father" (who art in heaven).[9] At Stamford Bridge, after the loss to Liddell, Sybil Gordon tells Abrahams "you ran like a God" and Abrahams replies: "And now God knows, what'll I aim for?" And in his crossing swords with the Master of Trinity (Father, Son, and Holy Ghost), representing the Church of England and King's Chapel, and the Master of Caius, pronounced keys (keys of the kingdom), representing the King of England, Abrahams ridicules their assumption that victory can be "achieved with the apparent effortlessness of Gods." Our heroes' vehicles are chariots of the gods in the heavens.

In the second and more important sense, chariots of fire are the steam engines that created and connected the dark satanic mills and the big industrial towns that befoul England's green and pleasant land, and the internal (infernal) combustion engines that extended "the great industrial maw" (Kazin 1946, p. 32). On the other side of this coin the chariot of fire is the vehicle of escape to the unspoilt English countryside from the satanic mills that the engines created. One scene in each of the movies makes the double point. In *Loneliness*, after stealing a car and going for a joyride ("I wanted a breath of fresh air"), Colin and his friends find a high vantage point above Nottingham, a patch of green grass that will soon be consumed by a gaping limestone quarry and cement factory. While they look out over the devastated industrial landscape—broken-down buildings, railway banks, gasometers, barbed-wire fences, terraced housing—a passenger train passes by on a viaduct, the hooting and shunting of the trains that ruined the landscape is heard in the distance, and the characters talk of means (engines) for getting "out of this dump."

Similarly in *Chariots*, Liddell takes his sister, Jenny, from the mission building, blackened with soot, up to the fresh air of the green pastures of Arthur's Seat high above Edinburgh, which he calls by its colloquial name "Auld Reekie" (foul-smelling and smoky). The sounds of a train, unseen in the murky valley below, remind us of the train's contribution to the yellow pollution, while Liddell talks excitedly of taking that train to glory, to Paris and the Olympic Games. Escape from the insensate industrial city to the beaches and sand dunes of Skegness is provided by a train blanketed by smoke and hissing steam in the gloomy half-light of dirty Nottingham Station in *Loneliness*. The characters are joyous and light-hearted as they leave, traveling first class. But in the tawdry railway station cafe they are dismal to the point of despair at the prospect of going back on the same track from the seaside to their Nottingham "prison," this time third class.

Everywhere the machine is winning against people and the countryside. Abrahams in training strives to keep up with a coupe. Liddell is paced on the beach by a motorcycle and sidecar that he never catches. Colin and Mike narrowly avert being run over by a charabanc hurtling through the city center of Nottingham. The American athletes train like machines, to a background of machinelike music on the soundtrack. The ultimate victory of the machine in the garden is the sight in the middle distance of the lawn at Highbeck House of the aged Marquess of Exeter, father of Lord Lindsay, trying with no success to ride a two-wheel bicycle with the help of two servants ("Father's never going to learn how to do that").

Trains take the heroes to their destinies: their major confrontations on and off the track. Abrahams is driven, and on a narrow track, like the train that propels him from London into the sleepy preindustrial town of Cambridge, there to confront the prejudice of the guardians of the English Establishment and to train successfully in rural England. Abrahams and Liddell, both well trained, travel by sea and by land on the boat-train to steamroller the English power elite and to confront the American athletics juggernaut that arrived in an ocean liner and a battleship! And both return in triumph to London's Victoria Station in a chariot of fire now also a chariot of gods.

The ultimate chariot of fire is the fastest passenger train in Britain: the Flying Scotsman. It runs between cities known colloquially for their metropolitan and industrial soot and smells, The Smoke (London) and Auld Reekie (Edinburgh). It carries Abrahams north to enlist the coaching skills of Mussabini and to scout Liddell, whom he finds to be as wild as the north country. It carries Liddell, nicknamed "the Flying Scot" because he runs like the world-famous express train, due south to London's Kings Cross Station.

Kings Cross: Place as Metaphor

Alongside London's St. Pancras Station (1868–74), with its Gothic Revival architecture beloved by Blake (Schorer 1946, p. 452) and submitted, so the story goes, as a design for the Houses of Parliament, Lewis Cubitt's Kings Cross (1850–52) stands spare, functionalist, supremely modern, and "one of the century's masterpieces in cast iron" (Brown 1966, p. 140). It can easily be taken for modern architecture of the mid-twentieth century rather than one of the great modern buildings of the mid-nineteenth century. It is, then, an early symbol of the modern industrial era standing in stark contrast to Ruskin's beloved Gothic Revival of England's pastoral and medieval past and at the opposite end of the track from Waverley Station in Edinburgh, named for Sir Walter Scott's novels that romanticized Scotland's Celtic and Highland past.

Kings Cross is the home and the hub of the trains that radiate outwards from England's capital city to dominate and despoil the English and Scottish countryside, and it is the modern antithesis of the pastoral of England's past and of the ancient city of faith epitomized by Jerusalem. Like Jerusalem in *Chariots* it is a place as metaphor, a code unobtrusively stated twice by a sleeping-car porter as the Flying Scotsman pulls into the station. The porter in his northern (industrial) working-class accent is proudly announcing the arrival of the country's greatest chariot of fire into one of the great symbols of modernism and of the future: the overarching shed of glass and iron that is Kings Cross. And in a double entendre he is also preparing the way for the crossing of the kings of English and Scottish athletics that afternoon at the AAA championships at Stamford Bridge, London: the clash between the chariots of the (future) gods, Abrahams and Liddell, the first kings cross of *Chariots*.

The use of the name of a place as a metaphor for the plot is explicit in *Chariots*. The hitherto separate trajectories of the two heroes cross for the first time on the day that the name "Kings Cross" is called twice by the porter. On the surface the story is about the result of that crossing and about the anticipated second crossing that for each athlete turns into a crossing of swords with American athletes at the Paris Olympics. Beneath the surface the real Kings Cross is the battleground between each of the young heroes and the power elite (kings) of the English Establishment bent on breaking their will and undermining deeply held principles and beliefs. Kings Cross is not mentioned in the film of *Loneliness*, but the crossing of the two athletic kings on a number of occasions is central to the plot as is the crossing of each of the heroes with the governor and the prison officials who represent power and the English Establishment. *Loneliness* is a rare film about a runner and a race. The filmmakers of *Chariots* obviously studied it closely and paid it many tributes within the film, including the adoption of "Jerusalem" as a code word. The screenwriter, Colin Welland, can hardly have missed the characterization of the hero, Colin Smith, as the "king of this borstal" (soon after he replaced Stacey on the throne). And the idea of the runner making a Faustian compact with the devil to ensure victory in his crossing of the English Establishment is central to *Loneliness* and incorporated and greatly elaborated in *Chariots*.

Her Majesty's borstal at Ruxton Towers is run by a governor who was obviously educated in an English Public School and who tries in every way possible to incorporate the methods and structure of the English Public Schools initiated by Thomas Arnold at Rugby and immortalized in Thomas Hughes's *Tom Brown's Schooldays* (1906). A critical component of the Arnold method is the prefect system, which gives some power of discipline to specially selected individuals in return for special privileges. The most powerful of the boys and those with the greatest privileges are the captains of the "houses" into which the student body of the school is equally divided. It is to one of these "house captains" or "kings" to whom Colin Smith takes an instant dislike, viewing him as a traitor to his class, cooperating as he does with "them" (the Establishment) in enforcing prison laws. The "king" (Stacey) advises the inductees to cooperate with "them" because "they've got the whip hand." Colin balks at this initially with words. But when he sees the privileges given to Stacey, it is inevitable that the two kings cross, for Colin has a history of taking the law into his own hands when faced with injustice. They cross first in soccer and then in cross-country, both of which Colin wins, gaining the governor's approbation.

Stacey's wrath at Colin's victories and his own prospective downgrading precipitates a vicious, law-of-the-jungle brawl that is on the surface inconclusive (the third kings cross). In effect, however, Colin emerges as the new "king" because Stacey, seeing the prospective loss of his privileged position to a better athlete, uses his long-distance running privileges to scarper (run away from the borstal).

Subsequent kings crosses are battles between the two kings and Her Majesty's (H.M.) Borstal Governor and prison staff, representing the Establishment. Stacey's escape, abetted by the prisoners' diversionary food riot during which a prisoner throws a plate full of food at an official portrait of Queen Elizabeth II who watches from on high on the prison wall, is the first crossing. But the governor, obsessed with his desire to win the Cross-country Cup presented by the trustees of the Public School with which the borstal boys will be competing, covers up the incident and allows the prisoners, among them Colin with two big black eyes from the fight with Stacey, to go ahead with an evening of entertainment. It is during the final hymn ("Jerusalem") that movie-viewers see the resolution of king Stacey's crossing up of the Establishment. He is brought back from his "honeymoon" by the police, taken down into the bowels of the prison, and thrown into a cell with bars.

The "whip-hand" of a prison guard, wrapped in prison keys, crashes into the solar plexus of the helpless, still handcuffed Stacey, just as the prisoners above sing the words "chariot of fire." With Stacey literally beaten in solitary confinement, the mantle of king is donned by Colin Smith who told his fellow prisoners earlier that he would use "cunning" to beat "them," without knowing quite how he would do this. He accepts H.M. Governor's (Mephistopheles') compact ("you play ball with us and we'll play ball with you"), appearing, at least to the governor, to promise to win the long-distance race and the cup. He is allowed outside the prison grounds to do his early-morning training runs in preparation for the race. He gets to enjoy his training runs and the attendant privileges of being king or, as the prisoners call him, "daddy." But he is brought up with a jolt when his mate from Nottingham, Mike, just sent down to Ruxton Towers and hearing about his privileged status, asks Colin on the eve of the big race: "Whose bloody side are you on, all of a sudden?"

The scene shifts to the rudimentary dressing rooms before the big race where the leading runner for the Public School, Gunthorpe, inquires about the opposition and, in learning that it is Colin, crosses the room to shake his hand and wish him "good luck."[10] The "king of this borstal" (Colin Smith) still does not know how he is going to beat the devil (H.M. Governor) when the race starts. But in a sequence of flashbacks, Tony Richardson shows the thoughts racing through Colin's head as he runs: the temptations of the athletics and middle-class life offered by the governor, the miserable conditions of his family life in the prefab in Nottingham, the vindictive detective and police threats of violence, his shop-steward strike-leading father dying a proud but pitiless death from cancer, the windfall life insurance monies that devolved to his mother, his own embryonic Marxist-Socialist thought about needed change with workers sharing the profits. The frames that finally bring him to the devilish conclusion of his thinking are, in sequence, Mike's questioning of his allegiances, the governor's enunciation of the Protestant work ethic, his dying father's refusal to go to a hospital ("I'm no bleeding guinea pig for anybody"), and the battery of the defenseless Stacey after his daring to cross the king's minions.

A furlong ahead of the rest of the field and only a few yards from the finishing line, with both sides urging him to win, he stops dead. With his face wreathed in a devilish smile, he bows in mock servility to Ranleigh School's official winner, Gunthorpe, and to the other runners who eventually pass him to cross the line. The camera pans first to the three symbols of the Establishment—the churchman/padre, the army general, and H.M. Governor of the Borstal—for whom incomprehensibility turns to disbelief and, in the governor's case, to angry frustration and the certain knowledge that he will not make the Queen's New Year's Honors List. In denying the governor his "one moment of perfect contentment" (*Random House Encyclopedia* 1977, p. 2166), Colin beats the devil at his own game and turns the tables on him, achieving his own "moment of perfect contentment" and a "cunning" and perfect solution to his problem. "Once the boys caught on to me losing the race on purpose [they] never had enough good words to say about me, or curses to throw out [to themselves] at the governor" (Sillitoe 1959, p. 46).

It is the memory of Colin Smith, antihero, champion of the underprivileged working class, and conqueror of the Establishment (social, religious, political, and military) that is evoked in *Chariots*. As with the crossing of kings Colin and Stacey in *Loneliness*, the first crossing of the kings in *Chariots* for the British and World 100-meters crowns is a petty fight compared to the kings' pitched battles (off the track) with the Establishment. The Jewish Abrahams is bitter in the face of anti-Semitism that he catches "in a look" or "on the edge of a remark" as we do in remarks of porters, student-spectators at the College Dash, and the masters of Trinity and Caius colleges, at Cambridge. Abrahams describes himself as "semi-deprived," which means that the "Christian and Anglo-Saxon" elite "who stalk . . . her corridors of power" and "guard them with jealousy and venom . . . lead me to water, but they won't let me drink." To beat them and to gain the privileges he is denied by his Jewishness, he sets out to use his speed "to take them on, one by one, all of them, and run them off their feet."

From the first revelation of his "ache, a helplessness, and an anger" in his Cambridge study with Aubrey Montague, he is seen, poker in hand, "playing with fire." This takes mild forms at first. As "our special correspondent" for a national newspaper he writes reviews and notices of his own athletic performances. And while denied a place in Cambridge University's world-famous Kings Chapel Choir by his Jewishness (College porter: "One thing's certain, name like Abrahams, he won't be in the Chapel choir, now will he?"), he delights in singing in the operettas of Gilbert and Sullivan: a Jew taking the lead in parodies of his antagonists, Christian England and particularly its upper classes.

Preparing for the first kings cross (his clash as king of English athletics with the Scottish king, Liddell) he travels north to scout the next hurdle in his path. On discovering Liddell to be awesome ("I've never seen such drive") he adds fuel to the fire by offering to pay the professional athletics coach, Sam Mussabini, to train him to beat Liddell, thus, in 1923, endangering his amateur status and risking the censure of his peers.

For the moment Mussabini refuses on the grounds that he doesn't yet know whether Abrahams has what it takes physically ("You can't put in what God's left out"). But all this changes with Abrahams's comprehensive defeat by Liddell at the first kings cross (AAA finals, Stamford Bridge, 1923). Sitting abjectly in the middle of the grandstand (purgatory) after the defeat, Abrahams interprets it as the death of himself as an athlete ("Well, that's that, Abrahams. . . . I run to win. If I can't win I won't run") and his fiancée, Sybil, chides him ("It's a race you've lost. . . . It's not someone who's dead"). It is "death" to Abrahams because he "can't run any faster." That he is dead and on the way to hell is proved with a brilliant piece of symbolism. A faceless man at the far end of the wooden stand smacks up each wooden seat with a loud bang (the hammering of nails into Abrahams's coffin) in the row in which Abrahams is sitting and we realize that, as the steady and insistent claps inexorably draw closer to Abrahams, "the clappers of hell are after him."

The voice of Mussabini (Mephistopheles) from below them (in the nether world of the stadium floor) offers Abrahams the compact rejected by Mussabini a few months earlier ("Mr. Abrahams, I can find you another two yards"). It is confirmed as a professional contract initially with symbolic money ("Have you got another two coins, Mr. Abrahams?") and then with three slaps of Abrahams's face ("overstriding . . . death to the sprinter . . . slap in the face each stride you take") to prove Abrahams's dependent status. Four frames with symbols of hell prove that the Faustian compact is translated to the track. Mussabini with his pointed rod (shooting stick) directs Abrahams's high stepping ("You're running on hot bricks. If you leave your feet too long on the ground they'll get burned") and, with smoking (starter's) pistol in hand, he choreographs Abrahams's starts. Abrahams races against an open convertible, a Phaeton (named for the son of Apollo who drove his father's sun chariot across the sky but lost control of the horses, causing the earth to burn and Olympus to smoke), and is exhorted by Mussabini to "pass the car, come on." And Abrahams follows the hounds (of hell) on a straight path.

In the original Faustian compact, "Faust promises to forfeit his soul to Mephistopheles in exchange for one moment of perfect contentment" (*Random House Encyclopedia* 1977, p. 2166). That this was the agreement between Mussabini and Abrahams is confirmed as Abrahams commiserates with Aubrey Montague (who fell badly and finished sixth in the Olympic steeplechase final) one hour before Abrahams's 100-meters Olympic final. "You, Aubrey, are my complete man. A content man . . . contentment. I'm twenty-four and I've never known it." For Abrahams in his Faustian quest, the problem in winning the Olympic 100 meters— his joint obsession with Mussabini for more than a year—is that it may not yield that "one perfect moment" ("I'm forever in pursuit [of contentment] and I don't even know what it is"). And if the victory does produce that perfect moment, then there is the certain forfeiture of his soul to Mephistopheles and prospectively to eternal damnation ("I've known the fear of losing, but now I'm almost too frightened to win").

But there are reassuring signs of Mephistopheles' prospective leniency to Faust before the final race. Both are kindred spirits in their censure by the guardians of shamateurism in athletics, and both are excluded: Abrahams from the corridors of power; Mussabini from the grounds of the Paris Olympics ("the Olympic Stadium . . . seeing as I'm persona non grada [*sic*] there"). Both are also kinsmen of sorts, for

Mussabini packs in Abrahams's athletics kit for the final race a gold chain and pendant that is not the expected cross but an Arabic charm with an inscription from the Koran cut out in it: a talisman from one Semite to another ("Please accept the charm, my old father swore by it"). In fact the bond between them is much more than that, for Mussabini in his ecstasy at Abrahams's victory whispers audibly "Harold, my son."

The night of the gold-medal victory, in a celebration de deux in a Parisian bistro, Mussabini reveals that Harold's victory was not only Harold's moment of perfect contentment but also his ("I've waited thirty bloody years for this . . . It means the world to me, this, y'know"). And instead of consigning Abrahams (Faust) to eternal damnation, he consigns the whole of unappreciative humanity to this fate, symbolized by the French waiter who is trying vainly to get the two of them out of the bistro ("And if all the world wants to do is go to bed, then they can all go to hell"). And Mussabini is quite specific in giving back Abrahams's forfeited soul ("Now you've got it out of your system, go home to that girl of yours and start some bloody living"). As in Blake, the devil turns out to be benign and on the side of revolution. "Heaven, Earth & Hell henceforth shall live in harmony" (Blake in Schorer 1946, p. 389).

In effect, both of them die as athletes after their joint moment of perfect contentment. On hearing the British national anthem that signifies Harold's victory, Mussabini, visibly aging, clutches his heart (heart attack?) and staggers across the room to the bed, and we recognize that "for old Sam Mussabini" the strain was too much and that the end for him is near. Abrahams, in real life, contracts a serious injury soon after the Olympics and never competes in international athletics again. His own death as an athlete, announced after the first kings cross in 1923 and from which he was briefly resurrected by his compact with Mussabini, was a lease of life of one momentous year.

Abrahams's battle with the guardians of the corridors of power and the English Establishment is precipitated by an attempted censure of his plebeianism ("playing the tradesman") in employing a professional coach, in adopting a "professional attitude," and in aiming to "win at all costs." The accusers are the masters of Trinity and Caius, representatives of the closely connected state religion ("priests") and political tyranny ("kings") against which Blake railed all his life. Both are guardians of the "way of the amateur" (affected French pronunciation), "esprit de corps," and the ideals of the English gentleman in one of the two universities of the English Establishment. They accuse Abrahams of losing sight of the ideals fostered by games at the university, notably "loyalty, comradeship, and mutual responsibility," and on concentrating "wholly on developing your own technique in the headlong pursuit . . . of individual glory." Unbowed, Abrahams ridicules their classical and Olympian delusions, pillories their "archaic values of the prep school playground," pities their self-deception, and forecasts correctly (as the American experience at the Paris Olympics proved) that the athlete with a professional coach will carry the future with him.

But this crossing of swords with the Establishment is inconclusive. Getting into the corridors of English power still depended, as Abrahams knew on the eve of the race, on how well he did "down that corridor four feet wide with ten lonely seconds to justify my whole existence." It was the newspaper banner headlines read by the Master of Trinity to the Master of Caius that announced the victory over the Establishment: "Abrahams Triumphant Caius College Athlete Wins Blue Riband at Games." The newspaper placard at London's Victoria Station announces his elevation to the position of national hero: "Abrahams The Toast Of The Land."[11]

In the memorial service for Abrahams with which the movie begins and ends, the large congregation includes "Protestant ministers and Jewish rabbis, (recognizable) statesmen and great athletes, Jews and Christians alike" (Weatherby 1981, p. 174). We are reminded of Blake's hope for "one 'right' religion . . . a cosmopolitanism so broad that no sect, no nation, no continent . . . could be allowed to claim a superior revelation or a pre-eminent historical function" (Schorer 1946, p. 130), something for which Blake chided the Jews who assumed great significance in Blake's mythology and cosmology. It is they who founded Jerusalem on "Albion's Ancient Druid Rocky Shore" (Blake in Kazin 1946, pp. 446–51), they who built Jerusalem in England's green and pleasant land, they who in Blake's "curious theory of the Hebraic origins of Britain . . . migrated from Britain in the primeval time (Schorer 1946, p. 364) taking Jerusalem with them. In Blake's cosmopolitan vision and universal religion of forgiveness, the Jews are central in the return of Jerusalem "to Albion's Land" and to the building of "Jerusalem among those dark Satanic mills." The ecumenical congregation and a boys choir that has Indian (subcontinent) and Caribbean "Commonwealth-immigrant" faces in it singing "Jerusalem," Abrahams's successful marriage to a Christian, and his success in the "corridors of power," all suggest the approach of a New Jerusalem in postwar Britain.

The service is held in the Church of St. Mary-Le-Strand, a very Christian church close to Fleet Street, synonymous with newspapers for which Abrahams wrote through much of his adult life. It is halfway between the financial City of London (base of Abrahams's "financier" father) and the political City of Westminster (base of Abrahams, "the elder statesman of British athletics.") Both are commemorated in the biblical text read at the service by Lord Lindsay: "Let us now praise famous men and our forefathers that begat us. All these men were honored in their generations."[12] Proof of Abrahams's elevated, if not exalted, status in England is provided during the singing of "Jerusalem." The camera swings to the back of the church, up past the royal coat of arms and mottoes (*Dieu et mon droit* and *Honi soit qui mal y pense*) and on to the heavens just as the choir sings "chariot of fire," and as the subtitle notes Liddell's death "in Occupied China in 1944. All Scotland Mourned." We are reminded of the two athletes' immortality, above kings and other mere mortals (God and Jesus Christ even?).

If we had any doubts about whether the screenwriter intended this implication, they are removed by the doddering Lord Lindsay as he leaves the church. He twice repeats words and phrases used earlier. And as the only other such case is the once-repeated code-phrase Kings Cross, it is clear that screenwriter Colin Welland intended the double underlining. One phrase proves that Abrahams did indeed use his running to attain all his objectives: "He ran them off their feet . . . He ran them off their feet." The other proves his immortality: "HE did it . . . HE did it."

In a movie that announces that "This is a True Story," the encounters with devils and the three kings crosses are all fictional for Eric Liddell. In the first kings cross, Liddell wins at Stamford Bridge, but Abrahams was not in that final (Magnusson 1981, p. 186). In the second kings cross, the Paris Olympics, Liddell withdrew from the 100 meters months before the race, and his immediate and adamant withdrawal obviated the need for the "inquisition" between Liddell and the British nobility (the third kings cross of *Chariots*.) The two central figures in Liddell's Faustian compact—Sandy McGrath and his sister, Jenny—did not exist as portrayed in the movie. Magnusson's biography of Liddell (1981, p. 30) makes no mention of his having a coach, and quotes Jenny's self-portrayal in her own words: "I was a naive, unsophisticated teenager at the time. I would never have dreamed of telling Eric what to do." But in the movie Jenny is the voice of Eric's Christian conscience and the flame-haired Sandy is the devil in the battle for Eric's soul.

The battle is joined on a hillside in the Highlands before we encounter Eric. Jenny warns off Sandy: "I don't want his work spoilt with all this running talk, you hear?" But Sandy, to Jenny's displeasure, appears not to hear, and first persuades "Scotland's finest winger to show us his paces" in the 200-yards open championship in the Highland Gathering and then, after Eric's victory, corroborates her fears that he has been filling Eric's head with running talk: "Didn't I tell ya, Eric, didn't I tell ya."

The first salvos in the battle for Eric's soul are fired the next day outside a kirk in the Highlands when Sandy, a Blakean devil on the side of revolution, pleads for "a touch of liberality" and "freedom of choice" in Christianity. But Eric's missionary father (on the side of the institutional church that Blake loathed) rejoins that "the kingdom of God is not a democracy" and contends that "God is a dictator, a benign king." That evening at the dinner table and amid the toasts, Mrs. Liddell, jokingly, makes the mistake of entrusting Jenny and Eric to Sandy's charge ("I'm relying on you now to keep them out of mischief"), and Sandy tells Eric, "I'm going to rule you with the rod of iron" (the devil's three-pronged spear) and "protect my investment," whereupon Jenny leaves the room in obvious displeasure.

In the parlor later that evening, the three Christians (Eric, his father, and Rev. D. P. Thomson, the evangelist) meet to discuss the implications for the church and the mission of Eric's God given speed, Thomson says: "Sandy reckons he'll run for Scotland before the month's out and after that the sky's the limit . . . the Olympic games maybe." The "muscular Christian" will use his running to proselytize for the mission (Rev. Liddell: "Run in God's name and let the world stand back in wonder"). And with some foreboding of the dangers ahead, his father tells him to be uncompromising, for "compromise is the language of the devil." Interestingly, soon after this at the AAA games in Edinburgh, Mussabini (subsequently Abrahams's devil) makes a sign to Eric (a hex?) and then after Eric's miraculous recovery from a fall to win the 400 meters, charges Eric's subsequent devil (Sandy) to "take good care of this lad of yours, Mr. McGrath," adding "because if you drop him you'll never find another one like him" (i.e., there's only one Jesus Christ—the ultimate conquest for a devil).

That Eric was at this stage running free and without the sin of pride is proved by his unselfconscious wink to the adoring schoolgirl in the mission congregation (whom we will see later) and by the interchange between the sleeping-car porter and the Flying Scot as he awakes on the Flying Scotsman in Kings Cross Station. To the porter's question about the soundness of his night's sleep Liddell replies, "like a log," thereby setting up the expected folk response: "You must have a clear conscience." And the clear conscience is proved later that day when Eric thinks about the Christian thing to do, crosses the AAA dressing room, and offers Abrahams his hand, wishing him "the best of success" (and receiving in return the ungracious reply: "May the best man win").

After Eric's victory in the first kings cross, he is seen running in long trousers in the fells and then doing crouching starts in white shorts on the beach, under the direction of Sandy. In the first of the beach shots, Jenny sits bored in a motorcycle sidecar with Sandy between her and Eric. In subsequent shots Jenny has dropped from the picture and Eric is seen running in front of a conspicuously empty sidecar on a vast and very empty beach with his hounds of hell: two greyhounds (an allusion to his actual training without any coach at Powderhall [dog] track in Edinburgh). The emptiness of the beach and of the sidecar is explained when Eric is seen hurtling up the steps to the black mission church, impiously raising his hat to the statue of a dour John Knox, obviously so late for evensong that he catches only the last line of the last hymn (the Twenty-Third Psalm) "thy dwelling place shall be" and missing the penultimate line: "And in God's house forever more." We come to the startling realization (an invention of the movie) that Eric, the evangelical Christian missionary, was training on Sunday and distancing himself from his principles, his people, his piety, and his God.

All this is confirmed in the mission where Jenny chides him for "training, training, training. All I ever hear is training. Do you believe in what we're doing here or not?" and accuses him of insulting the Lord. As mother Mary she tells him: "Your mind's not with us any more, son. It's so full of running and starting and medals and pace." Realizing she has lost brother Eric to the flame-haired devil she concludes with trepidation: "I'm frightened for you, I'm frightened for what it all might do to you" (an obvious allusion to the imminence of hellfire). Further proof of Eric's change for the worst is seen in his sin of pride in signing the autograph book of the hero-worshiping schoolgirl to whom he had winked, with an approving smile from Jenny, during his clear-conscience phase at an earlier mission service. This time a frowning Jenny watches as Eric stoops down from on high, with vanity offering his fan a selection of colored pens, signing with a flourish and a condescending "there y'are." The final proof of Jenny's and the mission's loss of Eric comes in his walk with Jenny above Edinburgh when he admits "You were right, it's not just fun," talks of his running objectives before going off to missionary work in China, and asks her to manage the mission without him. An unsmiling Jenny, set up to be let down and resigned to Eric's fate, gives his cheek a sisterly peck and walks away without saying a word.

Eric's moment of truth comes as he boards the boat crossing to

France and the Olympics. With his personal coach unexpectedly traveling with him (illegally) and towering above him on the gangplank ("I'm not your coach, I'm your valet . . . if they ask any questions, I'm not your coach" [Weatherby 1981, pp. 112–13]), Eric takes a burning question posed by an American reporter: "What about the qualifying heats on Sunday?" Nonplussed, he feels betrayed in discovering that his friend knew about this ("the heats for the 100 are on Sunday after the opening ceremony") and tried to minimize it ("It's only a heat. Does it make all that difference?"). Faced now with racing on the Sabbath and not just with training on Sunday, he is bedeviled with indecision and contemplates compromise ("the language of the devil") as he broods in sight of Dover Beach. But with a succession of flashbacks reminiscent of Colin Smith's during his moments of truth in *Loneliness*, Eric heeds Jenny's chiding ("Your head's so full of running you've no room for standing still"), her concern for his fate ("I'm frightened for what it all might do to you"), and his remembrance of stopping two boys from playing soccer on Sunday ("Sabbath's not the day for playing football, is it?") and decides not to run ("To run would be against God's law. I was mistaken").

In beating one devil (Sandy), Eric encounters a much dirtier devil when he relays his decision not to run to the chairman of the British Olympic Committee, Lord Birkenhead. Feigning sympathy and understanding ("My boy, as things stand you must not run"), Birkenhead persuades Eric not to broadcast his decision and to "leave everything to me," promising to try to persuade the unprincipled French to "shift that bloody heat of yours." But he does no such thing. Rather, on the pretext of having Eric simply meet the Prince of Wales and accusing him of "arrogance" when Eric demurs, he ushers him into a full meeting of the British Olympic Committee and to his final kings cross: Eric, the king of Scottish athletics and Christ-like leader of the Church of Scotland versus the future King of England (Prince of Wales, later Edward VIII) and his lay lords representing Ireland (Cadogan), Scotland (Sutherland), and England (Birkenhead).

The dirty devil (Birkenhead) uses every cheap trick to unsettle Eric, offering a cigar to a nonsmoker, alcohol to a nondrinker, and taking his legs from under him by pushing the chair in hard as he sits down, while Lord Cadogan withdraws his hand from a handshake, tossing a cigarette lighter from one hand to the other (playing with fire). The committee's unwillingness "to approach the French" about changing the heat is passed off as "a simple matter of national dignity" ("a guilty national pride" in the words of the Scottish lord, Sutherland, the only one in the room sympathetic with Eric's position). And they then appeal to his heritage and his allegiance to king and country, asking that he make sacrifices ("sever his running from himself . . . for his country's sake") in the name of loyalty, and demanding that he put "king first, and God after." But Eric stands his ground defiantly (newspaper headline the next day—"Athlete: I Won't Run On Sunday. God Before King"). Accusing them of calling "me up in front of this inquisition of yours," and of seeking "to influence a man to deny his beliefs," he lectures them on precedence and hierarchy: "God made countries. God makes kings and the rules by which they govern and those rules say the Sabbath is His." According to newspaper headlines the following day, he speaks for the spiritual king: "Man Of Principle, Says The Primate, We Should Be Proud." And on the Sunday of the disputed heat he stands high in the pulpit in the Church of Scotland in Paris and reads from Isaiah, Chapter 40: "Behold the nations are as a drop in the bucket . . . All nations before him are as nothing . . . He bringeth the princes to nothing."

In this crossing of kings the victory is Eric's, for it is an English lay lord (Lindsay) who cuts the Gordian knot by yielding his place to Liddell in the 400 meters. And it is an Eric confident in strength renewed by the Lord ("They that wait upon the Lord shall renew their strength"), with clear conscience rediscovered, who wishes the favored Americans good luck before the 400-meter final and adds: "I don't expect I'll see you 'til after the race." Presented with a note by a kindred spirit, the American sprinter Jackson Scholz, whose action symbolizes the overarching power of the spiritual over the national, Eric clasps it in his hand throughout a race that sees him overcome the difficult outside position, burn off the competition (the American kings?) at the halfway mark, and reach the tape 5 yards ahead of the opposition at a new world record.

The note, which reads "Mr. Liddell, It Says In The Old Book He That Honors Me, I Will Honor," contrasts with the motto of the English Order of the Garter (*Honi soit qui mal y pense*). We are positioned to remember that Edward VIII, head of the Order, by acting dishonorably in marrying a person unacceptable to Church and State, failed to practice the loyalty to country he preached to Eric, and was forced into exile. By contrast, Eric, after drifting into a barely comprehended (Faustian) compact with Sandy, had realized at Dover Beach (as did Faust much earlier) "that contentment lies in helping others" (*Random House Encyclopedia* 1977, p. 2167). He volunteers for exile, missionary service in China (Magnusson 1981, p. 75), and, in fulfillment of Part 2 of Faust, "pronounces himself perfectly contented and dies" a young man (*Random House Encyclopedia* 1977, p. 2167) with regrets but no doubts about the decision not to run in the 100 meters on Sunday. By failing to win the Olympic 100 meters Eric, like Faust, had lost his wager with Mephistopheles. Despite this, again like Faust, "his soul [was] taken into heaven" (*Random House Encyclopedia* 1977, p. 2167).

Kings cross when three young runners, kings among their peers, take on English royalty and H.M. Government. Each sells his soul to the devil, in some way, and wins, seemingly against insurmountable odds: one by turning the tables on the devil, another by rejecting the devil's counsel, and another by following the devil's instruction religiously.

Conclusion

It is the imagined world and cosmology of William Blake, epitomized in the poem/hymn called "Jerusalem," that pervades *Loneliness* and *Chariots*. "Jerusalem" is a microcosm of the great long poems "Milton" and "Jerusalem" composed at the end of a life lived dangerously in the wake of the American and French revolutions, which Blake supported fully, during the Napoleonic War, which he abhorred, and during a period of the most rapid social and economic change associated with the Industrial Revolution, which he saw to be a national tragedy (Williams 1961, p. 49). His attacks on the new condition of the working classes in the industrial north and on London anticipate Karl Marx and Friedrich Engels (Schorer 1946; Thompson 1968) and present the capital city in a new way, as "a systematic state of mind . . . an organized repression" (Williams 1985, p. 148). "I wander thro' each charter'd street, Near where the charter'd Thames does flow, And mark in every face I meet Marks of weakness, marks of woe. In every cry of every Man, In every Infant's cry of fear, In every voice, in every ban, The mindforg'd manacles I hear" (Blake in Frye 1953, p. 46). These ideas are deeply embedded in the socialism of Alan Sillitoe and Tony Richardson in *Loneliness*.

Blake's hatred of militarism and war ("And the hapless Soldier's sigh Runs in blood down Palace walls"), which brought him before the Chichester Assizes on the charge of sedition by a soldier/agent provocateur, is reflected in Colin Smith's rejection of the working-class army as a career and of the regimentation of the borstal in *Loneliness*. It is heavily underlined in *Chariots* in Colin Welland's baring of the power elite's guilty conscience in the face of the senseless killing and mutilation of the lost generation of British working-class soldiers in the World War I and in his exposing of the elite's attempt at glorification: the aftermyth of "a lovely war."

Jerusalem in Blake is above all the "symbol of freedom" (Schorer 1946, pp. 106, 308). The anarchist and libertarian in Blake castigated and pilloried authority as Colin does throughout *Loneliness* and as Richardson and Sillitoe do in invoking Blake by playing "Jerusalem" whenever the institutions that Blake loathed constrain and curtail individual freedoms. In *Chariots* the playing of "Jerusalem" at the end of the film invokes Blake in celebrating the achievement of two who resisted pressures of the institutions of the Establishment.

In the dangerous times of his lifetime, Blake was a self-styled "Liberty Boy" (Schorer 1946, pp. 164, 181) who got his friend Thomas Paine out of England half an hour ahead of government agents (Bronowski 1944, p. 68) but did not himself choose to escape. Rather he saved himself by clothing everything he said in "a system of mythological metaphor" (Schorer 1946, p. 267). "In a system of ever-widening metaphorical amplification," he explained "his story, the story of his England, the history of the world, prehistory, and the nature of all eternity" (Schorer 1946, p. 155). Jerusalem built "in ancient time" in Britain by the Jews and Druids was the holy city in Blake's "spiritual cartography, a symbolical map of England with a vast network of associations" (Schorer 1946, p. 429). Liddell and the muscular Christians aspired to build it wherever they proselytized, and Liddell, with his decision at Dover Beach, defended it against the secular institutions of England. With his stunning victory in the Olympic 100 meters and his acceptance into the upper echelons of English polity and society, Abrahams, symbol of the Jewish return to Albion's shore, made possible Blake's hope for a cosmopolitan New Jerusalem "among these dark Satanic mills." "And now the time returns again: Our souls exult, & London's towers Receive the Lamb of God to dwell In England's green & pleasant bowers" (Blake in Schorer 1946, p. 380).

By association with the landscapes of the ancient past, Jerusalem also symbolized the innocent pastoral of all preindustrial pasts when "the Holy Lamb of God in England's pleasant pastures [was] seen." Escape to the pastoral in Blake, in British literature in general, and in both movies meant happiness, renewal, and clear thinking. The antithesis of this Jerusalem is the machine that "became one with the mechanics of Newton and the mechanical society of Locke," and the "Satanic Wheels and Satanic Mills [that] are symbols for the planetary orbits and laws of gravitation which govern and constrain them . . . Blake saw in these laws symbols, in their turn, of an abstract and inhuman society of constraint" (Bronowski 1944, p. 128). The message of both movies is that when the runners get away from the modern mechanistic world, from the mills

and from the cities to the few surviving enclaves of the pastoral past
(albeit partly contaminated by the machine), their bodies, their minds,
and their whole beings are made the more sound.

Bronowski (1944, p. 138) maintains that Blake "strove for progression
of man from his society, to be man himself . . . beyond how man is to
live, to what man is to be. That is why the states of man symbolized in
his cities are not threefold but fourfold . . . In man the threefold reaches
the fourth state, Jerusalem," which assumes the "religious force of an
ideal for Blake." It is to this state that Colin Smith's "Fiery Chariot of
his Contemplative Thought" (Blake in Schorer 1946, p. 421) points in
Loneliness. The concluding frames of *Chariots* prove that Harold Abrahams and Eric Liddell attained the New Jerusalem.

Acknowledgments

I would like to acknowledge my colleagues in the Program of Humanistic Studies, Clark University, particularly Professor Marvin D'Lugo, for
teaching me how to read the film as text, and Professor Henry Steward,
cartographer at Clark University, for his insight and his bibliographic
contributions.

Notes

1. Quotations from the two films are my own transcriptions from the sound-
tracks of the American versions and are not cited in the running text. The character quoted is only indicated if the identification of the speaker is not self-
evident. W. J. Weatherby, *Chariots of Fire* (1981), "based on a screenplay by Colin
Welland" departs substantially in detail from the soundtrack of the American
version of *Chariots* and includes sections that were apparently cut from the final
version of the film. I have cited Weatherby wherever I have drawn on his version.

2. The joke is a wry one. The holiday camp became the highly regimented
alternative to the traditional week-at-the-beach staying-at-a-boardinghouse for
hundreds of thousands of the British working class after World War II. These
minicities made popular by Billy Butlin often housed as many as 10,000 "happy
campers" per week. Initially they were army barracks set up on the coast for the
Normandy invasion force, complete with Nissen huts like the ones the prisoners
slept in at Ruxton Towers. Holiday camps and borstals were similar in many
ways. They were both guarded by gates and perimeter fences. Working-class people were "inside" for a specific time, slept in Nissen huts or in little cells (called
"chalets" in the holiday camps), and caught up in the tightly scheduled world

of the factory that began with the early morning call ("Wakeywakey, rise and shine" over the loudspeaker in the holiday camp, the same phrase used to wake the prisoners at an "ungodly hour" in the borstal). Both originated in the aftermath of the war in the "period of Austerity" and of housing shortage and both were seen by the working classes as shorter term alternative prisons to the prison of the insensate industrial city where they lived.

3. Thomas Arnold, headmaster of Rugby School, introduced the philosophy, known now as "Arnoldism," into England. The Master of Trinity in the film echoes Arnold's ideas: "Here in Cambridge we've always been proud of our athletic prowess. We believe, have always believed, that our games are indispensable in helping to complete the education of an Englishman. They create character. They foster courage, honesty, and leadership." For a splendid view of the vast consequences of Arnoldism on the sports, polity, and society of the former British Empire, see James (1969, pp. 159–68). Baron Pierre de Coubertin was so impressed with British success in this area that he strongly encouraged France, with its imperial ambitions, to follow suit, reviving the Olympic games of the modern era as a forum for competition between the gentlemen athletes of the European imperial powers (Mandell 1971, pp. 18–23).

4. Rev. D. P. Thomson tells Liddell: "Running on the weekends, strong and true, the Mission cannot but gain by your success. What we need now is a muscular Christian to make folks sit up and notice."

5. Actually the huge crowds flocked to hear his message in the year that followed the Olympics; see Magnusson (1981, pp. 34, 75–79).

6. See the cartoon strip of "The Victor" reproduced in Magnusson (1981, facing p. 96).

7. Interestingly, the long, tree-lined drives in the Cheshire countryside used in the filming are within the estate of Lord Leverhulme, of Lever Bros. Ltd, like Abrahams's father a member of the nouveau riche and, in the 1920s, a recent entrant into the corridors of English power.

8. There is poetic license taken in the film both in the time and in the place of the decision. Liddell made the decision months before the Olympics and as soon as he heard that the heats for the 100 meters were on a Sunday (Magnusson 1982, pp. 40–41).

9. The filmmakers were also playing here with the favorite joke and calculated malapropism of the pupils reciting the Lord's Prayer in the morning assemblies in British state schools. "Our father who art in Heaven, Harold be thy name."

10. In a tribute to *Loneliness* in *Chariots*, Eric Liddell, like the Public School runner in having no ulterior motive for running, does the same to Harold Abrahams, a man like Colin with an ulterior motive: he had something to prove against the Establishment.

11. In a remarkable parallel following the 100 meters in the 1992 Olympics won by the black British runner Linford Christie, Christie told a commentator on the world satellite feed that his countrymen would be so happy about his victory they might "elect me King."

12. The first six words were made doubly famous by James Agee who chose them facetiously for the title of his bitter account of another case of "deprivation," that of three tenant families in the American South during the Depression.

References

Allison, L. 1978. Association Football and the Urban Ethos. In J.D. Wirth and R. L. Jong, editors, *In Manchester and Sao Paolo: Problems of Rapid Urban Growth.* Palo Alto: Stanford University Press.

Bowden, M.J. 1993. Theaters of Soccer. In K. Raitz, editor, *Theaters of Sport.* Baltimore: Johns Hopkins University Press.

Bronowski, J. 1944. *William Blake 1757–1827: A Man Without a Mask.* Harmondsworth: Penguin.

Brown, B.R. 1966. *An Art Guide to London.* New York: Anchor.

Darby, H.C. 1953. On the Relations of Geography and History. *Transactions, Institute of British Geographers* 19: 1–11.

Frye, N., editor. 1953. *Selected Poetry and Prose of William Blake.* New York: Modern Library.

Guttmann, A. 1978. *From Ritual to Record: The Nature of Modern Sports.* New York: Columbia University Press.

Hughes, T. 1906 (originally 1857). *Tom Brown's Schooldays.* New York: E. P. Dutton.

Hughes, Y. H., editor. 1935 (originally 1667). *Paradise Lost.* New York: Odyssey Press.

James, C.L.R. 1969 (originally 1963). *Beyond a Boundary.* London: Stanley Paul.

Kael, P. 1979 (originally 1970). *Going Steady.* New York: Warner Books.

Kazin, A., editor. 1946. *The Portable Blake.* New York: Viking Press.

Magnusson, S. 1981. *The Flying Scotsman: A Biography.* New York: Quartet Books.

Mandell, R.D. 1971. *The Nazi Olympics.* New York: Ballantine Books.

Mason, T. 1980. *Association Football and English Society 1863–1915.* Brighton: Harvester.

Oxford Companion to Music. 10th ed. 1970. Oxford: Oxford University Press.

Random House Encyclopedia. 1977. New York: Random House.

Schorer, M. 1946. *William Blake: The Politics of Vision.* New York: Henry Holt.

Sillitoe, A. 1959. *The Loneliness of the Long-Distance Runner.* New York: Signet Books.

Thompson, E.P. 1968 (originally 1963). *The Making of the English Working Class.* Harmondsworth: Penguin.

Trilling, L., editor. 1949. *The Portable Matthew Arnold.* New York: Viking Press.

Wallechinsky, D. 1984. *The Complete Book of the Olympics.* Harmondsworth: Penguin.

Walvin, J. 1975. *The People's Game.* London: Allen Lane.

Weatherby, W.J. 1981. *Chariots of Fire: A True Story.* New York: Dell/Quicksilver Book.

Williams, R. 1961 (originally 1958). *Culture and Society 1780–1950.* Harmondsworth: Penguin.

Williams, R. 1985 (originally 1973). *The Country and the City.* London: Hogarth Press.

Filmography

The Bridge over the River Kwai. 1957. Columbia Pictures. Director, Lean, D.

Chariots of Fire. 1981. Enigma Productions. Director, Hudson, H.

If . . . 1969. Paramount. Director, Anderson, L.

The Loneliness of the Long-Distance Runner. 1962. Woodfall Films. Director, Richardson, T.

Olympia. 1936. Leni Riefenstahl. Director, Riefenstahl, L.

5

Outside of Nothing: The Place of Community in *The Outsiders*

Denis Wood

> On the corner of the street he lived on, hung out
> a gang of Puerto Rican lads. One of them came
> with a shining new bicycle and all were soon
> wildly pedalling it. Jeremy was charmed by this
> generous camaraderie, as if all property be-
> longed to all. But he quickly saw that there *was*
> no community, no mutual pleasure or mutual
> concern, but each one was simply proving his
> prowess and demanding an equal go in order not
> to be belittled. All were so fearful of everything
> that they could not afford to be affectionate to
> anyone.—Paul Goodman (1960, p. 104)

When, many years ago, I stepped out into the bright sunlight from the darkness of the movie house, I had only one thing on my mind: what to make of Francis Ford Coppola's *The Outsiders*.[1] I've been thinking about it off and on ever since. The woman I was with hadn't liked it—teenage kids don't run away like that, she said. That didn't bother me so much: enough do. And besides, it was a film that seemed to me to go out of its way to make sure you didn't mistake it for a documentary or for a gang film or for anything else. I kept thinking about the *Gone With the Wind* (1939) quality of the color and the light when Ponyboy recited the Robert Frost poem and the way the camera dallied and panned in one of the scenes just after the credits, about the way the camera rotated just after the murder, and about the way the film never fooled around with my emotions when Johnny and Dallas died, about the Caravaggesque feeling to the close shots around the fire, about those close-ups, those huge close-ups. . . . It struck me as a film that insisted on being taken on its own grounds for itself, and what was bothering me was that I wasn't sure what those were.

Everything about the film put me off even as it attracted me: the Hinton novel on which it was based ("An Heroic Story of Youth and Belonging, Over Four Million Copies in Print"[2]), the pretty-boy stars from the pages of *16, Tiger Beat,* and *Superteen* ("Matt Shares His Private Thoughts With You!"[3]), the Stevie Wonder ballad, the lush Carmine Coppola score, the movieland gossip ("Will Coppola soon be in the market for another studio?"[4]). Exactly like the teenagers it's about. They have a tough, cocky self-sufficient style that warns one off, threatens one, denies the possibility of human intimacy, even as its transparent fragility and reactionary superficiality indicate its vulnerability and proclaim a yearning for community. Later I was to understand that by making itself in its subjects' image the film put itself precisely in their precarious situation, mirroring deeply its content in its form, for its ultimate subjects are all of us who do not resist the cleavage between form and content, ends and means. But I didn't understand this at first, because I was confronting rather than penetrating its style and that, as the film makes clear, leads only to a standoff.

The film permits few passive viewers. In order to see *through* the film it is necessary to see the *film,* not as a collection of parts, but as a superordinate emergent intelligence, in which context alone the parts make sense. Needless to say, this whole *is* embodied in its parts, but none of these fails to refer outside itself, not just to other parts, but toward the whole, toward *The Outsiders* and toward its makers' intentions. This filmic, as differentiated from scenic, self-consciousness is manifested in an apparent tension between *what* is on the screen and the *way* it is there—a tension resolved only within the frame of the film as a whole. *As experienced,* however, scene by scene, this resolution is continuously elusive, provoking endless reiterations of "What am I to make of this?" In answering these questions one inevitably chooses whether to be merely entertained by the film or to engage it in dialogue.

This provocation is present from the opening shot. Seated at a desk, a neat, blond, teenage boy bathed in an aureate light is caught in medium close-up staring off into the deep space of contemplation. The camera slowly pulls in on the boy's face (which comes to fill half the Panavision frame) before looking down. Adopting the boy's point of view, the camera watches his hand laboriously pen the words "When I stepped out into the bright sunlight . . ." into a school composition notebook (these words are simultaneously recited on the soundtrack). Both visual and sound tracks fade into the title, Stevie Wonder singing

"Stay Gold" over gilded clouds hovering around a golden sun, setting in a sky the red of all remembered sunsets. The implausibly golden light and patent innocence—almost vacuity—of the young face and carefully arranged hair drive the portentousness of the camera's slow movement into the close-up in the direction of . . . *what?* Pretentiousness? Sentimentality? But the inclination to snicker is suspended by a concurrent sense of simple and serious purpose. The boy is not camping it up. Neither is the camera. Yet . . . it is *so* stylized. *What is one to make of it?* The title only exacerbates the problem. Over Stevie Wonder and romantically dissolving shots of a medium-sized town suffused with the light of the setting sun, the title *The Outsiders* is a classic serifed typeface nearly the full height of the screen; the words take their own sweet time scrolling monumentally across it. The cast credits, Greasers on the right, Socs on the left, are each laid down, before zooming, in turn, to full frame and scrolling *up* the screen. It's a piece of technical flash thrown away, as often in this film, as if its makers felt compelled to assure us they knew what they were doing. Again, any inclinations to discount the film are held in abeyance. Predispositions to find sappy the dissolving sunset scenery are forced to contend with the classicism of the typeface, the pace, and the flash of the credits.[5]

These are subtle enough contradictions, and it is not clear that most audiences could articulate them. Yet no one I have talked to has proved to be immune to their effects. "At first I couldn't decide how to take it," they say, and they acknowledge little help from the scenes that follow. Three boys meet on a street corner. You think you recognize them immediately, the sleeves cut off the sweatshirt at the armholes, the denim jacket flapping in the breeze, the collar turned up on the black leather jacket. They're street-corner punks, Dead End kids. "What's happening, Dallas?" one asks. "We're early." "What do you want to do?" "Nothing legal . . . let's get out of here." They slouch off down the street with insouciant grace. Killing time. The camera tracks with them as they glide left across the screen toward a drive-in diner, moves with them as they array themselves around a car to talk with the greasers inside. A fight starts near them—as stylized as a ballet. The boys move, circling right across the screen; the camera, crouched, dallying and panning. In the fight a knife snaps open. The three boys continue their circular movement around the fight. Against their motion a cruiser pulls into the lot, the cop, also pulling against their motion, drawing his nightstick as he gets out of the car. It's such a fluid scene, currents and countercurrents, choreographed icons of low teenage life. The icons are so pat, but the camera's so fresh! The boys shamble into a gas station, hassle friends, get money, head on. They swagger down a street. "What's the movie about, Dallas?" "I don't know, it's one of those beach movies, they made a lot of them," says Dallas (Matt Dillon), grabbing the other's head with his right arm, bopping it with his left. They look into a store window, shielding the glass against the glare with cupped hands. They're moving, burning calories, getting-out-of-here wherever they are. Punk . . . but okay kids. *You can tell.* Three younger kids kneeling in the grass with playing cards occupy the right-hand side of the screen. The three older boys saunter through a hole in the fence in the background. "Did I say you could use my grass?" asks Dallas. The kids, terrified, shake their heads. Dallas demands the cards, interprets some gesture as a wisecrack. His friends stand awkwardly behind him. "I don't like little kids . . . I just don't like them." His profiled face fills the screen and it's obvious he's not kidding. He throws the cards in the air, chases the little kids across the grass, long and golden green in the low sunlight. Panting, the three lurch large into the frame, bobbing and weaving like kids who don't run for the hell of it. Idyllic violence. Terrifying humor. They're not nice, these kids. They've hearts of—*what?* Gold? Or stone? "It's getting dark enough," Dallas says, and they crawl under a fence and into a drive-in movie.

The whole sequence doesn't take five minutes, but the camera set-ups have been inspired, the superficial simplicity of the action masks a breathtaking complexity, and the acting is so refined that it seems, well, natural. In fact, the whole thing has the effortless grace of one of those endlessly rehearsed dances of Fred Astaire and Ginger Rogers, "Isn't This a Lovely Day" from *Top Hat* perhaps, though what sticks in the mind about what follows are the references to, and parallels with, the work of Caravaggio, not just because most of his early sitters were adolescent boys indistinguishable from these, but because the film takes on an increasingly Caravaggesque tone as it unfolds.[6]

Among the scenes in the drive-in sequence are some that strike me as direct quotations. The mellow chiaroscuro and tight framing of Dallas, Cherry (Diane Lane), Ponyboy (C. Thomas Howell), Marcia (Michelle Meyrink), and Johnny (Ralph Macchio), for instance, are more than an echo of the Metropolitan's *Music Party* (see Gregori 1985, especially p. 30). The subsequent fire-lit scene in the lot is later Caravaggio sieved to an attitude: the highly dramatic chiaroscuro, the shallow picture plane, the heightened emotional tension, and the deliberate casualness of Ponyboy and Johnny embracing are all hallmarks of Caravaggio's style. It is no surprise that it is this latter scene that most disturbs viewers, forcing them finally to cease asking "What am I to make of this?" and come to some decision.[7] Johnny and Ponyboy, the two young greasers palling around with Dallas in the opening vignettes, and their friend Two-Bit (Emilio Estevez) have picked up—or been picked up by—two somewhat older girls from the right side of the tracks (Socs, which is short for Socials and rhymes with *gauches*). This unexpected idyll has been shattered by an unpleasant encounter with the girls' boyfriends and later by a drunken brawl between Johnny's mother and father. Pony and Johnny have fled to an empty lot where they have built a fire whose light plays on close-ups of their faces, completely filling the screen. Johnny's head leans on Pony's shoulder, but their minds are elsewhere. When Johnny reveals the surface of his thought with "Man, that was a tuff car. Mustangs are tuff," Ponyboy abruptly moves to the fire, returning to comfort Johnny only when he speaks of killing himself. "Don't—you can't kill yourself, Johnny." "Well, I won't. But I gotta do something. It seems like there's gotta be someplace without greasers or socs, with just people. . . ." They lean back against an old car seat and look up at the stars. The camera slowly moves in on their faces, closing in on Ponyboy—on C. Thomas Howell, on a *boy*—so unrelentingly that the whole screen comes to be occupied by only a part of his face, his right eye dead center. The viewer has no choice but to come to terms with these faces on which the film is lavishing such meticulous attention, both in themselves and as metonyms for the very subject of low teenage life. The carefully asymmetrical composition, the Caravaggesque lighting caressing nothing but their skin, insists on the intrinsic value and beauty of these teenage boys—something as difficult to insist on in Coppola's twentieth century as in Caravaggio's seventeenth, when the unquenchable beauty of the boy in the Berlin *Amor Victoris,* then in the collection of the Marchese Giustiniani, was discreetly veiled by a green curtain.[8] Nothing so bold as Caravaggio's *puer lascivus* is essayed in *The Outsiders.* As a boy in the audience at a $2 matinee shouted when the girls packing the house began to squeal at the spectacle of a BVD-clad Matt Dillon bouncing around on his hospital bed, "Don't worry, girls, you won't see nothing!"[9] In any case, neither Hinton's nor Coppola's interest is even marginally focused on the triumphs of any kind of love, but rather on a more elusive . . . *failure of community.* So what are these faces, these bodies, that even had reviewers *defending* Coppola's heterosexuality? Means run amok? Uncontrollable sentimentality? Sops to the market that month after month lays down a couple of dollars apiece for *Teen Bag*—"Color Pin-Ups"—*16*—"Glorious Color Pin-Ups"—or *Superteen*—"18 Eye-Popping Color Pinups" (including "Yummy Matt Dillon" and "Dynamite Bob Lowe," the latter of whom plays Sodapop, Pony's older brother in the film)?

None of these. On the contrary, they happen to be nothing less than the cinematic, nay, filmic—even using the word in the strict sense of Barthes's "third meaning"—figuration of the Hinton novel taken as a whole.[10] In the world of *The Outsiders,* where social roles maim and finally even kill, the only good body, the only sane, healthy body, is the body unadorned, unstigmatized, unalienated, meaningless, free. . . . And Ponyboy, whose skin lies so large on the theater wall, is the only one who has one.

The temptation is powerful to take Ponyboy as the epitomical outsider, pure body because, standing outside (he has no parents, he is not a Soc, he's too young to drink), he has no place within. And clearly this is how most viewers chose to read the film (the title is *The Outsiders* and these are the guys the film's about, so these guys must be the outsiders). Given such a reading, the close-ups of Pony and Johnny are patronizing at worst, sentimental at best. But to be an outsider is to stand outside something, and when that something does not exist, *everyone* is an outsider. In *The Outsiders* this something is community, and its signal absence in the recognizable world of this film suggests that *everyone is an outsider,* we no less than the characters in the film. In such a world everyone seeks community where it cannot be found, in small groups incapable of coalescing into anything larger, clinging to such group membership the more tenaciously as there is no perceptible alternative. Everyone is trapped outside their own humanity by allegiance to signs of membership in these groups substantially less than the human whole, which frustrates the possibility of the human whole emerging. Eventually signs of identity themselves come to acquire greater significance than anything they might have stood for, and the ensuing confusion of means with ends leads to the tragic spectacle of people hungry for community ripping it apart in the attempt to defend no more than phantom visions of its existence. The tissues and organs of our body lose not only their role but their very being when our body dies. In *The Outsiders* the body of the community is dead (or has never come to life), and that community cannot be found in any of its parts (Socs or greasers) alone. The film's point is not, as some have had it, that everybody dies, but that nobody lives, at least not with anybody else.[11]

It is common to use the word "community" in two senses. The first of these makes reference to a group of people with some common identity of fellowship characterized by mutual aid, concern, and pleasure. The second makes reference, in an increasingly general way, to the location of that community. The former is a bunch of human beings who care for one another; the latter is a geographical entity like a neighborhood, town, or city. Because we have created organizations that enable the functioning of these geographical entities in the absence of any sense of fellowship, and because we use one word to describe two different things, we have a predisposition to take community for granted. Because many things—like the telephone—seem to work with unfailing precision, and the buses run on time, and the hospitals are stocked with blood, we accept that we have a community and so make no effort to achieve one. The "community" chest is full and the "community" college overenrolled and the volunteer fire department never fails to put out the fire. In *The Outsiders* this "community" is taken absolutely for granted. There is no question about the electric company providing the energy that lets Pony, Johnny, and Dallas watch *Beach Blanket Bingo* at the drive-in. Darry (Patrick Swayze) and Dallas use the telephone as casually as another limb. The freight train that takes Pony and Johnny to Windrixville is the 3:15 and there is no question of its not being on time. There is no surprise about the ambulance that takes Pony, Johnny, and Dallas to the hospital, nor doubt about their being admitted and well cared for, despite their vagrant status and patent lack of Blue Cross cards. Pony and Two-Bit don't fret about the bus that takes them home being late or unreliable. Schools and jobs—like Darry's, Sodapop's and Steve's (Tom Cruise)—are simple givens. Convenience stores are open all night. The firemen and police are on the job. Supposedly set—and actually shot—in Tulsa, this point is not made in the film (or for that matter the Hinton novel). The name of a factory in the background of a shot four-fifths of the way through the film does contain the word "Oklahoma," and the test-pattern of a TV in the corner of a frame even later in the movie does say "Tulsa," but most of the references in the Hinton novel to horses have been dropped, and the city, the region, don't really matter. Neither does the era. Supposedly set in 1966, coffee's pretty cheap and the cars aren't this year's models, but if the film isn't set in the galloping all-consuming present, it's not a costume picture either. The action does unfold in a real gritty and coherent place and time, but it's anyplace and anytime, any medium-sized contemporary town. It is America.

Anonymous and faceless. In the convenience store that is open all night the owner calls the youth of his town punks. And the kids do fight, do kill each other. There are no parents to see their kids to bed: Johnny's parents brawl, Pony's are actually dead, Dallas lives with friends. In the hospital where Dallas and Johnny are taken, only their bodies are addressed. In the end the cops kill Dallas. There is little community in this "community" built of Socs and greasers. On the South Side the

Socs have it made. They are the cheerleaders and the lettermen, and they drive Mustangs and drink whisky out of flasks. They wear their pants as short as their crew-cut hair. The greasers live on the North Side, and they don't have it made and they never will. They are the dropouts who end up pumping gas, and they walk and drink beer and smoke unfiltered Camels. They wear their blue jeans as long as their pomaded and carefully sculpted hair. The social world of the Hinton novel *is* marginally more complex. There, a middle class stands between the Socs and the greasers, themselves a cut above a subclass of hoods. Of Dallas, for instance, Hinton writes that "the shade of difference that separates a greaser from a hood wasn't present . . . He was as wild as the boys in the downtown outfits, like Tim Shepard's gang" (1967, p. 19). Coppola largely ignores these complications, creating for his anytown a stripped-down social environment exactly as a physicist specifies the conditions of an ideal gas, or a geographer postulates a homogeneous and infinitely extended plane on which to model the development of urban systems. Just as these scientists are thereby enabled to speak of the behavior of any molecule or any city, so Coppola would seem enabled to refer to any group of people. *The Outsiders* thus seems to assume the explicit intentions of its narrator (Ponyboy) and the novel's author to take on the character of a morality play in which Socs and greasers are to be accepted as any pair of mutually exclusive groups.

The behavior of the Socs is not well limned in *The Outsiders*, but—except with respect to the signs they exhibit to evince the fact that they are indubitably Socs—there is every reason to believe it is similar to that of the greasers on whom the film is centered. This is not the case, again, with the Hinton novel, in which Socs gratuitously assault the greasers in a manner that is not reciprocated. Though Coppola shot such scenes—in fact the whole book page by page—he drops them in the film as released.[12] This behavioral distinction having been abolished, the action of the film is constrained to evolve out of no agent specific to either group, but out of the failure of community alone. Some pains are taken to establish the similarity of the two groups in this respect. It is the aggressive shoving of the chubby greaser in the line at the drive-in concession stand that precipitates the tiff that follows, but it is Dallas's crude and insulting attempt to pick up Cherry that precipitates, ultimately, the Soc attack on Johnny and Ponyboy. It is this attack that causes Johnny to kill Bob Sheldon (Leif Garrett), which leads to the rumble. There Socs and greasers are perfectly matched, from the face-off of Darry and Paul to each of the carefully choreographed kicks and punches. When, in Ponyboy's description of a Soc attack on Johnny, Cherry hears an implication that all Socs are like that, she retaliates with a description of generally similar behavior on the part of Dallas. Counterpoint, Pony assures Cherry that one can see the sun set equally well from north and south sides of town. Repudiation of Soc–greaser tension similarly comes with equal force from both sides, as Johnny's early plea for a world without Socs and greasers is echoed faintly in Randy's (Darren Dalton) monologue to Pony, and Randy's insistence that fighting solves nothing is repeated in Johnny's dying words to Dallas. Identical in their behavior, equally (if incompletely) convinced of its inanity, Socs and greasers nonetheless persevere in it, because all are so afraid of being nobody and so incapable of being somebody on their own that they are forced to hew to the identities vouchsafed them by the "communities" of their fellows, where identity derives not from being somebody, but merely from not being somebody else, Soc merely not greaser, greaser merely not Soc.

They are, then, communities of signs, not substance, redoubts against the world, not propositions for its forging. This is not to say that the superficial camaraderie that Jeremy—in the epigram—sees in the Puerto Rican lads hanging out on his street is absent. Far from it. It is present in such touching abundance—especially among the greasers— that it has moved Richard Corliss to describe it as "familial, embracing and unselfconsciously homoerotic" (1983, p. 78), although he failed to add that it is also superficial, reactionary and fatally incomplete.[13] The film permits no doubt about either of these points. The camaraderie is everywhere, in mutual association, mutual affection, and mutual aid. Ponyboy, for instance, from whose point of view the film is largely shot, is alone *only* in the framing shots that open and conclude the film. He is always palling around with someone, Johnny, Two-Bit, Dallas, or his brothers, who are themselves always palling around with others, Sodapop with Steve or Darry, Steve with Two-Bit, or all of them together (around the gas pumps, at breakfast, before, during, and after the rumble). Their affection for one another, openly expressed only between Pony and Johnny and among the brothers in their reconciliation in the hospital, is otherwise exhibited by constant touching (as when Dallas takes Johnny's head under his right arm and bops it with his left), arm wrestling (as between Steve and Sodapop) and taunting banter. I count no less than twenty-eight instances of mutual aid in the film, from Pony helping Johnny climb under the fence into the drive-in, through the constant sharing of food, clothing, and cigarettes (property might as well be communal), to Johnny's willingness to kill in defense of Pony. But neither Hinton nor Coppola makes too much of this, and far from idealizing it, they reveal it as ultimately empty, an inadequate substitute for the real thing.

Consider one of the most beautifully put together scenes in the film, Pony's reintegration into this community of comrades after his flight from the law. Pony is frying eggs when Steve and Two-Bit enter his house as freely as though they lived there, which in a sense they do. Glad to see Pony after his absence, they roughhouse him, causing him to throw the eggs on the walls and the floor. Kidding him about his short bleached hair and his new hero's status, they casually pull a beer from the refrigerator and a chocolate cake from a shelf. Darry emerges in response to a jibe from Steve, and Sodapop pops out of the bathroom draped in a towel. Steve reminds him to put on his pants ("there's a law or something") and later to get his shoes. Two-Bit watches Mickey Mouse on television, across which Pony and Darry hold a stuttering conversation about their future as a family and whether Darry should leave Pony home alone, before Darry, Steve, and Soda dribble off to work, leaving Two-Bit to care for Pony. Granting that this incredibly fluid piece of filmmaking manifests friendly familiarity, there is nothing terribly positive about it. It is not just—or even especially—that in welcoming him home, Steve and Two-Bit cause him to throw away the eggs he's been cooking, nor that they don't bother to help clean up the mess, but that they are incapable of saying "Welcome Home!" in a direct and supportive manner (everything is so *heavily* coded they can't speak straight), incapable of recognizing that Darry and Pony have important things to say to each other (in a world where nothing matters . . . *nothing matters*), and incapable of aiding Pony in his recovery (especially whenever it would violate anything coded . . . *cool*). Worse, Two-Bit violates Darry's explicit instructions to keep Pony at home, and all conspire in permitting him to join a rumble that leads to his nervous breakdown. But all their behavior involving one another is like this, from the least action (the "playful" hurts required to manifest action) to the most global (the failure of family that leads Pony to run away, the compulsive violence of the "rumbles," the cheapness with which life is held).

Evidently, then, the camaraderie *is* superficial and the "communities" of Socs and greasers are merely signatory. But if nothing but signs keeps them apart, and if being at odds is so destructive, why cannot Socs and greasers, in the great tradition of American liberalism, *get over their differences and get together on what they share in common?* Clearly, this is what Pony and Cherry and Johnny and Randy are on about with their observations on sunsets and their comments on the futility of fighting. Why doesn't it work? Why doesn't Coppola conclude his film with Socs and greasers pulling together to . . . *clean up the environment?*

Because even signs must be embodied.

Since signs *necessarily* weld a signified to a signifier, and since the latter is unavoidably substantial, the sign—at least an expressive pertinence— is unavoidably substantial as well.[14] It is here that Coppola's Caravaggesque gloss has to be taken for the materialist polemic it is. Precisely because his camera has insisted on the fleshy reality of the boys it caresses, it forecloses the possibility of their being no more than cards in a game of social poker. Endowed by the camera's scrutiny with an inescapable naturalism (the naturalism of the bug beneath the entomologist's lens), their bodies are thereby granted the dignity of the history that produced them.[15] Coppola's gaze *does not* universalize them, it particularizes them, it grants them the uniqueness of their situation in time and space, a situation scarred by the no less observable sociospatial realities of an American class system. With their short hair the Soc boys get the cars the greasers with their long hair make do without. With their madras jackets come the good-looking girls that the leather jackets seem unable to attract. With the whisky comes the big houses on the South Side of town. In the refrigerators of the shacks in the north there's only beer. The differences between the Socs and greasers are superficial— they do constitute a sign system—but in Coppola's hands they are signs that point to substantial, material, *historical* differences as surely as topographic differences on the surface of the earth point toward differences at the core-mantle boundary.

To embed these differences as deeply in his film as he could, Coppola attempted to replicate in his young cast *off-stage* the differences Hinton had described for her hometown: "Coppola wanted to create a tension between the Socs and greasers even off the set," reported Leif Garrett. "He did this by paying more per-diem to the Socs. He also gave better covered scripts to the Socs. He even made sure that their hotel rooms were better than the greaser's. This really made us into rival gangs" (Weiss 1982, p. 33).[16] Darren Dalton noted the spatial dimension when he said that "greasers and Socs didn't mix even off the set" (Weiss 1982, p. 20).[17] Lacking any sense of real community, too different to regard one other as no more than variant styles, Socs and greasers are not even "communities" of . . . *signs*—blue jerseys opposed to white and switch at halftime—but . . . *kids stirred by history*—that of Tulsa in the fictional world of the film, that engineered by Coppola in the real world of making the movie—into distinctive mélanges locked into mutual loathing by the asymmetry of their situation, a symmetry, it must be insisted on, generated by the exploitation of *greaser parents* by *Soc parents*. By insisting on the material substance of flesh and the history that shapes it, the film's Caravaggesque naturalism propels it beyond the poignant morality tale the sixteen-year-old Hinton wrote out of the anguish she experienced over the unmotivated beating of her boyfriend (Weiss 1982, p. 47).

Yet the narrative structure her story provides at the same time saved *The Outsiders* from being trapped at the (remarkable) level of documentary achieved by Larry Clark in his contemporaneous *Tulsa*, a despairing insider's view of teenage speed freaks. If Hinton's suggestion that "because our differences are only skin deep we can be whatever we want to be" is empty, so is Clark's "once the needle goes in it never comes out" (Clark 1971).[18] The elusive truth—dialectically suspended between dark despair and luminous promise—is better caught in Coppola's refusal to commit himself either to the story, which the actors would no more than "flesh out," or to the body, which the story would no more than justify. Forced to see the story *in* the body—in the bodies of the adolescent boys—we are forced to acknowledge that if the action in the film does evolve out of no more than a failure of community alone, this failure is not *original* with these bodies but inscribed in them by the sociospatial milieu of which, after all, they are no more than ambulatory incarnations.

With their "bodies caught in the toils of parcellized space," to use Henri Lefebvre's (1991, p. 98) words—the only way out is . . . *out.* At the remarkable heart of this film, Pony and Johnny hop the 3:15 to Windrixville where in sociospatial milieu of neither Soc nor greaser they remake themselves . . . as humans. In a world of rabbits, owls, and racoons— Johnny's place "without greasers or Socs"—they cut and dye their hair from which they've washed the eponymous grease. Freed from the taken-for-granted greaser *Weltanschauung* they not only read to each other from *Gone With the Wind,* but watch sunsets and recite the poetry of Robert Frost.[19] When in response to Pony's complaint that their new looks are "like being trapped in a Halloween costume you can't get out of," Johnny responds with "It's our looks or us," the apparent retreat to a historical world of brothers-under-the-skin blocked by the question their situation begs. After all, in Tulsa their looks *were* them; why is it here an either-or choice? Because here, as the alert animals and protracted sunsets make evident, they've escaped from the places scarred by history to an Eden of prelapsarian grace (they even live in a deserted—hence nondenominational—church). Privileged to incarnate here a "natural" world, finally freed of allegiance to signs of membership in any group, their latent humanness is released to let them form a genuine community, that is, one characterized by mutual aid, concern, and pleasure.

When the history does reintrude itself—as in all but dreams it must—it is impossible for Pony and Johnny to wholly revert to their original greaser personas. Having been reintegrated into some world—however marginally—they try to save the lives of the little kids caught in the burning church to whom they now feel connected. This reimmersion in history, of course, claims Johnny's life and plunges Pony back into the "parcellized space" of Soc and greaser. There he will fight in a rumble that will precipitate the death of Dallas and his own nervous breakdown.

At the end, Pony, bathed in aureate light, is seated at his desk, his dark hair still dyed blond, inwardly grappling with the reality of Johnny's and Dallas's deaths. As he reads Johnny's deathbed letter, the camera slowly pulls in on his face. Far from vacuous, it is now suffused with the tragic awareness that in a world parceled out between Socs who have and greasers who have not, there is no space to escape into to realize the promise of escape Johnny's letter makes, that there can be no community among those who exploit one another, that though we can to some extent make our own history, we cannot do so free of the constraints of the history we embody. Like those who created him (Hinton, Coppola), Ponyboy will cope with this realization by transmuting it into art. After his face—in which this is all inscribed—has filled half the screen, the camera adopts his point of view, watching as he laboriously pens the words that open both book and movie: "When I stepped out into the bright sunlight from the darkness of the movie house. . . ."

Notes

1. *The Outsiders* was based on the novel of the same name by S. E. Hinton (1967) and the screenplay thereon by Kathleen Knutsen Rowell. It was produced by Fred Roos and Gary Fredrickson and directed by Francis Coppola for Warner Brothers for release in 1982. It didn't, however, make the theaters until the spring of 1983.

2. The sales figures are from the cover of the paperback released to coincide with the release of the film.

3. No teenage-oriented magazine of the period failed to carry stories about the film and its stars.

4. This is from an unsigned paragraph from *American Film* (1982). It's probably relevant to recall that Coppola had just bombed disastrously with the over-budget *One From the Heart*, was entangled in the production of *Hammett*, and was losing/had lost Zoetrope Studios in the process. *The Outsiders* had, in many senses, to be a comeback for Coppola.

5. Not irrelevant here is Roland Barthes's (1977, p. 116) observation about

some of the ways bourgeois society attempts a kind of naturalism: "Generally, however, our society takes the greatest pains to conjure away the coding of the narrative situation: there is no counting the number of narrational devices which seek to naturalize the subsequent narrative by feigning to make it the outcome of some natural circumstance and thus, as it were, 'disinaugurating' it: epistolary novels, supposedly rediscovered manuscripts, author who met the narrator, films which begin the story before the credits. The reluctance to declare its codes characterizes bourgeois society and the mass culture issuing from it: both demand signs which do not look like signs."

6. Reacting against both the idealism and the mannerism of sixteenth-century art, Caravaggio (Michelangelo Merisi) introduced both a revolutionary naturalism and a dramatic realism, the latter typified by a shallow picture plane and a startling chiaroscuro. See Friedlander (1955) and the essays and plates in the catalogue *The Age of Caravaggio* (1985).

7. There are really two issues here. One revolves around the fact that *The Outsiders* was, to begin with, a teen flick. How seriously was one to take it? Many critics dismissed it out of hand, on this ground alone. Godfrey Cheshire, for example, complained that "from telling morally complex tales for adults, Coppola has regressed—that's the only word for it—to the level of the Hardy Boys" (Cheshire 1983, p. 16). But as frequently as not, this was prompted by an uneasiness over the homosexual implication of what Cheshire glossed as "pretty teenage boys gazing sensitively and spouting over poetry at each other." What *was* it? Homoeroticism on the big screen? Pin-ups for teenage girls? A stupid teen flick? Or was it, as the evident craft and intelligence of the movie-making and script insisted, something else altogether?

8. There seems to be little middle ground in our thinking about the display of nude teenage males. Here, for example, is Jacobs (1979) on the *Amor Victoris* (or *Amor Vincit Omnia*): "Another artist with a line of blatant 'pin-ups' was Caravaggio, but his sexual inclinations, like those of his clientele, were exclusively homosexual. The male nude in art, usually athletic and well-developed, seems absurd as simply a languorous object of passive sensual contemplation. Exceptions are the bodies of young boys, which served as subjects for many of Caravaggio's early paintings, destined for such notorious paedophiliacs as Cardinal del Monte and Vinccenzo Giustiniani" et cetera et cetera (Jacobs 1979, p. 45–59). For another reading, all but ignoring (or denying) the homosexual implications of the painting, and stressing instead the way it illustrates the Vergilian "Omnia vincit amor, tu pictor, et omnia vincis,/Scilicet ille animos, corpora tuque animos," see Gregori 1985, pp. 277–81), which also provides a history of the painting's shifting interpretations.

9. Here's Cheshire (1983, p. 16) on this scene: "Clad in his BVDs, Dillon is made to move around the bed unnecessarily but relentlessly, showing us his glorious pubescent physique from every angle; in one emphatic composition, the boy lies prone and the camera cuts off his face at mid-forehead, so that screen-center is dominated by his statuesque torso. What, one inevitably won-

ders, is going here? But had it been a girl cavorting on the bed, would Cheshire have even raised the question?

10. Barthes (1977, pp. 69–78) introduced the notion of the *third* (or *obtuse*) meaning, where it is distinguished from informational and symbolic (or *obvious*) meanings. The third meaning is that which . . . *lies beyond*, which works apart from the narrative without destroying it, which lends itself to a . . . *vertical reading*. With respect to the cinema, he writes, "In other words, the third meaning structures the film *differently* without subverting the story and for this reason, perhaps, it is at the level of the third meaning, and at that level alone, that the 'filmic' finally merges. The filmic is that in the film which cannot be described, the representation which cannot be represented. The filmic begins only where language and metalanguage end." And this is the significance of these boys . . . about which . . . *I cannot write.*

11. That everyone dies is the moral drawn by Corliss (1983).

12. But why? It was not, probably, to achieve the thematic intelligence I think the loss of these scenes gives the film. Apparently Warners found the film too violent for the audience of young teen girls it assumed would comprise its major audience and they requested and got another cut. This did not necessarily make everybody happy. Rob Lowe, for example, was all but cut from the film (Farber 1984, p. 18): "It's difficult for me to watch that movie. The only reason I watch it is to see the other people in it. I can't watch it to see myself because I'm not in it. We just bastardized that book. A lot of irate young kids have come up to me and asked what happened to the movie. I hope the people responsible for the way it turned out get the same complaints I do."

13. Though he found the film "not quite a good one," he liked it better than just about anyone else reviewing it at the time (anybody, that is, who wasn't writing for one of the teen magazines).

14. Strictly speaking, the *"sign is not a physical entity*, the physical entity being at most the concrete occurrence of the expressive pertinent element" (Eco 1976, p. 49). See also de Saussure (1959), especially pp. 65–78, Barthes (1968), and Cullers (1981).

15. As Barthes (1982, p. 478) writes, "I then realized with stupefaction (only the obvious can stupefy) that *my own body was historical.*" This historicity of the body—its historically created particularity—is, since it cuts against the *ideal*, precisely what fueled Caravaggio's naturalism and scandalized his contemporaries notoriously in his *Death of the Virgin* (Gregori 1985, p. 43).

16. In an interview, Rob Lowe—a greaser—added that "*They* were on one floor of the hotel and got their beds turned down at night while *we* were on another where Francis had forbidden the maids to touch the beds. *They* went to live for a while with Tulsa oil families . . . while *we'd* get into wardrobe and hang out at this local park and try to carry on convincing conversations with the local kids in our Oklahoma drawls" (Chase 1983, p. 10). What is all this but an attempt to create in an actor's body some of the history required by his role?

17. Speaking for the greasers, especially C. Thomas Howell and Rob Lowe,

Patrick Swayze notes, "While filming this movie, we all got very close . . . like brothers. We could play football and just have good times together whenever we had time off which was rare when you are working six days a week. The socs got better treatment than the greasers in order to create a natural tension between us for the film. It worked" (Weiss 1982, p. 27).

18. Unpaginated, the quotation appears following the copyright page in this context: "I was born in Tulsa, Oklahoma in 1943. When I was sixteen I started shooting amphetamine. I shot with my friends everyday for three years and then left town but I've gone back through the years. Once the needle goes in it never comes out." Green (1984, p. 126) describes *Tulsa* in these words: "Larry Clark's *Tulsa* shows the quiet atrocities of a very real war. Tulsa is the battlefield. For Clark it was 'shaking' with violence, guns, sex, and drugs, and he was determined to get to the action. The needle, the vein, the penis, and the breast were the weapons. The stakes were life and death." Clark's *Teenage Lust* (1983) is even more devastating. It covers Tulsa in the early 1970s.

19. Namely, "Nothing Gold Can Stay" from Frost (1951, p. 85). Ponyboy's recitation of this poem to Johnny after watching a sunrise drives critics as nuts as the close-ups of their faces or the shots of Matt Dillon on his hospital bed. Corliss (1983, p. 78) states: "left to their better selves, [the greasers] can easily go all moony over sunsets, quote great swatches of Robert Frost verse, or fall innocently asleep in each other's arms. Their ideal world is both a womb and a locker room: no women need apply to this dreamy brotherhood." The "great swatches" of verse consist of eight, short, rhymed lines.

References

Anonymous. 1982. The "Outsiders." *American Film* October: 77.

Barthes, R. 1968. *Elements of Semiology.* New York: Hill and Wang.

Barthes, R. 1977. *Image–Music–Text.* New York: Hill and Wang.

Barthes, R. 1982. *A Barthes Reader.* New York: Hill and Wang.

Chase, D. 1983. A new Lowe. *Ampersand* April: 10.

Cheshire, G. 1983. New and noteworthy. *The Spectator* April 14: 16.

Clark, L. 1971. *Tulsa.* New York: Larry Clark.

Clark, L. 1983. *Teenage Lust.* New York: Larry Clark.

Corliss, R. 1983. Playing tough, going nowhere. *Time* April 4: 78.

Cullers, J. 1981. *The Pursuit of Signs.* Ithaca: Cornell University Press.

de Saussure, F. 1959. *Course in General Linguistics.* New York: Philosophical Library.

Eco, U. 1976. *A Theory of Semiotics.* Bloomington: Indiana University Press.

Farber, S. 1984. Rob Lowe. *Moviegoer* September: 18.

Friedlander, W. 1955. *Caravaggio Studies.* Princeton: Princeton University Press.

Frost, R. 1951. *Complete Poems of Robert Frost.* New York: Holt, Rinehart and Winston.

Goodman, P. 1960. Jeremy Owen. In P. Goodman, *Our Visit to Niagara.* New York: Horizon Press.

Green, J. 1984. *American Photography: A Critical History.* New York: Abrams.

Gregori, Mina. 1985. The Musicians. In *The Age of Caravaggio,* edited by Metropolitan Museum of Art. New York: Rizzoli.

Hinton, S. E. 1967. *The Outsiders.* Viking: New York.

Jacobs, M. 1979. *Nude Painting.* New York: Mayflower Books.

Lefebvre, H. 1991. *The Production of Space.* Oxford: Basil Blackwell.

Metropolitan Museum of Art, editor. 1985. *The Age of Caravaggio.* New York: Rizzoli.

Weiss, H. 1982. *An Inside Look at All the Stars of the "Outsiders": Superteen Special No. 6.*

Filmography

Gone With the Wind. 1939. M.G.M. Director, Fleming, V.
The Outsiders. 1982. Warner Brothers. Director, Coppola, F.

6

Sunshine and Shadow: Lighting and Color in the Depiction of Cities on Film

---

Larry Ford

In Woody Allen's *Annie Hall* (1977), when Marshall McLuhan steps out from behind a theater poster and settles a dispute concerning the interpretation of his work, Alvy Singer (Woody Allen) turns to the camera and asks if it wouldn't be nice if life were always that simple—clear-cut answers direct from the proper source. This seems like an appropriate scene to keep in mind for those of us who would attempt to interpret films. Since McLuhan is not likely to pop in and give us the answers, our musings can best be seen as tentative speculations. This is not to say that they have no value, because art is created to be interpreted. By expanding the contexts in which we view films, we may enliven and enrich our understanding not only of the films themselves but of the places depicted in them.

The purpose of this chapter is to trace the ways in which cities have been depicted in films over time with a special focus on the roles of lighting and color. More specifically, I hope to affirm with this focus some recent theories that suggest that the role of cities in film gradually changed over time from serving as mere background scenery to acting as the equivalent of major characters in many stories. My contention is that lighting and color are of major importance in this development. Second, I hope to show that in recent years, cities have been illuminated in increasingly complex and often contradictory ways in films and that by examining this topic, we may add an additional layer of understanding to our knowledge of place-making and place representation. Sense of place is of vital concern to geographers, yet it remains a nebulous concept. Films provide controlled and replicatable visual experiences that can enable us to study the ways in which people and places interact as stories unfold.

The City as a Backdrop

In the early days of American silent films during the 1920s, cities were used as random, often unidentified, stages for action. City scenes appeared in many of the early film comedies. Memorable images include Harold Lloyd hanging from a clock tower (*Safety Last*, 1923) and Laurel and Hardy pushing a piano up a steep hillside stairway (*The Music Box*, 1932), but the city was a stage, not a player. It did not influence unduly the psyches of the human participants in the stories. There were tall buildings, traffic jams, busy sidewalks, and so forth, but Harold Lloyd and Laurel and Hardy took them all in stride. The city was just "there." For technical reasons, most films had to be shot in bright daylight and so the mood of the films was not much affected by changing levels of lighting. In America, the focus of early films was on the actors. A strong tradition of stage comedy and Vaudeville meant that famous stars could transfer their antics to film and be presented to an even wider and more appreciative audience. One could argue that America was naive and unsophisticated in its demand for entertainment compared to European *haute couture* and that Charlie Chaplin doing slapstick comedy was what people wanted to see. City scenes were used most often because they were handy. Much invaluable footage of early Los Angeles is found in these films, but the city as a purposeful character is not fully developed. Neither was the role of nature carefully contrived since much of the scenery of the "wild west" was actually within the city limits of Los Angeles, but that is another story.

This casual concern for the role of place and setting was less prevalent in Europe where early films were seen as part of artistic movements rather than as mass entertainment. During the early 1920s, for example, German Expressionist filmmakers were creating urban worlds (on artificial sets) that were carefully contrived to contribute to a sense of mood and to enhance the emotional valence of films. In many, cities are depicted as brooding, tension-filed places that actually participate in the character's descent into nightmarish predicaments. Dark shadows are often contrasted with tense, malevolent light. The city was depicted as having an uneasy ambience that contributed mightily to human despair. In films such as *The Cabinet of Dr. Caligari* (1919) and *The Blue Angel* (1930), the claustrophobic, isolating settings are important in creating the mood of the stories. In Fritz Lang's *Metropolis* (1926), the city itself becomes a monster villain contributing directly to the misery of the human characters. It was as if the filmmakers sought to recreate the intense impact of Edvard Munch's painting *The Scream* in moving form

(Hirsch 1981, p. 54). In Europe, films were often made for a relatively small audience by directors who sought to author a piece of art. In America, the goal was more often to create a blockbuster that would make lots of money and showcase a star.

The chaos in Europe during the late 1920s and early 1930s brought an end to the creative period in German filmmaking, and many German directors and actors sought refuge in America. By the mid-1930s, Hollywood was the undisputed film capital of the world, but by then everyone was preoccupied with the advent of sound, and experimentation with lighting took a back seat to finding actors who could speak in sentences and perhaps even sing. Early talking pictures involved a great deal of talking. Many films look like live theater captured on celluloid. Actors were recruited heavily from the theaters of Broadway, and fast-paced stagelike dialogues dominated the screen. Dazzling, larger-than-life musicals became very important money-makers in Depression America. Interior scenes came to dominate exterior settings as films moved inside, at least in "city films" (less so in westerns, etc.). Fred Astaire and Ginger Rogers dance around ballrooms, and Chicago gangsters argue and fight in hotel rooms. The city itself was still largely a backdrop—something to be seen from restaurant windows or speeding cars. Outdoor urban scenes often feature the decks of luxury liners or penthouse patios. During the 1930s, big cities were seen as fantasy lands full of tuxedo-clad dancers and cigar-chomping gangsters but the presence of the city was lightly felt. *Forty-Second Street* (1933) was not really a place as much as a state of mind. There were, of course, some exceptions. When King Kong (*King Kong*, 1933) meets his fate climbing the newly completed Empire State Building, the symbolism is powerful—the best and biggest of the modern world defeats the best and biggest of the traditional world. Four decades later when King Kong once again visits New York, in 1976, it takes TWO skyscrapers to defeat him.

Night and the City: German Expressionism and Film Noir

By the 1940s, carefully contrived city scenes were becoming more important in many American films. World War II shortages made big, expensive films difficult to produce and actors and directors turned to lower budget dramas to fill the theaters. It may also be that audiences were simply ready for a change. The endless Broadway extravaganzas full of tap dancers with feather boas were becoming somewhat predictable and the novelty of sound and music was wearing off. In the absence of big orchestras and chorus lines, many directors sought to create a stronger film atmosphere through creative lighting and camera angles. Directors such as Billy Wilder, Otto Preminger and Fritz Lang had been trained in the German Expressionist tradition of the 1920s and were ready to show what they could accomplish with low-key lighting, a few dark alleys, and rain-slick streets. These dark and brooding urban dramas were later dubbed "Film Noir."

It is difficult to say just when Film Noir (and the Film Noir city) first emerged. The term was coined after the fact in France during the late 1940s and did not come into wide usage until the mid-1950s. The earliest date often suggested is 1941 when *The Maltese Falcon* and *Casablanca* appeared. The latter in particular developed the theme of people watching their lives and their worlds go slowly out of control. Others would put the beginning closer to the mid-1940s with the production of such classics as *Double Indemnity* (1944) and *Scarlet Street* (1946). The latter view holds that fully developed Film Noir was too bleak and morally ambiguous to be accepted by the wartime public. At any rate, the heyday of the genre was the late 1940s, a time when new philosophies of the individual and concern with anomie came to the fore. Film Noir and existentialism went hand in hand. By the late 1940s, audiences knew that the world was a complex and often evil place and that some discussion of this was in order. Tap dancers could sugarcoat the Depression for a while, but Nazis and Iron Curtains eventually wore them down. It was time to examine the depths of human nature.

Isolation and anomie in the midst of the city was a favorite theme, although different directors and different national contexts sometimes suggested other ways of depicting the increasing concern for these existential effects. British filmmakers tended to focus on the importance of social class, often with neo-Marxist overtones. In *The Loneliness of the Long-Distance Runner* (1962), for example, a reform school inmate becomes a working-class hero to the Establishment because of his ability to win races against "better" schools. In the end, he recognizes the idiocy of his role (and society?) and refuses to finish a race he can easily win. The coding of class-related socialist ideals in *Loneliness* is well articulated in Martyn Bowden's essay (Chapter 4).

It is very possible that the development of new styles of music during the late 1940s and early 1950s also played an important role in the creation of moods of urban tension. Compared to the often schmaltzy background music of the 1930s, the hard-edged, nonlinear sound of the bebop sax could contribute to a sense of unease. In some cases, as in *The Man with the Golden Arm* (1956), hard-driving theme songs became as popular and recognizable as the films. Television theme songs such as those from *Dragnet* and *Peter Gunn* immediately conjured images of Film Noir scenes.

Deciding when Film Noir began may be easier than deciding just what Film Noir is and just what films belong in the genre. In its purist form, however, the type is fairly easy to describe: Film Noir usually features a psychological drama in which seemingly normal people are drawn ever deeper into a very personal, isolating nightmare. Mistakes are made, crimes are committed, and characters gradually lose touch with their normal lives and friends. There is moral and ethical ambiguity in the sense that everyday people may gradually become criminals as if by fate. Many of the actors associated with the genre were selected to epitomize ambiguity in contrast to the swashbuckling heroics of the films of both the 1930s and the late 1950s. Handsome, flawless people such as Alan Ladd and Veronica Lake were directed to "sleepwalk" toward their dooms with a minimum of emotion. In a world that seemed out of control, it seemed appropriate that individuals might suffer similar fates. Everyday people became allegorical explanations. "If it could happen to Alan Ladd, then I guess it could happen to Germany."

Even strong characters like Humphrey Bogart and Robert Mitchum exhibited a sort of tight-lipped resignation as they were drawn into their respective fates. Why fight it when night comes to the city. Night scenes, usually very dark and shadowy, dominate the films. Low-key lighting and strong black and white contrasts, often provided by streetlights shining through venetian blinds, are also used to create the dark psychological moods that led to the term Film Noir. The city plays an important role in the development of a nightmare atmosphere. In the best films, however, the role is subtle. The city itself is not depicted as horrible or nightmarish but rather as a setting that gradually contributes to the development of such feelings.

The Film Noir city is a tense, brooding, lonely, isolating place that tends to push people over the edge. Typical titles were *Night and the City* (1950), *The Naked City* (1948), *Side Street* (1950), *The Street with No Name* (1948), *The Asphalt Jungle* (1950), *The Dark Corner* (1946), *Cry of the City* (1948), and *Nightmare Alley* (1947). Lines such as "It's the city that's getting to us" were often used to explain the actors' otherwise unexplainable descent into a personal hell. Film techniques borrowed heavily from the German Expressionists but the urban images were also derived from American Realist artists such as George Bellows, Reginald Marsh, and Edward Hopper. City scenes were presented as strangely stark and aloof. Still photography may have also had an influence—especially the stark urban scenes of artists such as Alfred Steiglitz.

In *Scarlet Street* (1946), Chris Cross (Edward G. Robinson), a solidly middle-class clerk leading a humdrum life in a small apartment with a dominating wife, chooses to walk home alone after an award dinner. The night is dark and rainy and he becomes disoriented and confused in the mazelike streets of Greenwich Village. He witnesses a man hitting a woman, and in coming to her rescue he begins his descent into mayhem and, finally, murder. In such a setting, he is helpless to resist. "It's the city that's getting to us." He enters a shadowy, claustrophobic world with no light at the end of the tunnel. The atmosphere is not all-pervasive evil as in later terror films, but rather gives the feeling of ambiguous tension and uneasiness. I contend that this mood has stuck with us and that American cities have been associated with ambiguous tension for the past fifty years. But that is getting ahead of the story.

Like *Scarlet Street*, most of the early Film Noir dramas were filmed in soundstages rather than real city streets. The sense of isolation could thus be complete with designed-in emptiness and foreboding. Lighting was often blatantly allegorical with happy times bathed in the noonday sun while the worst moments occurred in almost total darkness with perhaps only a flashing neon sign to illuminate the scene. The fact that everything was artificial and could be controlled contributed to the nightmarish emptiness in Film Noir atmosphere. Back and side lighting could create just the look of uneasy weariness on the face of the hapless victim of life in the big city.

By the late 1940s, however, the stage set was beginning to lose some of its appeal and the trend was toward films made "on location," especially if the location was nearby. Documentaries had become increasingly important during the 1930s as American filmmakers sought to describe and explain Dust Bowl migrations and other aspects of the Great Depression (see Chapter 9 by Arthur Krim). During World War II, Americans came to expect a continuous dosage of war footage complete with waving Churchills and Roosevelts. By the end of the war, documentaries had become popular in Europe as liberation revived the possibility of real news and the accurate filming of rapidly unfolding events. In Europe, artistic directors were also intrigued by the documentary approach, partly because elaborate soundstages were simply not available and also because the Nazi era had made people suspicious of contrived and unauthentic art. There was a need to film real people in the real world in order to establish credibility. In Chapter 11 John Gold and Stephen Ward discuss some of this neorealism with regard to documentary footage of New Town phenomena of postwar Britain, but nowhere was the need for "real world representation" more vital than in Italy where many postwar films were seen to represent a movement dubbed Italian neorealism. The influence of Italian neorealism was being felt in America by 1948 as directors began to seek a more documentary approach in urban crime dramas. Capturing, but at the same time controlling, the real city became the challenge of the day. Who knows, with enough cameras rolling through the city streets, maybe a few Communist spies could be uncovered.

Realism and the City

Postwar Italian neorealism films such as *The Bicycle Thief* (1948) and *Open City* (1945) demonstrated to American directors that real urban scenes could be just as conducive to the creation of an atmosphere of lonely uneasiness as the stage set had been. In addition, the use of real settings could lend a sort of exposé/documentary quality to the dramas that could take advantage of the public's familiarity with the newsreels being shown widely in theaters. Location films such as *The Naked City* (1948), *Criss Cross* (1948), and *Kiss of Death* (1947) used neorealist techniques to create a city that is more than a merely neutral and uninflected backdrop. The city is molded into a powerful neurotic element in the story. According to Hirsch (1981, p. 17), for example, "In the brilliant *Night and the City* (1950), a real London, oozing with slime and enshrouded with fog, becomes a maze of crooked alleyways, narrow cobbled streets and waterfront dens; a place of pestilential enclosure." Similarly, New York in *The Window* (1949) is depicted by Hirsch as "an infested environment that seems to be a breeding ground for crime."

While Film Noir on location still used the motif of "it was a dark and stormy night," new settings for crime gradually emerged. Tenement rooftops are a favorite scene because the theme of isolation and separateness in the midst of the big city can be developed fully there. In *The Naked City* (1947) the rooftop epitomizes the Film Noir ambience even on a sunny day. Seemingly empty and abandoned warehouse and industrial districts are also perfect for Film Noir. Loading docks and alleys are ideal lonely spots for crime even with the glittering city skyline in the background. These places are also perfect for Film Noir lighting because glaring spotlights can be contrasted with dark spaces and backlighting techniques can be heavily used. The strong contrast between light and dark can be perpetuated.

The City of Monsters and the Death of Film Noir

Classic Film Noir was done in black and white, and whether true Film Noir can be done in color is a hotly debated point. Color changed everything. To a very real degree, however, Film Noir was on its way out well before color films took over. While the heyday of the genre was the late 1940s and early 1950s, variations on the Film Noir theme continued until at least 1960 when *Psycho* and *The Hustler* (1961) were released. By that time, however, such films were becoming few and far between. Black and white films remained predominant through the 1950s but Film Noir gradually gave way to other types of films as the decade progressed. Westerns were particularly popular, as were films featuring an assortment of oversized monsters. Perhaps inspired by concerns over atomic war and possible associated mutations, moviegoers were treated to visitations from giant ants, spiders, space creatures, and blobs. The city (once again an artificial city) became something to be either stepped on or eaten. The depiction of the city as a major character diminished as more scenes were designed to simply blow up in a picturesque and exciting manner. Lighting still played a role in creating desired effects, but artistic subtlety waned.

Film Noir died in the early 1960s but vestiges of the Film Noir city live on. The remainder of this chapter focuses on the ways in which new color and lighting technologies have been used to reproduce, redefine, modify, and occasionally reverse the image of the city as created in Film Noir.

The Technicolor City

Directors experimented with color almost as soon as films were invented. Some tried hand coloring but that proved to be too expensive and tedious. Others tried tints such as blue for night and amber for fireside romances. For the most part, however, filmmakers stuck with black and white until color film was invented in the 1930s. Because it was expensive and difficult to use, color films were rare until the 1950s. Blockbusters such as *Gone With the Wind* and *The Wizard of Oz* came out in 1939 but World War II brought a hiatus to further production. It was not until the late 1960s that color films became the norm. It was also not until the 1960s that color films looked truly accurate as Technicolor brightness gave way to more varied and sophisticated experiments with hue and tone.

The Technicolor films from the late 1930s to the 1960s emphasized overly bright primary colors. When *She Wore a Yellow Ribbon* (1949), it was indeed yellow. Technicolor was best suited to lively musicals and colorful westerns. City scenes simply looked too good for the expected Film Noir ambience. By the time *West Side Story* was filmed in 1960, it was hard to make New York look as menacing in color as it had looked in black and white. A dark and rainy night looks like fun in *Singing in the Rain* (1952), and the (stage-set) alleys of Paris look absolutely delightful in *An American in Paris* (1951). Directors reveled in color as cities from New York to Rome were filmed in bright sunlight and depicted as wonderful and exciting places for Doris Day, Rock Hudson, Tony Randall, and Audrey Hepburn to romp. Sunlight reflected from the new glass towers of Manhattan showed a very different kind of city and there was almost no way to get around this. Even a dark and foggy Paris looked good in the noir-like *Phantom of the Rue Morgue* (1954).

It is interesting to ponder whether some types of films should be made only in black and white or only in color. It is generally accepted that grand musicals and films featuring magnificent scenery are best shot in color, but for other types of films there is no consensus. Would *Dr. Strangelove* (1963) have had the same impact in color? Would *Catch 22* (1970) have been a stronger film in black and white? Can any true Film Noir picture be shot in color? Perhaps the best attempt to create a Film Noir ambience in color was Hitchcock's *Rear Window* (1954). In this film, the dark and claustrophobic atmosphere is enhanced by the fact that the main character is immobilized by a leg cast. He cannot escape from his fate. To a very real degree, however, the Film Noir city was put on hold during the late 1950s to be reinvented or at least redefined at a later date. Meanwhile, Sgt. Friday still roamed through a kind of Film Noir Los Angeles on black and white television. Perhaps we had become so used to the dark urban setting as appropriate for moody crime dramas during the first decades of film that colorful rural locales could not be used convincingly. *Bonnie and Clyde* (1967), driving brightly colored vehicles through small towns on sunny days, simply cannot be that bad. For one thing, shooting in color required a lot of light, and so bright, sunny days predominated. Nights were unconvincing because they were really daytime scenes shot with a blue filter. Night scenes became incidental rather than essential as they had been in Film Noir.

By the late 1960s, color techniques had become more sophisticated. Primary colors gave way to more somber and subtle greens and grays. A neo-Film Noir quality appeared along with a new emphasis on realism in *Midnight Cowboy* (1969). A darker New York of nighttime scenes and somber grays replaced the pervasive brightness of *Lover Come Back* (1961). Later, Franco Zeffirelli put nylon stockings over the camera lens in his 1975 version of *The Taming of the Shrew* in order to achieve a painterly effect reminiscent of the Dutch Masters and to emphasize the dark, muted colors of the late medieval city.

Perhaps the final and most pervasive attempt to create a Film Noir city occurred in the making of *Blade Runner* in 1982. Set in Los Angeles in the year 2020, the dark, oppressive cityscape plays such a powerful role in the film that it all but overwhelms the characters. The sky is always dark and polluted, the streets are always wet and foggy, the alleys always narrow and claustrophobic, and the lighting is strong and focused. In addition, there are the ingredients of moral and ethical ambiguity, despair, and isolation. The connection between *Blade Runner* and its Film Noir heritage is solidified by the use of Los Angeles' historic Bradbury Building, an oft-used setting in the detective stories of the 1940s. The role of the city is so rich and powerful in *Blade Runner* that any further attempts to recreate the Film Noir city as a major dramatic element may seem trite and underwhelming. The otherwise effective setting used in *Brazil* (1985), for example, seems to have less impact than it might have as a result of the impact of *Blade Runner*. New images of the city were needed. It was no longer enough to pit darkness against light. The Film Noir city was in danger of becoming hackneyed.

Woody Allen's *Annie Hall*: A Reversal of Images

Woody Allen, according to Woody Allen, likes cities and dislikes the countryside, likes New York and dislikes Los Angeles, likes somber colors and dislikes bright colors. This all comes together in his 1977 film, *Annie Hall*. The main character, Alvy Singer, loves a New York that is filmed almost entirely in dark and subtle greens and grays. New York is seen as visually calm with few strong contrasts or bright accents. Gray-green trees and green-gray buildings provide a comfortable background for chameleonlike, gray-green-clad Alvy Singer. Nighttime is also depicted as comfortable—a time for strolling and chatting. The city has a role in the film but it is a muted, subtle role like a favorite old sweater. The cityscape contributes to a mood of serenity.

Bright lights and colors appear chiefly when there is conflict. Arguments between the characters often occur in association with the appearance of bright colors such as yellow taxis or bright red doorways. In the scene where Annie and Alvy finally break up, both characters are (uncharacteristically) wearing red. When the story shifts to the West Coast, it is in Los Angeles that the city as ambiguous tension reappears.

Los Angeles is awash with blazing sunshine in *Annie Hall*. The antipathy that Alvy Singer has for California is symbolically represented by a pervasive, glaring sunlight. Sunlight is reflected off bland buildings, automobile windshields, and residential patios. Characters are often backlit as they stand in front of windows or patio doorways. An interesting reversal of Film Noir lighting occurs as the characters appear darkened while a halo of bright light surrounds them. At other times, the actors are depicted as sort of fading away and/or washing out into the inescapable sunshine. Most of the characters wear white or a variety of bright clothing that makes the brightness even more pervasive (*Film Soleil?*). At one point, a character dons a space suit in order to safely drive a convertible into the blazing California sun as Alvy Singer asks, "What are we, driving through plutonium?" In the "environmental" 1970s, excessive sunshine could even be dangerous. Maybe shadowy cities were not so bad after all.

Reflected sunlight seems to represent Allen's view of the lack of depth of Southern California culture as if the glaring sun limits access to subtle meaning and deeper truths just as it limits access to subtle colors and shading. Everything is surface/superficial. In "shallow" Los Angeles, the characters wear bright colors and romp in the sunshine but the setting is somehow less serene than subtle, gray-green New York. The roles of light and dark are not only expanded but reversed.

The films of Woody Allen represent a purposeful reorienting of our image of the (traditional) city. He admittedly tries very hard to select scenes that will portray Manhattan in a positive light and to emphasize the pleasures of urban life. In a sense, he is reflecting an emerging pro-urban ideology associated with the pervasive gentrification and yuppification of many cities during the 1970s. Woody Allen films such as *Annie Hall, Manhattan* (1979), and *Hannah and Her Sisters* (1986) are not so much blatant "boosterism" films for the city as illustrations that normal people can live good, interesting lives in the midst of comfortable but very urban landscapes. The city itself is more a calming influence than a menacing one. When interpersonal tension arises, there is always a friendly coffeehouse or a good street to walk down. The city is still a major player in the film but in a more subtle, complex way. It is backdrop but it is not mere backdrop.

Woody Allen has continued to experiment with lighting and color. In 1979, he presented Manhattan in black and white (by now a daring thing to do). In the opening credits, Allen makes it clear that he feels

New York City is BEST seen in black and white. "He adored New York City . . . to him, no matter what the season was, this was still a town that existed in black and white and pulsated to the great tunes of George Gershwin" (Allen 1980, p. 181). Once again, the shadowy city is depicted as a friendly place. A decade later, in *Scenes From a Mall* (1991), he represents the (for him) polar opposite Los Angeles as a brightly lit, almost totally white shopping mall, which is nothing more than a bland backdrop for the trials and tribulations of the main characters. Woody Allen and Bette Midler are in the mall but somehow they cannot interact with it. It is all surface. It is as though "whiteness" and sunshine now contribute to the isolation and anomie that were once the forte of dark and rainy nights. The characters can interact comfortably with green-gray New York but the white glare of Los Angeles is isolating. In a sense, Allen perceived the increasingly negative image of Los Angeles and perhaps California as a whole, which is now pervasive.

Uneasy Sunshine, a Continuing Tradition?

Over the past decade, there have been a number of films that have helped to perpetuate the reversal of day and night and light and dark in the creation of a disturbing urban atmosphere. In *Choose Me* (1984), for example, the characters seem at home in the friendly confines of a dark and dreary Skid Row but in the light of day, they seem awkward and disoriented. The city at night seems warm and comforting whereas sunshine seems strangely oppressive. The light and dark reversal here is perhaps related to character development in that the people in the story have night jobs and are more used to night living, but there is more to it than that. Dark and rainy "claustrophobic" alleys just do not threaten anymore. White heat does.

In *White Palace* (1990) the city at night is comfortable and exciting, whereas tension and conflict arrive with the sunny dawn. The characters are at home in dark city scenes and even the stark light–dark contrast of the diner at night is comforting. Problems occur only when the unconventional couple meet the family in full daylight. A similar sense of comfort was found a few years earlier by the characters who frequented the dark and rainy city streets surrounding *Diner* (1982), supposedly set in an industrial slum on the Baltimore waterfront.

In *Edward Scissorhands* (1990), an overly colorful, sunny suburban landscape is seen as sterile and superficial. The people there are generally amiable but their lives are bland and empty. Edward Scissorhands, a Frankenstein-like creation, adds depth and meaning to life in suburbia. His home is a classic Psychoesque abandoned Victorian on the top of a hill. Significantly, the castlelike compound is depicted as dark and nearly devoid of color. The images of good and evil (or at least good and not-so-good) are completely reversed.

In other films the reversal is not quite so blatant. In *Grand Canyon* (1991), for example, Los Angeles is a very disturbing city but there is no difference between night and day. Some of the most obvious criminal encounters take place in classic Film Noir settings but bright, sunny days bring little respite from the tension. They almost seem worse simply because crime is supposed to happen at night. We are so used to the allegorical use of light and dark that tension on a pleasant, sunny street can be particularly disturbing, especially when people are gunned down in their neighborhoods. The same undiminishing uneasiness is masterfully accomplished in *Boyz in the Hood* (1991). Once again the sun plays a role in the creation of a "tense and brooding" city and provides no escape from the evils of the night.

Although the picture is more of a spoof than the ones mentioned above, sunshine brings little in the way of soothing effects to Steve Martin and the other characters in *L. A. Story* (1991). The opening of "Drive-by shooting season" for example, begins on a brilliant day.

Now that sufficient time has passed since the heyday of Film Noir, some of the settings from the Film Noir city can be revived safely and even parodied in ways that can appeal to both new audiences and those who remember the originals. In *The Player* (1992), for example, a film set in an otherwise sun-filled Los Angeles, the murder takes place in a dark, wet, gloomy, brick-filled alley. Film Noir strikes again. In *My Own Private Idaho* (1991), sunny rural scenes are presented as a dreamlike escape from the dark, rainy city tenements. In *Blue Velvet* (1986), a made-to-order Film Noir world complete with dreary apartment building, smoky nightclub, and grotesque characters is somewhat incomprehensibly plunged into the middle of an idyllic small town. In the opening scene, the camera pans the sunny village but then suddenly swoops under the green lawn as if to uncover the evil that lurks there. The message is clear. Even in the most unsuspecting places, the Film Noir city lives.

New Uses for Color and Light: The Influence of Theater and Comic Strips

The cinema thrives on change. As technology and art have progressed together, there have been continuing attempts to utilize light and color in novel and entertaining ways. Two important sources of ideas of late have been the London and New York stage and the newspaper comic strips.

In the 1980s, live theater began to experiment with color themes in clothing and sets. For example, all the players might wear light blue, or all the men one color and the women another. In other cases, the good guys and the bad guys might be depicted in appropriate colors. The color themes could be used to enhance other aspects of the play's direction. While this blatant approach has not yet found its way into movies, there have been signs that it has had an influence. In *The Fisher King* (1991), for example, warm people wear warm colors such as browns and oranges while the nasty, hard-edged folks wear steel gray. As people change their demeanors, they change clothes. The settings have the same color theme with cozy apartments and restaurants shown in orange-brown while office towers and less friendly settings are black and gray. New York is depicted as a city with both good and bad people and places and you can tell them apart by their colors.

Color coding is much more obvious in the comic book-inspired *Dick Tracy* (1991). Although the picture takes us through the dark streets and rainy alleys of the Film Noir city, the characters are, to some degree, protected from the setting by their colors. Dick Tracy himself wears bright, sunny yellow while his girlfriend and "the kid" wear orange and red respectively. The "bad guys" wear dark indigos and purples and blend in with the shadowy city.

The characters are also colorful in *Batman* (1989) and, as in *Annie Hall*, the symbolism is reversed. The Joker wears bright and garish colors as if bad taste was an important part of villainy. Batman, of course, saves the day while wearing nothing but stylish blue-black. Batman also lives in a dark and shadowy "cave" reminiscent of the bleak mansions of Film Noir. Gotham City in Batman is a pastiche of Film Noir stereotypes similar to what might be expected in a comic book version of *Blade Runner*. Derelict Deco towers emerge from the fog, and the grimy streets seem perfect for breeding crime, prompting the Joker to quip "Decent people shouldn't live here." Batman gets things straightened out but he does it under the cover of darkness. There is no need to bring sunshine into the picture.

The Increasing Variety and Complexity of City Images in Film

Cities are now depicted in a variety of ways in films. During the early days of American films, cities tended to be depicted as neutral backdrops for the antics of the stars. This was due in part to the fact that film in America grew out of Vaudeville rather than "serious art" as was the case in Europe. Gradually, as European-trained immigrant filmmakers began to influence American production in the 1930s and 1940s, the city emerged as an additional participant in films as city scenes were used to create and enhance moods of tension and isolation. This played to both a widespread anti-urban bias in American culture and the existential environment of the immediate postwar world. I have dubbed this depiction the "Film Noir city." The golden age of Film Noir lasted only a decade or so, from the late 1940s to the late 1950s, but its influence lingers on. While the classic Film Noir city still appears occasionally in many American productions, it is now as likely to be parodied as emulated. In films such as *Blade Runner, Batman,* and *Dick Tracy,* the Film Noir city plays a powerful but blatant comic book role in the dramas. In others, such as *Blue Velvet,* the Film Noir city appears as only one of a variety of important settings and contexts.

In recent years, the city of bright sunshine has begun to compete successfully with the Film Noir city in the area of brooding urban tension. The "city of uneasy sunshine" has been perfected so that there is no longer a consensus way to create an atmosphere of urban tension or, conversely, an atmosphere of jolly goodwill. In films such as *Grand Canyon* (1991) and *Boyz in the Hood,* the city by day offers little respite from the tensions of the night. Cities can now be depicted with a complex combination of color coding as well as with combinations of stereotypical and reversed images. Relatively muted colors have been developed to the extent that lighting can sometimes dominate color to a degree unknown since the black and white films of the 1950s.

Over the past eighty years, films have been one of the most important sources for images of the city and urban life. It is important, even imperative, that we geographers begin to examine the roles that films have played in shaping our understanding of and attitudes toward the city. While the role of the urban scene as a character in films may be less obvious and stereotyped today than it was at one time, it is still useful and fun to ponder how the city is being depicted and portrayed. We will never really understand the ways in which Americans perceive cities unless we pay attention to the roles that cities have played in films.

References

Allen, W. 1980. *Four Films of Woody Allen.* New York: Random House.

Hirsch, F. 1981. *Film Noir: The Dark Side of the Screen.* New York: Da Capo Press.

Selected Bibliography

Allen, R., and Gomery, D. 1985. *Film History: Theory and Practice.* New York: Random House.

Allen, R. 1980. *Vaudeville and Film 1895–1915: A Study in Media Interaction.* New York: Arno.

Balio, T., editor. 1976. *The American Film Industry.* Madison: University of Wisconsin Press.

Barlow, J. 1982. *German Expressionist Film.* Boston: Twayne.

Boggs, J. 1991. *The Art of Watching Films.* Mountain View, Calif.: Mayfield.

Bordwell, D., and Thompson, K. 1986. *Film Art.* New York: Alfred A. Knopf.

Braudy, L. 1976. *The World in a Frame: What We See in Films.* New York: Doubleday.

Casty, A. 1971. *The Dramatic Art of the Film.* New York: Harper and Row.

Dick, B. 1990. *Anatomy of Film.* New York: St. Martin's Press.

Everson, W. 1972. *The Detective in Film.* Secaucus, N.J.: Citadel Press.

Gross, L. 1976. Apres Film Noir: Alienation in a Dark Alley. *Film Comment* (July–August).

Jacobs, L. 1968. *The Rise of the American Film.* New York: Teachers College Press.

Kracauer, S. 1947. *From Caligari to Hitler.* Princeton, N.J.: Princeton University Press.

Overbey, D., editor. 1978. *Springtime in Italy: A Reader on Neo-Realism.* London: Talisman.

Place, J.A., and Peterson, L.S. 1976. Some Visual Motifs in Film Noir. In B. Nichols, editor, *Movies and Methods.* Berkeley: University of California Press.

Schatz, T. 1981. *Hollywood Genres: Formulas, Filmmaking and the Studio System.* New York: Random House.

Silver, A., and Ward, E. 1979. *Film Noir: An Encyclopedic Reference to the American Style.* Woodstock, N.Y.: Overlook Press.

Sklar, R. 1976. *Movie-Made America: A Cultural History of American Movies.* New York: Vintage.

Wood, M. 1975. *America in the Movies.* New York: Basic Books.

Filmography

An American in Paris. 1956. M.G.M. Director, Minnelli, V.

Annie Hall. 1977. United Artists/Jack-Rollins-Charles H. Joffe. Director, Allen, W.

The Asphalt Jungle. 1950. M.G.M. Director, Huston, J.

Batman. 1989. Warner Bros. Director, Burton, T.

The Bicycle Thief. 1948. Italy: P.D.S.-E.N.I.C. Director, de Sica, V.

Blade Runner. 1982. Warner Bros. Director, Scott, R.

The Blue Angel. 1930. U.F.A. Germany. Director, Pommer, E.

Blue Velvet. 1986. De Laurentis Entertainment Group. Director, Lynch, D.

Bonnie and Clyde. 1967. Warner/Seven Arts/Tatira/Hiller. Director, Penn, A.

Boyz in the Hood. 1991. Columbia Pictures. Director, Lee, S.

Brazil. 1985. Universal Studios. Director, Gilliam, T.

The Cabinet of Dr. Caligari. 1919. Decla-Bioscop Productions. Director, Wiene, R.

Casablanca. 1942. Warner Bros. Director, Curtiz, M.

Catch 22. 1970. Paramount. Director, Nichols, M.

Choose Me. 1984. Island Alive. Director, Rudolph, A.

Criss Cross. 1948. U-I. Director, Siodmak, R.

Cry of the City. 1948. T.C.F. Director, Siodmak, R.

The Dark Corner. 1946. T.C.F. Director, Hathaway, H.

Dick Tracy. 1991. Touchstone Pictures. Director, Beatty, W.

Diner. 1982. M.G.M./United Artists. Director, Levinson, B.

Double Indemnity. 1944. Paramount. Director, Wilder, D.

Dr. Strangelove; or, How I Learned to Stop Worrying and Love the Bomb. 1963. United Kingdom: Columbia/Stanley Kubrick. Director, Kubrick, S.

Forty-Second Street. 1933. Warner Bros. Director, Bacon, L.

Gone With the Wind. 1939. M.G.M/David O. Selznick. Director, Fleming, V.

Grand Canyon. 1991. T.C.F. Director, Kasdan, L.

Hannah and Her Sisters. 1986. Orion. Director, Allen, W.

The Hustler. 1961. T.C.F./Robert Rossen. Director, Rossen, R.

King Kong. 1933. R.K.O. Directors, Cooper, M. C., and Schoedsack, E.

King Kong. 1976. Dino de Laurentis. Director, Guillermin, J.

Kiss of Death. 1947. T.C.F. Director, Hathaway, H.

L. A. Story. 1991. Capaloco Pictures. Director, Kassar, M.

The Loneliness of the Long-Distance Runner. 1962. British Lion/Bryanston/Woodfall. Director, Richardson, T.

Lover Come Back. 1961. U-I/Seven Pictures/Nob Hill/Arwin. Director, Mann, D.

The Maltese Falcon. 1941. Warner Bros. Director, Huston, J.

Manhattan. 1979. United Artists. Director, Allen, W.

Metropolis. 1926. Germany: U.F.A. Director, Lang, F.

Midnight Cowboy. 1969. United Artists/Jerome Hellman. Director, Schlesinger, J.

The Music Box. 1932. M.G.M. Director, Roach, H.

My Own Private Idaho. 1991. Universal Pictures. Director, Van Sant, G.

The Naked City. 1948. Universal. Director, Dassin, J.

Night and the City. 1950. United Kingdom: T.C.F. Director, Dassin, J.

Nightmare Alley. 1947. T.C.F. Director, Goulding, E.

Open City. 1945. Italy: Minerva. Director, Rossellini, R.

Phantom of the Rue Morgue. 1954. Warner. Director, del Ruth, R.

Psycho. 1960. Shamley/Alfred Hitchcock. Director, Hitchcock, A.

Rear Window. 1954. Alfred Hitchcock. Director, Hitchcock, A.

Safety Last. 1923. Harold Lloyd. Directors, Taylor, S., and Newmeyer, F.

Scarlet Street. 1946. Universal/Diana. Director, Lang, F.

Scenes From a Mall. 1991. Touchstone Pictures. Director, Allen, W.

She Wore a Yellow Ribbon. 1949. R.K.O. Director, Ford, J.

Side Street. 1950. M.G.M. Director, Mann, A.

Singing in the Rain. 1952. M.G.M. Directors, Kelly, G., and Donen, S.

The Street with No Name. 1948. T.C.F. Director, Keighley, W.

The Man with the Golden Arm. 1956. Otto Preminger. Director, Preminger, O.

The Taming of the Shrew. 1967. Columbia/Royal/F.A.I. Director, Zeffirelli, F.

West Side Story. 1961. Mirish/Seven Arts. Directors, Wise, R., and Robbins, J.

The White Palace. 1990. Universal Pictures. Director, Mondok, L.

The Window. 1949. R.K.O. Director, Tetzlaff, T.

The Wizard of Oz. 1939. M.G.M. Director, Fleming, V.

7

Of Pelicans and Men: Symbolic Landscapes, Gender, and Australia's *Storm Boy*

Leo E. Zonn and Stuart C. Aitken

Symbolic landscapes have been a pervasive subject in geographic literature, but the forms in which they have been presented by media have elicited little sustained research attention, perhaps with the exception of a set of provocative and yet theoretically limited research that has developed around literature (Tuan 1976; Pocock 1981; Silk 1984). Recognition of the nature of a symbolic landscape's portrayed image should be especially important to the geographer (Meinig 1979), at least partially because it may be an important source of the lacunae in individual and collective images of the world's landscapes, but more importantly for this volume, because it can be an essential ingredient in the creation and perpetuation of nationalistic myths. This chapter is concerned with a prominent national symbolic landscape of Australia that perpetuates an image of the dominance of man in Australian environments, places, and society. Our focus is on the crafting of a film's immediate narrative in terms of the juxtaposition of image-events that may contest or reify a broader cultural narrative (cf. Aitken 1991). We attempt to show how a film that is heavily influenced by the federally created Australian Film Commission helps to perpetuate and bolster rather than subvert a series of myths of male dominance in Australian culture.

Storm Boy is a financially successful and award-winning Australian film made and released in 1976, the sixth year into the government-inspired and government-supported renaissance of the national film industry. The film was unusual in that it portrayed an environment rarely considered by the industry—an isolated coast. It was also the first major film of the new era to state a strong conservation perspective in its environmental themes, and it was one of the very few national-level films to be directed explicitly toward family audiences, especially children. None-

137

theless, this chapter contends that the filmic experience of *Storm Boy* differed little from the primary segment of mainstream national film production in that it helped to perpetuate a mythical national symbolic landscape, complete with archetypal Australian characters who were assigned gender roles and values that are purported to be a part of the Australian psyche. Parts of the chapter emphasize this fact by drawing from feminist theory, with particular emphasis upon some recent speculation on the role of women in many mainstream films. Several feminist writers suggest that women are either represented as the "other," the dark continent, or they embody societal structures and norms against which the hero is rebelling (e.g., Mulvey 1975; Silverman 1988). In short, this view states that women in commercial narrative cinema have little relevance beyond their representations as sexual objects or symbols that help to establish an "essential" set of societal values. We take this theme further by exploring this essentialism as latent in the characters and environment in *Storm Boy*. Finally, the fact that the veiled portrayal of a gender-biased nationalistic myth was aimed at children and family audiences makes the film's intentions all the more insidious. Whereas it is relatively easy to discern the value-laden patriarchal discourses embedded in many early children's films, particularly timeless Disney cartoons such as *Bambi* and *The Jungle Book*, it is much more difficult to differentiate hidden gender biases in contemporary productions for children such as Bluth's *The Land Before Time* (1987) and *Rock-A-Doodle* (1990). In the case of *Storm Boy*, we feel that it is important to acknowledge the nationalistic and masculine context that underlies the sponsorship of the film's production, and thus an essential and underlying theme is that federal and state support for the purposes of promoting an Australian identity is at least partially responsible for the nature of the film's representation.

Australian Identity, a Symbolic Landscape, and a Male Credo

Three closely related aspects of the place must be considered for this study. The first is the unique environmental circumstances of Australia and the interpretation and use of this setting by Europeans and Australians. The second is the search for the nation's social and cultural identity, which by definition must include those elements of place that individually and collectively provide a self-identifying distinctiveness to its own people. The third is the relationship among environment, national identity, and gender distinctions in the ways men and women are portrayed as part of particular environments and events (cf. Aitken and Zonn 1993).

The search for Australia's identity has involved a historically complex interaction between the nation's physical setting and interpretation of that setting, the Australian people, and British institutional influences, which have more recently been complemented by an increasing American presence and the institutions associated with high levels of Asian immigration. The Australian's historical interpretation of the nation's rural environment envisions it as a place that is vast, distant, usually inhospitable, and often uninhabitable. The form and character of this landscape may vary dramatically from the more pastoral settings of rolling hills and gum trees to vast stretches of uninhabited desert. This broadly defined landscape is simultaneously a source of national strength, beauty, and eventually, the Australian personality (Heathcote 1972a). "The bush or outback," writes Lowe (1974, p. 4), "stands as a symbol of the Australian way of life, of man's triumph over the elements, and is a purifier of man's soul, a spiritual place with redemptive powers, a place of salvation with a healing mystique."

The image of a rural national symbolic landscape, which has been held by a population that has always been overwhelmingly urban, has been perpetuated as part of the national identity, from poetry to literature to painting, since before federation in 1901 (Heathcote 1972b; Bolton 1976; Elliot 1976; Thomas 1976; Eagle 1982). "In the fine arts," says Thomas (1976, p. 158), "there has been . . . [an] impulse towards what is rather remote from the daily big-city lives of most people, but although . . . inland Australia might be little visited by city-dwellers . . . [it is] known to be vast in area and also to be a source of much of Australia's wealth. The pastoral landscape is therefore a symbolic landscape, rightly understood to be the most characteristically Australian of landscapes."

Quite importantly, this landscape includes as an essential ingredient the nature of the Australian—a man with strong proclivities toward mateship, egalitarianism, and antiauthoritarianism. These distinct characteristics of the purported Australian personality have been seen to evolve in a strongly deterministic fashion. He rarely owned the land he worked, unlike his American counterpart, while he often moved from one rural station to another, and most social interaction was with men like himself. He was rarely accompanied by women. The outback or bush was his place; it was an essential element of the symbolic landscape where he became man and experienced life as only an Australian could. Thus, man and landscape possessed a synergistic energy. In this archetypal man, formalized in Russell Ward's (1965) classic *The Australian*

Legend, the personality, "although exaggerated and romanticized, has reality, not only because it is rooted in a nation's past, but because it influences present-day ideas of how Australians ought 'typically' to behave." In Ward's view, the model is

> a practical man, rough and ready in his manners, and quick to decry affection . . . He is a great improviser . . . willing to "have a go" at anything, but . . . content with a task done in a way which is "near enough." Though capable of great exertion in an emergency, he normally feels no impulse to work hard . . . He swears hard and drinks constantly, gambles heavy and often, and drinks deeply on occasion . . . He is usually taciturn . . . stoical . . . and skeptical about the value of religion, and of intellectual pursuits generally. He believes that Jack is not only good as his master, but probably a good deal better, and so he is a great "knocker" of eminent people, unless, as in the case of his sporting heroes, they are distinguished by physical prowess. He is a fiercely independent person who hates officiousness and authority—especially when . . . embodied in military officers and policemen. Yet he is very hospitable and, above all, will stick to his mates through thick and thin . . . He tends to be a rolling stone, highly suspect if he should chance to gather much moss. (1965, pp. 1–2)

The importance of this national symbolic landscape to the nation's identity is still powerful (Carroll 1982; Clancy 1982; Hutton 1981; Turner 1986; Ryan 1990; Rattigan 1991), but its precise character has been challenged over the past two decades. In particular, the relation between the rural setting and the purported elements of the Australian personality—mateship, egalitarianism, and antiauthoritarianism—nearly always represented in masculine terms, is no longer unequivocally accepted (cf. Monk and Norwood 1990). Debate has revolved around the inclusion of these elements as integral to the symbolic landscape, and thus the very nature of the landscape is questioned.

Many writers have contended that truth and legend have not been synonymous, and in fact, the long-term need for an identity has helped to produce one. Thus, the national symbolic landscape of Australia has reflected an imposition, rather than recognition, of national values (Hodges 1982). Graeme Davison (1982) represents a widespread view, in fact, when he contends that many features of the Australian character were creations of late-nineteenth-century discontented urban intellectuals, most of whom lived in Sydney or Melbourne and who wrote for *The Bulletin,* which was considered to be quite nationalistic.

Contemporary Australian cinema has tended to ignore these views, and in its attempt to portray a national identity has embraced the symbolic landscape for its "Australian content," complete with the folk history of the Australian personality. The primary catalyst and mechanism for achieving this end was the federal government's Australian Film Development Corporation, its related successors, and similarly structured state bodies.

Federal Legislation and Australian Cinema

The Australian Film Development Corporation (AFDC) was conceived in the late 1960s during a period of renewed nationalism. This rejuvenation was at least partially a reaction to the country's involvement in Vietnam, and thus much of the sentiment against foreign influence was directed toward the United States, rather than the United Kingdom. The war was only one of several increasing American impositions; American cinema could be counted high on the list. The Australian market of the 1960s was dominated by American films while the Australian industry was experiencing its lowest ebb. "We need a film industry," said Phillip Adams, "because our emotions were being lived for us by American experts" (1984, p. 70).

Development of a viable film industry explicitly required federal support. Accordingly, the Australian Parliament passed the Australian Film Development Corporation (AFDC) Act in 1970 and the AFDC became functional in 1971. It was superseded by the Australian Film Commission (AFC) in 1975 with no major changes in intent or practice. The AFDC legislation created an investment bank from which financial assistance for "Australian Films" could be provided, and a board was formed to administer such assistance. The form of aid has ranged to the present day, from direct grants at various stages of production to tax incentives. Importantly, an Australian film was defined as

> a film that had been made, or will be made, wholly or substantially in Australia . . . and in the opinion of the corporation, has or will have a significant Australian content. (Ginnane 1984, p. 66)

The term "Australian content," which is of considerable importance here, was defined as follows:

> In forming an opinion whether a film has or will have a significant Australian content the corporation will have regard to the subject matter of the film; the place or places where the film was or is to be made; the places of

residence of the persons taking part in the making of the film, including authors, actors, musical composers, and technicians; the source from which the money to be used in the making of the film will be derived; the owner-ship of the shares or stock in the capital of any company concerned in the making of the film; the ownership of the copyright of the film, and any other matters that it thinks relevant. (Ginnane 1984, p. 66)

The first state film commissions were created in South Australia in 1973 and New South Wales in 1977, and to the present day these are the two most successful in the country. The criteria utilized by these state bodies for support of respective films are very similar to those of the AFDC and its successors, and so subsidies and tax breaks from these commissions have often complemented federal support (McFarlane 1987, pp. 25–26).

An increasingly accepted view of Australian cinema is that its "renais-sance," which dates from federal support in 1970 and state support in the early and mid-1970s, has been preoccupied with historic and rural subjects (Hutton 1981). Recognition of these efforts does not deny con-siderable contemporary and urban works, only that the major produc-tions, including those that have been successful in national and interna-tional markets, have had these proclivities. Clearly, those who have supported and made films were looking for an identity model, and it was in the historical-rural genre, complete with an intact symbolic land-scape, that they found help. This emphasis has been lamented by Pau-line Kael (Beilby and Lansell 1983, p. 48), who has called the nation's films "slow, ponderous, and old fashioned" and "careful, laborious re-stagings of the past," by P. P. McGuiness (1977), an Australian reviewer who stated that "there is great danger that the renaissance in the Aus-tralian Film Industry . . . will founder in a wave of nostalgia," and by Phillip Adams (1984, p. 70), chairman of the Australian Film Commis-sion, who said, "I just hope that filmmakers won't feel any more that they have to dress people up in crinolines or have a mandatory merino or gum tree in every scene." Nonetheless, when *Cinema Papers* polled Australian critics in 1984 to rank the best films produced since forma-tion of the AFDC (Anon. 1984, 62–65), eight of the resulting top ten were historical, one was futuristic (*Mad Max II/The Road Warrior*, 1982) and only one (*Lonely Hearts*, 1982) had a contemporary and urban set-ting. As important is the fact that the most prominent and successful films made in the first fifteen years were dominated by men in historic rural settings—men who exuded the Australian character, and thus men who crystallized the Australian symbolic landscape. All of these films were supported by the federal government and, in fact, the film board usually premised support upon approval of the subject matter. What could have greater "Australian content" than films about a man's experiences in the outback or bush? Clearly, the chosen films tended to typify such content and thus demonstrate a national identity, despite the neglected fact that they were relying upon questionable premises. The culprit was multidimensional, therefore; it was the government, filmmakers, as well as the Australian public. The fact that these films were the ones that tended to be accepted by the international markets reflects careful promotions by the Australian government and a recognition that the genre was what international film-goers, especially British and American, wanted to see.

Aboriginals are often included in the settings of mainstream Australian films, although it is difficult to tell if they function aesthetically—as an environmentally charged backdrop—or as characters in their own right. The fact that the quasimystical visions of rural settings as seen by blacks and interpreted by whites are so often included suggests that they have been accorded a modest place in the Australian character. Women in mainstream Australian cinema are largely absent or portrayed as playing supporting roles to a masculine ethos. They are portrayed as the love or fear inspired in the male character, or they represent the societal strictures or mores against which the male character is struggling. It is noteworthy that in his recent book *Images of Australia* (1991), Neil Rattigan establishes, through a review of one hundred films of the new Australian cinema, a reification of myths about the bush, bushman, pioneers, the Anzac, and the ocker (redneck) image without one mention of feminist issues or women's films. In short, the purveyor of the Australian character is overwhelmingly male. This point should not ignore women in film, only that, with the exceptions of a few select period-pieces like *Picnic at Hanging Rock* (1975), *My Brilliant Career* (1979), and *We of the Never Never* (1984), man-in-historical-rural-landscape was the overwhelmingly popular theme for major productions. With the notable exception of *Walkabout* (1971), children were rarely seen.

What follows is a discussion of *Storm Boy* in the light of the national discourse within which it is situated and the concomitant male-dominated ethos that enables the construction of a broader narrative that encompasses a large part of the Australian identity. That the film holds a significant debt to environmental conservation subtly subverts the familiar ecofeminist theme of "man is to culture as woman is to nature" (cf. Griffin 1978; Merchant 1979; Keller 1985; Davis 1988; Spretnak 1990; Rosser 1991). Women, although largely absent in *Storm Boy*, represent urban, civil society—a society from which the main adult male characters (one Aboriginal and one white) find sanctuary in the natural preserve of the Coorong. It is within this environment that "Storm Boy" (Mike, the son of the white male) grows up, and it is with the tension of urban-society-female versus nature-freedom-male that he and his father are forced to come to terms.

The Coorong and Storm Boy

The Australian coast varies dramatically in character over its 12,000 miles. The population is, of course, peripheral in location, but most of the coast is remote and relatively unspoiled, from rocky and abrupt edges to discontinuous beaches to unencumbered stretches of shoreline to tidal coasts of salt marsh and mangrove. Located in southeastern South Australia, the Coorong is a narrow strip of water that runs parallel to the coast for nearly 60 miles. The region is situated between the dunal peninsula that faces the Southern Ocean and a series of older dunes and interdunal flats, the latter often characterized by mangrove swamps and lagoons. The coastal plain extends to the east and southeast of the shoreline. The foredunes that separate the Coorong from the sea can be quite significant in height and usually include a discontinuous cover of mangroves, dune grasses, and other vegetation. Finally, it should be noted that the term Coorong is often used in reference to the area's complex of dunes, swamps, lagoons, and flats.

The Coorong has intrigued visitors for many years. More than a century ago, George French Angas wrote of the Coorong:

> After toiling for nearly a mile over these sandy mountains, the roar of the surf grew nearer and nearer and more distinct; and as we gained the summit of the final ridge, the first sight of ocean burst upon our view. It was a grand and solemn scene; a dull haze shut out the horizon, and the utter and almost awful solitude was unbroken by any living thing. (Faulkner 1983, p. 199)

A descendant of the Ngarinjera tribe presents a different perspective on the same place:

> The Coorong means to me what Ayers Rock means to those in Central Australia . . . The Coorong represents a bond with the past, a closeness to the earth. I know what it means to say that "this land is mine." It is an inseparable part of me and mine. I love nothing better than to run through the bush and sand dunes, to climb high enough to see the Coorong, the

Southern Ocean and Lake Alexandria and I hope that one day I may return with my family to the place I call mine. For it was amongst nature itself that I was taught my identity. For to know one's past and who one is, and where one fits into all this, is the most satisfying experience of a lifetime. (Faulkner 1983, p. 200)

Only a handful of Aboriginals are left in the area. The sparse white population can be found in a few settlements scattered along the lightly traveled two-laned road that runs parallel to the Coorong. The clearing of land and the imposition of cattle, sheep, the rabbit, and the creature known as the dune buggy have irrevocably altered the fauna, flora, and morphology of the place, although its nature still seems remote. Thiele and McKelvy (Faulkner 1983, pp. 200–201) have stated "and so man may destroy the Coorong as he has destroyed so many other places in the world . . . despite lip service and protest, half hearted legislation and surveillance, the spirit of the Coorong will die."

Storm Boy was taken from the children's book written by Colin Thiele and was directed by Henri Safran, a French immigrant to Australia. Supported by the Australian Film Commission and the South Australian Film Corporation, the production was part of a larger promotional package that included a twenty-minute documentary on the making of the film, a "Storm Boy Picture Book" for preschoolers, and the "Pic-a-Pak Study Guide" for schools. Most of the shooting of the film took place in the more isolated area of the Coorong southeast of Goolwa. It cost $320,000 to make. *Storm Boy* opened in Adelaide in late 1976 and became an instant success throughout the country. Five years later it was counted among the ten top grossing Australian films ever made. It was shown at Cannes, won several major awards at the Moscow Film Festival, and received Australian Film awards for best picture, cinematography, and screenplay (Faulkner 1983, pp. 194–95).

Storm Boy is about a boy and his father who live in an isolated area of the Coorong near a game reserve. Their home is a humpy, a small dwelling that is nearly a shack. It is set between a 20-foot-high dune and a quiet lagoon; the open sea is within sight. There are no neighbors and few visitors. Alone, the father fishes and the boy scours the shoreline for any usable debris that may have washed ashore during storms. Their life is simple, quiet, and isolated. The story of *Storm Boy* revolves around the boy's relationship with his father, Tom, and an Aboriginal called Fingerbone Bill. The fourth character is a pelican, Mr. Percival.

The opening shot of the film is of a flight of pelicans; we then see an oblique view of the Coorong. The camera then focuses on a boy walking

Figure 7–1. Storm Boy
learns the way of the land
through the eyes of his
Aboriginal friend,
Fingerbone Bill. Courtesy of
the National Film Archive,
National Library of
Australia.

Figure 7–2. Storm Boy on the beach with his pelican friend, Mr. Percival. Courtesy of the National Film Archive, National Library of Australia.

down the beach, evaluating every piece of debris for its potential useful-
ness. Mike has found a water-logged radio. Upon returning to the
humpy, he shows it to his father, who says tersely, "You can throw that
in the rubbish." "What is it?" asks Mike. "A radio, we don't want it,
son!" "Why don't we keep it, Dad? Could have some music, couldn't
we?" The father does not reply. A little later, Mike asks, "Why do we live
here?" To which the father replies, " 'Cause it's the best place there is!"
These lines comprise the only dialogue in the first ten minutes of the
film. The initial images of the Coorong have already established its presence in the film; these lines establish the relationship of the father to
technology and society, and a tension between the father and son. Later,
Mike is shown guiding a raft, like Huckleberry Finn, along the Coorong's quiet waters toward a camp, complete with a fire, located on the
bank. He stops, and soon meets the owner, Fingerbone Bill. A friendship
develops.

An evening soon after, Mike is seen on a dune watching the sunset,
which soon changes into night, which in turn dissolves into dawn. Mike
is shown collecting shells in the early-morning light, when he is startled
by gunshots. Pelicans flee, while a few unlucky birds fall, shot by the
intruders. More gunshots ring out and the perpetrators run from shots
fired from some unknown place within the dune grasses; Fingerbone
Bill has chased them away. Mike and Fingerbone find three baby pelicans, orphaned by the shootings. Fingerbone looks to the sky and says,
"Big Blow come tonight . . . you kill pelican, the sky comes up with a
storm." Mike saves the pelicans, and the one he names Mr. Percival not
only becomes his companion but also a symbol in the film of the tension
between nature and (wo)man, freedom and society.

Over the following months, the pelicans grow. Mike's friendship and
happiness with the birds is obvious, but it soon becomes apparent that
the birds have become unmanageable. The father insists on returning
them to the wild. After releasing them far from the humpy, father and
son return home, the latter clearly dejected from the loss of friends.
However, Mr. Percival soon returns and several subsequent scenes are of
Storm Boy and Mr. Percival playing among dunes, beaches, and lagoons.
The image-event that captures Mr. Percival's return is of interest to some
central themes in the film and we will discuss it more fully in a moment.

The rest of the film deals with Storm Boy, his pelican, the Aboriginal
friend, and the father's growing realization that his son must be
"brought up proper." There is a nighttime scene where a group of men
in dune buggies terrorize the boy who is sleeping alone in the humpy.
There is the noise of revving engines and shouting men, and the image

of multiple headlights and spotlights, smashed equipment, and skidding tires. The association between these images and those of unbridled violence, mayhem, and dune buggy terror in *Mad Max II/The Road Warrior* is quite clear and deliberate. In *Storm Boy*, we have the representation of a different kind of male. Tom, Fingerbone, and Mike shun technology and unnecessary violence, and they are sensitive to nature and know its moods. In another sequence of images, Tom and Mike prepare for a coming storm of which only they and Fingerbone seem to be aware (the initial scenes show their preparation against a backdrop of cloudless skies). Although it is not entirely clear from the narrative, it is possible that Fingerbone's ritualistic chanting summoned the storm. Meanwhile, a large, expensive, radar-equipped yacht sets sail with a crew of beer-swilling mates. Inevitably, the yacht's crew gets into trouble and is saved by Fingerbone, Tom, and Mike, with the help of Mr. Percival who, rather improbably, drops a line to the crew trapped on the sinking boat. Once saved, the crew offers Tom the money that he will eventually use to buy the petrol station he once managed.

After hearing his father talking to Fingerbone about how he left his wife, Mike runs away from the Coorong to seek out a school and urban life in Goolwa. The teacher, who has been trying to pry Mike away from his father and the Coorong, embraces the child and leads him over to the other children in her class. Prompted by the teacher, the class talks of nature and pelicans, and we sense that there is some considerable coercion being instigated by the teacher. Mike looks quite happy until the image-event is broken by Tom and Fingerbone appearing at the classroom door. With the next immediate scene, Tom is portrayed as embarrassingly out-of-place and awkward. Mike, on the other hand, seems quite comfortable with the school environment and he also seems to be accepted by the other students—a surprising turnaround of narrative convention that usually requires a struggle between the "wild" and the "civil." As Mike leaves to return to the Coorong with his father and Fingerbone, and after he has been told how much Mr. Percival misses him, we sense that a precedent has been set with Mike's newly established relationship to the town and society.

Days later, Mike is shown talking with Mr. Percival about the possibility of his moving to the town, when abruptly the bird flies off across the dunes. Shots are heard. Storm Boy, panic written across his face, is seen rushing through the vegetation and over the dunes trying to find Mr. Percival. He is not successful. Days later, Fingerbone appears, and solemnly takes Mike to the grave site of Mr. Percival. He then motions to Mike; located behind some swamp reeds are several pelican chicks. The two friends then look upward to a flight of pelicans and smile. The final image is an aerial view of Mike running along the beach. The camera then shows a single pelican in flight, a sunset, and then credits.

The film's story leaves the Coorong on only a few brief occasions, and that is to the small town of Goolwa. The portrayal never forgets that the nature of the Coorong is of utmost importance. Dunes are captured from many angles and are often seen through zoomed lenses and dune reeds and grasses. Sunsets and sunrises are not missed. The presence of place given to the viewer is not as soft and visionary as the clearly impressionistic view of so many rural Australian films, *Picnic at Hanging Rock* being the standard, and yet it does not opt for the surreal that some post-Impressionistic Australian painters have borrowed for the land and that surprisingly few filmmakers have adopted. Nonetheless, the straightforward realism garnered Geoff Burton accolades from many reviewers, including Hall, of *The Bulletin*, p. 196, who said:

> The film was shot in the Coorong, South Australia's windy coastal wilderness, an area of sudden storms and silvery light, brought beautifully to life through Geoff Burton's photography . . . there has always been a lot of talk in the industry about ways in which the uniqueness of the Australian landscape can be put on film, but this is the first picture since Picnic at Hanging Rock to do it with any real sense of the unusual. (Faulkner 1983, p. 196)

Purdon, of *Cinema Papers*, said, "Geoff Burton's photography, full of air and light, makes considerable use of low and wide angle in the exteriors, giving the winter land and seascapes an almost surreal space and presence"(Faulkner 1983, p. 196).

The three characters of *Storm Boy* are inextricably intertwined with their environment. The integration of these three people with the Coorong is more complex than relations between the bush and the portrayed drover or shearer or any other man, if for no other reason than the fact that the film is a clear plea for preservation. The linkage between man (boy) and environment is clear in Thiele's book and is quite apparent in the film. Dermody, of *The New Australian Cinema*, reports:

> One of the strengths of the film is the way it manages to admit the Coorong as a presence, as idiosyncratically influential as any of the three main characters . . . This is partly achieved through bridging passages of images of the landscape itself, but, more importantly, the Coorong infiltrates the characters. (Faulkner 1983, p. 203)

Heinrich, of *The Age*, wrote:

> Compared with the book, Sonia Borg's screenplay has better used the re-
> moteness of the Coorong by investing the characters with a haunting sense
> of loneliness, the longing of people in exile. (Faulkner 1983, p. 203)

The three characters are outcasts of a sort, and the environment provides them a solace they have basically chosen for themselves. Tom has
withdrawn from city life and has severed most ties; Mike is the dependent of Tom and has evolved his own sense of isolation and independence; and Fingerbone has been exiled from his tribe: "they would kill
me . . . they'd point the bone at me." The Coorong has provided them
the needed refuge, but it has also allowed development and expression
of basic forms of mateship, egalitarianism, and antiauthoritarianism.
The power of the larger authority that attempts to invade their place,
and thus lives, is represented by the ranger who is looking for Fingerbone, the female teacher who wants to coax Mike into school, and the
shooters, polluters, and other destroyers of the environment. These are
people against whom our heroes, all of them men or soon-to-be-men,
can take a stand.

The Coorong's version of these classically Australian traits of the bush
is clearly illustrated by the comments of Tom. The ranger has heard that
a shot was fired at the dune buggies (it was actually Fingerbone), and
he has come to inform Tom that the law against guns in the Coorong is
strict. Replies an enraged Tom: "And when is there going to be one
against lunatics and buggies. After they have ruined the Coorong and
they have churned up every blade of grass?" No respectable sheep
shearer from the outback would ever make such a comment!

The relation between Fingerbone and the environment is, of course,
far easier to document. When speaking of Fingerbone, Heinrich said:
"He is seen striding across sand dunes and through reeds with an incredible grace, dancing on the beach in a transfixing rhythm, and singing up a vengeful storm in a scene of extraordinary menace" (Faulkner
1983, p. 202). Fingerbone knows the place of the pelican in the uni-
verse, the place of the pelican in the Coorong. Sitting on the beach,
with white paint patterned across his face, he tells the following story to
an attentive Storm Boy:

> Longtime ago, all the men were animals
> First Konai Man
> It was a pelican

He came long way,
Long, long way from the hills
Carry a bar canoe
On his head
and he goes and he goes and he goes and he goes and he goes
Hear tut tut tut
Sound like knocking
Looks here
Looks there
Where's the tut tut coming from?
Comes to a river
Put down the canoe
What's inside?
Mas Duck
Mas Duck sit there
Go tut tut tut all the time
Pelican happy
Marries duck
Start Konai people

Mike may not understand Fingerbone's association with the setting, but he certainly appreciates it. Fingerbone sees Mike's clarity of vision and flatters him when referring to Mike's familiarity with the Coorong: "You run like a black man." Tom understands, though not as clearly, perhaps because the man's way is irrevocably set by his stage in the life cycle. When he asks Fingerbone where he will go next, the Aboriginal says, "Go Walkabout." Replies Tom: "That's what I'd do if I was on my own. I'd like that."

Discussion

Several aspects of interpersonal and person-place relations in *Storm Boy* deserve scrutiny. Women are not overtly part of this film but their influence upon the narrative is extremely important. We have already discussed the teacher (the only woman in the film with lines) who comes to the humpy with concern over Mike's education. Her role is to establish the urban-based value system and the essence of a society from which Tom is trying to escape. But Tom's capitulation to the system is seen in the number of times he corrects his son's use of English with quite apparent dismay on his face. By the end of the movie he has (happily) resigned himself to going back to work at a petrol station (oil, technology, dune buggies) for the sake of the boy's education; the viewer is led to feel quite good about this resolution.

Women relate face-to-face, they discuss and talk about their feelings, whereas men stand side-by-side intent on "doing" rather than "saying." By the same token there is not much conversation in *Storm Boy*. Tom is taciturn to the point of noncommunication, and Mike tends to be a mute observer. The film is usually content to let the narrative speak for itself rather than spell itself out in dialogue. One of the few times that Tom does speak at length is to Fingerbone over a campfire when they exchange information (underlying feelings are only implied) about their women. Tom has told Mike that his mother is dead (the society embodied by motherhood is now dust), and it is upon hearing Tom tell Fingerbone that he left his wife that Mike is prompted to run away to the teacher (mother-figure) in Goolwa. The portrayal of Tom as a principled man cannot tolerate this dark lie, however, and we are soon reassured that Tom's wife was killed in a car accident shortly after he left her. Nonetheless, the breakup precipitated Tom's move to the Coorong. Fingerbone is an outcast from his society because he had slept with the wrong "gal" and consequently had the (finger) bone "pointed at" him and had to flee the tribe. Apparently, his woman now belongs to a white man and Fingerbone prefers to be alone. In both cases, these men sought sanctuary from women and community, while searching for self, in the Coorong. It seems that women are the reason for men being alone, being in the middle of nowhere, being mates and apostate against society. The teacher is used as a narrative device, of course, to tell us we know how men should really behave. The women in *Storm Boy*, then, are objects that establish the context of the men in the film. They are cast in the role of civil homemaker and the embodiment of societal values with no identity in and of themselves. As such, "female essentialism" is much more poignant in this film than in other mainstream Australian films of "males searching for self," such as *Mad Max II/The Road Warrior* and *Gallipoli* (1981), where the "female" is apparent only in a covert homoeroticism (Aitken and Zonn, 1993). *Storm Boy* is, of course, decent family entertainment. The conclusion we are drawn to with this reading echoes some recent feminist perspectives on mainstream cinema's preoccupation with various kinds of male regression—physical, psychological, and historical—that establish the essential nature of women, because this is the only means whereby men can find themselves (Mulvey 1975; Silverman 1988; Modleski 1991). Although women do not feature largely in the immediate narrative of *Storm Boy*, the need to represent women as *other* is still part of the film's broader narrative. Women are not imaged (looked at) in *Storm Boy* in the same voyeuristic sense that Mulvey (1975) suggests, but they are (re)presented as something from which the male characters find definition. In fact, *Storm Boy* buys into a patriarchal discourse that establishes not only the image of woman as *other*, but also woman as symbolizing societal values and cultural mores. What remains to be fitted into this scenario are the Coorong and the pelican.

Storm Boy's narrative overturns some important past myths of Australian cinema that pit men against the environment in an adversarial relationship. Films like Peter Weir's *Gallipoli*, for example, establish the outback as something to be overcome and dominated in a confrontational manner that forges the male character. The landscape in *Storm Boy* is not included for its mythic resonances, nor is it visual support for the thematic expression of the narrative. In a very real sense, the Coorong is a character—passive, active, and reinforcing—with many moods that contextualize in an aesthetic sense the actions of the drama. The character of Fingerbone, in particular, resonates with the landscape. Without the need for elaborate narrative exposition because of the latent image of the Aboriginal in the Australian cinematic landscape, Fingerbone can immediately represent a mythical figure whose place in nature serves to initiate Mike into communion with nature, thereby justifying the many sequences of the boy (and the pelican) and man (Mike) and as a social mediator between father and son (Rattigan 1991, pp. 288–89). Fingerbone, however, is not so mystical and supernatural as to be able to define himself without the help of a woman. Even his name signifies a relationship with a woman and the community. Ironically, also, it is Fingerbone's intervention to bring Tom and Mike closer together that ultimately removes them from their physical intimacy with nature.

It is Fingerbone who teaches Mike how to feed and raise the pelicans, and it is with Mr. Percival that we discover the "solution" to the running tension between the antinomies of nature/freedom and (wo)man/society. In two scenes, the behavior of Mr. Percival symbolizes how Mike and Tom are meant to resolve their dilemma. Mike is depressed over his father's decision to free the birds. The image-event that encompasses this part of the film comprises well over five minutes of Mike walking alone on the beach and in the dunes. Eventually he returns to the humpy where his father is waiting. In an attempt to soothe his son's broken spirit, Tom says, "Wild things ought to be free." At that exact moment, Mr. Percival returns. Clearly this symbolizes a choice of the bird between nature/freedom and the community of Mike and Tom. This image-event portends the decision that Mike and Tom will make at the end of the movie. The second important symbolic action of Mr. Percival is when it flies away to be a target for the "shooters." Mike and Mr. Percival are walking among the dunes and Mike is musing over what the future will bring. Should he go to boarding school and visit his Dad in the Coorong during the holidays, or should he go and live with his Dad in Goolwa and attend regular school, or should they stay in the Coorong? He turns to look at Mr. Percival for inspiration, "Maybe I'll just stay here with you." With that, the pelican flies off and, a few moments later, we hear gunshots. We are left with a protracted series of images of Mike frantically running across the dunes after Mr. Percival. When he eventually stops, he is looking down at the humpy. It is time to move on!

Mr. Percival symbolizes more than just a pointer toward the decisions that Mike and his father should make. When Mike runs away to school after feeling betrayed by his father, the schoolteacher gives him milk and cookies and welcomes him into the classroom with the other children. The next image-event is in the classroom with Mike sitting near the front with a look of delight in his face. The teacher is standing by the blackboard upon which is drawn the outline of a pelican. The teacher is finishing a story not about pelicans, but about Percival, the knights of the Round Table, and the search for the Holy Grail. Mr. Percival, then, is clearly linked to a mythical male search for the meaning of life itself. And the Holy Grail that Mr. Percival points to is "community and societal values" epitomized by women.

Conclusions

Media have the ability to select, neglect, reject, emphasize, and distort a vast range of symbols that reflect the nature of a place. The degree to which these symbols and their arrangement reflect the experiences and realities of the places is dependent on the nature of the medium, the intentions of the image maker, and the nature of the audience toward whom the image is directed. Images of Australia portrayed in the cinema have reflected a tripartite association between the Australian government, its moviemakers, and the public. The need and search for a national identity and the moviemakers' attempts to satisfy that demand through the portrayal of select environmental and personality characteristics have had a great impact on the character of portrayed images of Australia.

Storm Boy presents an image of Australia that differs from other rural films in that the coast is the primary locale for promoting the Australian character, the concept of conservation of select environmental attributes is of immediate concern, and children are a primary focus of the intentions. Nonetheless, the individuals of the story clearly exhibit features of the Australian character. In fact, the young Australian viewer may have been presented a primer on the nature of the national psyche. The relation between Mike and his pelican, which is of foremost interest to many children, was clearly a form of mateship and antiauthoritarianism. Best of friends, they seemingly were bonded by the environment, and together they oppose the world of those people who can harm them—from the teacher and ranger to the hunters and others who harm the environment. But it is the pelican that ultimately, and subtly, reinforces a patriarchal societal ethic. Mr. Percival returns to Mike and Tom, suggesting that it is all right to shun nature and freedom, ostensibly, for friendship, but also for the constraints of community. It is only through the pelican's death (sacrifice) that Mike accepts the move to Goolwa and the values of the school. And it is through the pelican's heroic efforts in saving the yacht's crew that Mike's father receives remuneration sufficient to purchase a petrol station (and a new life) in Goolwa. Maybe he will marry the schoolteacher? Regardless, we have a happy ending! Finally, while *Storm Boy* opened a new type of landscape for Australians to embrace as part of their identity, it did not instigate a major new environmental ethic. Perhaps, however, the film's greatest contribution as judged by "Australian content" was a reinforcement of patriarchal forces behind a masculine national identity.

References

Adams, P. 1984. Two views: Phillip Adams. *Cinema Papers* 44–45:70–72.

Aitken, S. 1991. A transactional geography of the image-event: The films of Scottish director Bill Forsyth. *Transactions, British Institute of Geographers* 16:105–18.

Aitken, S., and L. Zonn. 1993. Weir(d) Sex: Representation of Gender-Environment Relations in Peter Weir's *Picnic at Hanging Rock* and *Gallipoli*. *Environment and Planning D: Society and Space* 11: 191–212.

Anon. 1983. The top ten films. *Cinema Papers* (March–April):62–65.

Beilby, P., and R. Lansell, editors. 1983. *Australian Motion Picture Yearbook*. Melbourne: Four Seasons Press in association with Cinema Papers.

Bolton, G. 1976. The Historian as Artist and Interpreter of the Environment. In *Man and Landscape in Australia: Towards an Ecological Vision*, edited by G. Seddon and M. Davis, pp. 113–24. Canberra: Australian Government Publishing Service.

Carroll, J., editor. 1982. *Intruders in the Bush: The Australian Quest for Identity.* Melbourne: Oxford University Press.

Clancy, J. 1982. Film: The Renaissance of the Seventies. In *Intruders in the Bush: The Australian Quest for Identity,* edited by J. Carroll, pp. 168–79. Melbourne: Oxford University Press.

Davis, K. 1988. What is ecofeminism? *Women and Environments* 10:4–6.

Davison, G. 1982. Sydney and the Bush: An Urban Context for the Australian Legend. In *Intruders in the Bush: The Australian Quest for Identity,* edited by J. Carroll, pp.109–30. Melbourne: Oxford University Press.

Eagle, M. 1982. Painting an Australian Identity. In *Intruders in the Bush: The Australian Quest for Identity,* edited by J. Carroll, pp. 180–91. Melbourne: Oxford Univeristy Press.

Elliot, B. 1976. Emblematic Vision: Or Landscape in a Concave Mirror. In *Man and Landscape in Australia: Towards an Ecological Vision,* edited by G. Seddon and M. Davis, pp. 125–44. Canberra: Australian Government Publishing Service.

Faulkner, C. 1983. A Geography of the Screen: Landscape in Australian Cinema. Unpublished M.A. thesis, Bedford Park, South Australia: Flinders University of South Australia.

Ginnane, A. 1984. Two Views: Antony I. Giannane. *Cinema Papers* 44–45:66–70.

Griffin, S. 1978. *Women and Nature: The Roaring Inside Her.* New York: Harper and Row.

Heathcote, R. L. 1972a. The artist as geographer: Landscape painting as a source for geographical research. *Proceedings, Royal Geographical Society of Australasia* (South Australian Branch) 73:1–21.

Heathcote, R. L. 1972b. The Visions of Australia: 1770–1970. In *Australia as Human Setting,* edited by A. Rapaport, pp. 77–98. Sydney: Angus and Robertson.

Hodges, E. 1982. The Bushman Legend. In *Intruders in the Bush: The Australian Quest for Identity,* edited by J. Carroll, pp. 3–13. Melbourne: Oxford University Press.

Hutton, A. 1981. Nationalism in Australian cinema. *Cinema Papers* 97–100:152–53.

Keller, E. 1985. *Reflections on Gender and Science.* New Haven: Yale University Press.

Lowe, B. 1974. Australian film esthetics. *Lumière* (March):4–7.

McFarlane, B. 1987. *Australian Cinema: 1970–1985.* Richmond, Victoria: William Heinemann Australia.

McGuiness, P. 1977. *The National Times.* August 1–6.

Meinig, D. W. 1979. Symbolic Landscapes: Some Idealizations of American Communities. In *The Interpretation of Ordinary Landscapes,* edited by D. W. Meinig, pp. 164–92. New York: Oxford University Press.

Merchant, C. 1979. *The Depth of Nature: Women, Ecology and the Scientific Revolution.* New York: Harper and Row.

Modleski, T. 1991. *Feminism Without Women: Culture and Criticism in a "Postfeminist" Age.* New York: Routledge.

Monk, J., and V. Norwood. 1990. (Re)membering the Australian City: Urban Landscapes in Women's Fiction. In *Place Images in Media: Portrayal, Experience, and Meaning,* edited by L. Zonn, pp. 105–21. Savage, Md.: Rowman and Littlefield.

Mulvey, L., 1975, Visual pleasure and narrative cinema, *Screen* 16(3): 6–18.

Pocock, D. 1981. *Geography and Literature.* London: Croom Helm.

Rattigan, N. 1991. *Images of Australia: 100 Films of the New Australian Cinema.* Dallas: Southern Methodist University Press.

Rosser, S. 1991. Eco-feminism: Lessons from feminism and ecology. *Women's Studies International Forum* 14(3):143–51.

Ryan, K. B. 1990. The "Official" Image of Australia. In *Place Images in Media: Portrayal, Experience and Meaning,* edited by L. Zonn, pp. 135–58. Lanham, Md.: Rowman and Littlefield.

Silk, J. 1984. Beyond geography and literature. *Environment and Planning D: Society and Space* 2:151–78.

Silverman, K. 1988. *The Acoustic Mirror: The Female Voice in Psychoanalysis and Cinema.* Bloomington: Indiana University Press.

Spretnak, C. 1990. Ecofeminism: Our Roots and Flowering. In *Reweaving the World: The Emergence of Ecofeminism,* edited by I. Diamond and G. Orenstein, pp. 3–14. San Francisco: Sierra Club Books.

Thomas, D. 1976. Visual images. In *Man and Landscape in Australia: Towards an Ecological Vision,* edited by G. Seddon and M. Davis, pp. 157–66. Canberra: Australian Government Publishing Service.

Turner, G. 1986. Film and Fiction: Dealing with Australian Narrative. In *Diversity Itself: Essays in Australian Arts and Culture,* edited by P. Quartermaine, pp. 109–20. Exeter: Exeter University Publications.

Tuan, Y. 1976. Literature, Experience, and Environmental Knowing. In *Environmental Knowing: Theories, Research, and Methods,* edited by G.T. Moore and R. G. Golledge, pp. 260–72. Stroudsburg, Pa.: Dowden, Hutchinson and Ross.

Ward, R. 1965. *The Australian Legend.* Melbourne: Oxford University Press.

Filmography

Bambi. 1942. Walt Disney Studios. Director, Hand, D.

Gallipoli. 1981. Associated R & R Films. Director, Weir, P.

The Jungle Book. 1942. United Artists. Director, Korda, Z.

The Land Before Time. 1987. Spielberg/Lucas Films. Director, Bluth, D.

Lonely Hearts. 1982. Adams Packer Film Productions. Director, Cox, P.

Mad Max II/The Road Warrior. 1982. Kenedy Miller Entertainment. Director, Miller, G.

My Brilliant Career. 1979. Margret Fink Films. Director, Armstrong, G.

Picnic at Hanging Rock. 1975. Picnic Productions. Director, Weir, P.

Rock-A-Doodle. 1990. Samuel Godwin. Director, Bluth, D.

Storm Boy. 1976. South Australian Film Corporation. Director, Safran, H.

Walkabout. 1971. Max L. Raab-Si Litvinoff Films. Director, Roeg, N.

We of the Never Never. 1982. Film Corporation of Western Australia. Director, Auzins, I.

8

The Myth of Heroism: Man and Desert in *Lawrence of Arabia*

Christina B. Kennedy

Some of the evil of my tale may have been inherent in our circumstances. For years we lived any-
how with one another in the naked desert, under
the indifferent heaven. By day the hot sun fer-
mented us; and we were dizzied by the beating
wind. At night we were stained by dew, and
shamed into pettiness by the innumerable si-
lences of the stars.

—T. E. Lawrence

T. E. Lawrence's autobiography, *Seven Pillars of Wisdom,* is replete with
the kinds of person-environment passages exemplified in this introductory quote. It seems to establish a sense of the effect a place can have
on human actions and events. This sensitivity to person-environment
relationships is carried through into David Lean's film, *Lawrence of Arabia* (1962), which is purportedly based upon Lawrence's autobiography.
It is the desert, the opportunities, and the challenges afforded by the
"landscape," as well as the clash of English, Arabic, and Turkish cultures, that create the situations in which the portrayed events occur. This
chapter draws upon a transactional framework in order to examine how
the different layers of textual representation—environment, culture,
politics, and individual experience—interpenetrate one another to effect a representation of Lawrence's life as portrayed in Lean's film.

Lawrence was a success in America not only in the early 1960s, but also
when rereleased in 1971 and again in 1989. This success suggests that
the film was able to sustain a level of meaning that transcended significant changes in American values and politics. In the 1960s the film may

have resonated with the decline of colonialism and anti-Vietnam senti-ments, whereas by 1989 it could be seen as a statement against imperial-ism. I believe, however, that the major reasons for the movie's continu-ing success lie not so much in the social and political climate of the times, but in the strength and artistry of the movie, and in its portrayal of deeply human characters. Above all, the film's success may be attrib-uted to the portrayal of intense human interactions with the Arabian desert. Lean's Lawrence is a charismatic leader and a fallible, tormented man trapped in the role of a hero. The movie portrays a man who is inalterably changed by his experience of the desert and the political culture of the time through the veils of two conflicting cultures: premod-ern Arabic and modern British.

The desert has always been a crucible for intense experience. Equated with wilderness in Judeo-Christian accounts, the desert was "a cursed land, associated with the absence of water" where "God sent men for punishment." It was also a place of refuge, redemption, and spiritual uplift (Kay 1989). In the desert, people were humbled and purged, and then prepared for a better or higher existence (Ittelson et al. 1974, p. 30). There is an ambiguity, then, reflecting the dualism of hell, yet the possibility of redemption. This dualism is used effectively by Lean in his portrayal of the special relationship Lawrence had with this environ-ment. At yet another level, the concept of desert is ambiguous because its defeat is a marker of human progress but it is also a marker of an earthly paradise, the place of "before the fall" where people lived in close harmony and deep sympathy with nature (Short 1991, p. 10). In Lean's film, Lawrence's souring relationship with the desert becomes a metaphor for the capitulation of the Arab nations to British hegemony that, ostensibly, represents progress.

Clearly, in *Lawrence*, the desert is not simply a backdrop, a stage on which the story or action takes place. Integral to the movie is a continu-ing interaction between the desert and Lawrence, resulting in the pro-found change that takes place in Lawrence's relationship with himself and his relationship with the desert. It is a change from love to fear. Lawrence embraces the desert and through the intensity of his experi-ences is transformed, a transformation that results in a destruction of a part of himself. It is upon this change, this intense person-environment interaction and its effect on the continuing creation of "self," that I will focus.

Person-Environment Interaction and Change

It has been postulated that our environment is important to the kind of self we create through the opportunities it affords and the meanings we impart to our transactions with it (Altman and Rogoff 1987; Russell and Snodgrass 1987); that "we are, in an important sense, the places that we inhabit" (Little 1987, p. 221). Transactional theorists recognize this dynamic person-environment interdependence and use transactions, or events that precipitate change between people and environments, as the basic unit of study (Altman and Rogoff 1987; Wapner 1987; Aitken and Bjorklund 1988; Aitken 1992). Behavior is assumed to be embedded in and strongly influenced by the environmental context in which it occurs (Ittelson 1973; Russell and Snodgrass 1987; Stokols 1986). The spatial and temporal environment or "place" that surrounds the person is composed of both a physical and a social milieu imbued with "symbolic meaning and motivational messages" (Ittelson 1973, p. 14). It also, however, is concurrently defined by personal action and by what we attribute to it from our own experiences (Ittelson et al. 1974; Zonn 1984). Although place is viewed as an *active* entity, affording specific opportunities for "large scale, complex actions" (Little 1987; Russell and Snodgrass 1987, p. 246), a person's fitness, psychological and physical needs, expectations, goals, and emotions all affect person-place transactions (Wapner 1987). As these aspects change, or as the environment itself changes, there is a consequent alteration of our transactions with place. Behavioral changes include transformations in both cognitive and overt behavior and can be rapid and dramatic or incremental, until a new transactional pattern (homeostasis) is achieved (Stokols 1986; Aitken and Bjorklund 1988). We may tease out separate aspects of our experience—physical setting, culture, social conditions, politics, situation—for discussion and study, but we cannot separate them from our experience itself. They interpenetrate one another and form the context in which the dynamic person-environment system of a specific historic moment and location is embedded (Altman and Rogoff 1987; Aitken 1992).

Transactional Theory and Film

If we assume that the primary elements in movies are people and their environments, then they clearly offer a unique opportunity for the study of person-environment transactions (Aitken 1991). Much of what we know of the world, and of specific places in the world, comes not from firsthand knowledge, but what we are taught through secondary information (Ittelson et al. 1974). We can assume, then, that many of our place images are derived from cinematic representations. The degree to which place portrayal in film affects our mental image depends upon a variety of factors: whether we have had personal experience with that place, the skill with which it is portrayed, the context of the media representation, the purpose of the director, as well as the filters that director and audience bring to the filmic event (Zonn 1984; Zube and Kennedy 1990).

Drawing on some of the early work on montage by Russian film theorists, Aitken (1991) suggests that if transactional theory is concerned with the events that constitute change in person-environment relations, then the "image-event" is an important focus for the study of narrative and contextual change and incoherences in film. Image-events are defined as a sequence of shots that violate or enhance the rhythm of a film and, as such, provide a fundamental level of communication between filmmaker and viewer (Aitken 1991, p. 106). Aitken argues that the representation of person-environment transactions showing ordinary and extraordinary behavior in extraordinary environments can heighten the audience's involvement in the narrative (p. 109). Much of the action in *Lawrence* is extraordinary and is in an extraordinary environment. Aitken further concludes that the juxtaposition of ordinary and extraordinary image-events can create an atmosphere whereby characters and environments transact in interesting and provoking ways. Thus, the changes in portrayed relations between Lawrence and the desert in Lean's film can be read as transactions that authenticate and make "real" the narrative fiction.

Heroic Transactions: The Portrayal of Self and Myth

Lean understood "the hold [the desert] had exercised over Lawrence. This is why the film itself expresses so remarkably the feelings of Lawrence and the spirit of that time" (Pratley 1974, p. 158). Each of Lawrence's actions takes place within a specific environmental context. It is not enough to talk about a "monolithic" desert, for the desert is comprised of a myriad of moods and faces. Lean uses these superbly as an integral part of the microcontext for specific actions (finding a solution to taking Akaba, an execution, a massacre). The desert is also the large-scale environment in which events take place, and it is only on a "scale" such as the Arabian desert that Lawrence's grandiose schemes can be carried out. Pratley sums it up nicely:

> The setting that Lean has thoughtfully created and emphasized for Lawrence's deeds is so magnificent and noble that his very audacity at stepping somewhat hesitantly into the role of an epic and romantic leader is sanctioned by his awesome surroundings. Here away from all procedures, laws, systems and restraint, it is possible for Lawrence to develop into a hero. . . . (1974, p. 158)

Was the heroism of Lawrence an illusion fabricated by Western media? Did Britain need a "lone Romantic, framed heroically against the clean desert sand of Arabia" to help erase the "appalling carnage of World War I" (Gray 1989, p. 80)? The British and Americans were seeking a "warrior" hero, and in a military sense heroism is

> an artifice . . . in which some combination of moral courage, staunchness, idealism, fraternity, love of fellows, recklessness, nihilism, morbidity, a suicidal will, simple stupidity, and insensibility before danger triumphs over the powerful natural impulses of fear and the urge to survive. (Pfaff 1989, p. 105)

The Lawrence portrayed by Lean is certainly a hero in this light.

Lean's Lawrence is, however, more than a military hero. A hero embodies our beliefs and values and takes risks we are not brave enough to take for "things we believe in" (Lubin 1968, p. 5). A hero's role is to guide and save society. In the hero's journey he surpasses personal limitations, encounters incredible forces, wins a victory, and returns with the "power to bestow boons on his fellow man" (Campbell 1949, p. 30). The hero may find, however, at the end of his journey that the world doesn't know how to receive or institutionalize the gifts that the hero has struggled to bring it (Campbell and Moyers 1988, p. 141). To a large degree, this is the case with the freedom and technology Lawrence offers the Arabs. The Lawrence portrayed by Lean is a modern tragic hero who is on an internal as well as an external journey. Lean's Lawrence is an existential man "caught in a state of becoming and therefore perpetually in crisis" (Glicksberg 1963, p. 359). The tragedy for the character of Lawrence revolves around the conflict between his idealistic aims and what he construed to be the Arabs' limitations.

Because Lean's Lawrence is clearly human, his heroism takes on elements of a personal myth. In this sense, myth implies illusion but it also provides a model for human behavior and thus "gives meaning and value to life" (Eliade 1963, p. 2). Myth "is a system of [personal] communication" (Barthes 1957, p. 109), a filter that provides order and coherency to information that passes through it, a language that provides a context in which to fit new experiences (Ausband 1983). Myth represents our striving to make sense of the world, to find meaning in our lives (Campbell 1949; Ausband 1983; Campbell and Moyers 1988). In myths, the "themes are timeless" but how they are expressed and the values they represent are specific to a culture (Campbell and Moyers 1988, p. 11). In *Lawrence*, Lean captures the importance of the creation of a mythic Lawrence as hero for both British and Arabic cultures, but it is clear that his heroism is sparked by the catalyst of the desert. And it is the desert as much as the British and Arabic cultures that destroys the man while reifying the myth.

The Evolution of the Portrayed Lawrence/Desert Transactions

The development and the destruction of interpersonal and person-place relationships are integral to the image-events in *Lawrence*: to Lawrence's experience of the Arabian culture, and to his conflicts with his own. The image-events enhance the contradictions in Lawrence himself: hero, intellectual, warrior, exhibitionist, masochist, and possible homosexual. He is a man with great internal conflicts—one tormented by self-doubt. These images derive from Lawrence's own writings and are skillfully executed in Lean's movie. Integral to the movie is Lawrence's attempts to define himself; to understand who and what he is through his actions, and through his relationships with the desert and its people.

The character of Lean's desert changes along with the nature of Lawrence's interaction with it and with the Arabs. The portrayed desert differs dramatically from the first half to the second half of the movie. Originally, it is a clean, heroic landscape full of challenge and beauty where Lawrence is alone or with allies or friends. Panoramic shots show the scale of the landscape. In medium-range shots, Lean makes extensive use of triangular composition—reflecting the forms in the landscape and indicating stability. Modern technology is largely absent. There is a testing of individuals in a direct intimate relationship with the desert. It is a time of building relationships and of achieving remarkable things, such as crossing the Nefudh or taking Akaba. By the end of this time Lawrence has recognized his own extreme nature and doesn't feel "fit" to continue his role in Arabia, but is persuaded to return by Colonel Allenby of the British Army.

In the second half of the movie the desert is decentered from the narrative and, importantly, it loses its beauty. There are few panoramic shots, and those mostly of retreating armies or massacres. The narrative focus shifts to battles and destruction. Modern technology is more in evidence. Triangular composition is gone. Vertical and diagonal lines meet at odd angles, giving a sense of instability and chaos. The landscapes are harsher, rocky, flat, full of dust, war, slaughter, suffering, death, and flies. No longer does Lawrence interact with the desert on his own, but in groups of people. Moreover, within these groups his

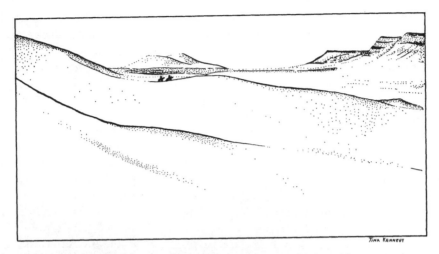

Figure 8–1. Early panoramic scenes showing Lawrence crossing magnificent open vistas and golden sand dunes exemplify Lean's portrayal of the desert as a clean, heroic landscape in the first half of the film. Drawing by Tina Kennedy.

interpersonal relationships are disintegrating. Extreme events and conditions are imposed on an unwilling Lawrence and they last over an extended period until his strength and will begin to break. Lawrence participates in events over which he has little control, in which he loses control of himself, or which result in doubts about his efficacy and honor. In the rest of this chapter, I look more closely at the changing representations of person-environment relations in the two halves of *Lawrence.*

The film begins with Lawrence's death through a motorcycle accident in England. Rolling hills, green fields, trees, stone walls, and cottages provide a confining landscape that he expands and, in a sense, escapes from through the speed of his motorcycle. After this introductory sequence most of Lawrence's interaction with the British culture is institutionalized, taking place within the confines of headquarters in either Cairo or Jerusalem. These are limited, controlled environments in which Lawrence is portrayed as being uncomfortable and where he exists in relative social isolation.

When relieved from duty as a mapmaker in a "dark, dirty, little room" in Cairo where he is "not happy" and given the opportunity to seek Prince Feisal for the Arab Bureau, Lawrence's reaction is "Oh thanks, Dryden, this is going to be fun." Dryden replies, "Lawrence, only two kinds of creatures get fun in the desert—Bedouins and gods, and you're

neither. Take it from me, for ordinary men it's a burning, fiery furnace."
But Lawrence says again, "No, Dryden, it's going to be fun." Indeed,
the very next scene shows a broad desert sunrise and exquisite open
vistas, accompanied by the augmented 7th chords of composer Maurice
Jarre's main musical theme for the movie. The desert, the Jebel Tubeig
in southeastern Jordan, is "vast, awe-inspiring, beautiful with ever changing hues" (Silverman 1989; Sweeney quoting Crowther 1989, p. 10) and
is comprised of magnificent red-gold sand dunes and black basaltic features. The first close-up of Lawrence shows him looking out over the
vast expanse, a content expression on his face.

Lawrence and his guide, Tafas, travel in unlimited landscapes. At
night they camp by a dead, ghost-white tree, with little else but sand and
stars. Making friends with Tafas, he explains that England is not a desert
country but a "fat country full of fat people." When the guide points
out that Lawrence is not fat, he responds, "No, I am different."
Throughout the movie, as his character grapples with the desert, Lean
explores this difference.

Despite the heat and harshness of the desert environment, Lawrence's experiences during this time are predominantly positive—a testing in which he prevails regardless of the hardships or odds. Lawrence
is shown drinking only when the guide drinks, resting when the guide
rests. Tafas shows him how to gallop on a camel and he gallops over the
horizon and falls off laughing. He welcomes the challenges offered by
the desert and in becoming involved in a different culture. Although
the scale of the portrayed landscape is so grand that humans are as
nothing, in this early stage Lawrence is not overwhelmed. He is in love
with the desert.

The first change toward the desert becoming traumatic for Lawrence
is in the death of Tafas, a Hassimi of the Beni-Salem, for drinking at a
Harif well. This is also the first point in the movie where the desert fails
to be gloriously rich in color with interesting forms of dunes and cliffs
or rock formations. The desert at the well is a mud flat, alkali-caked,
with a single withered plant. Sherif Ali rides out of a mirage, intensifying
the sense of heat and dryness, and shoots Tafas. There are no strains of
background music during this sequence; the only sounds are wind in
the guide's clothes, the clopping of the camel's feet, and Lawrence's
footsteps as he trips. We sense that Lawrence can overcome this first
assailment, but a mood is set by Lean's image-event and we suspect that
it will return.

Lean sets the stage for the underlying conflict between British and
Arab approaches to technology with Lawrence's entrance to Prince Fei-

sal's camp at Wadi Saffra during an attack by Turkish airplanes. With the introduction of modern technology—weaponry—the desert becomes a place of explosion, smoke, fire, and destruction. Prince Feisal urges his people to "stand and fight." On a white stallion, with drawn sword, he charges an airplane. No match for bombs and machine guns, he halts and, head bowed, struggles with defeat. As he raises his head and looks through the smoke, he finds himself facing Lawrence, who is looking at him compassionately. With this image-event the would-be "savior" of the Arab army and nation is introduced. Prince Feisal asks, "Who are you?"—a question repeated throughout the movie.

Later, Prince Feisal questions Lawrence's ability to be loyal to both Britain and Arabia and asks if he perhaps thinks the Arabs are something he can play with. When Lawrence tells Feisal it is time for the Arabs to be "great again," Feisal claims that "To be great again it seems that we need the British . . . or . . . what no man can provide, Mr. Lawrence. We need a miracle." Feisal fears British intentions for Arabia, noting that "The English have a great hunger of desolate places." He recognizes Lawrence's fascination with the desert and warns him, "I think you are another of these desert loving English. Stanton, Gordon of Khartoum . . . No Arab loves the desert. We love water and green trees. There is nothing in the desert. No man needs nothing." With this dialogue, Lean articulates differing British and Arab attitudes toward the desert.

For Lean's Lawrence there are many things in the desert, including answers. The sequence in which Lawrence realizes how to take Akaba is an important turning point. Lawrence's mission of "appraising the situation" for the British turns into a personal quest to "save" the Arabs and to help them gain their own objectives: independence from the British. This realization signals a change in Lawrence's relationship with the Arab people and with the desert. Lean creates an image-event of Lawrence walking over waterlike sand ripples as he retreats into moonlit dunes. This metaphor—signifying that he can "walk on water"— represents Lawrence's determination to seek Feisal's miracle. The wind thunders and washes sand from the dunes' crests like spray from ocean waves. Throughout the night, in the blue-white dunes accompanied by sounds of skittering sand, Lawrence seeks a way to take the strategic port of Akaba from the Turks. Finally, at midday, it occurs to him that Akaba should be attacked from the impossible landward side. The seed for the miracle is planted.

Lean portrays Lawrence's journey with Feisal's men to take Akaba as both a time of endurance and one of building personal relationships.

Akaba lies on the other side of the Nefudh Desert, "the worst place God created." The extreme character of the Nefudh is clearly portrayed. Here desert stereotypes are reflected in the harshness of the environment: cracked and parched earth, hot rock and sand, dust devils and deadening monotony. Men and camels travel through mirage. The land is hypnotic. Just when it seems that the most desolate of places has been traversed, the small army reaches the Sun's Anvil, which must be crossed before sunrise. One of the men, Gassim, is lost in the crossing. Ali, focusing on group survival and on the success of the mission, refuses to return and search for him. Lawrence, with typical Western emphasis on the individual and a desire to behave heroically, against reason and Ali's will, starts back. A furious Ali accuses Lawrence of "blasphemous conceit," questions his motives for bringing them there, and predicts he will not be at Akaba. Lawrence promises, "I shall be at Akaba. That *is* written," pointing to his head, "in here."

The Sun's Anvil is portrayed in blazing white—a perfectly flat, cracked, baked salt pan. The sound of Gassim's shuffling steps alternates with shrill electronic notes and the tapping of drums from Jarre's score. Gassim collapses, a bundle of dark rags on a limitless, pitiless, white and blue landscape. In this struggle with the most extreme face of the desert, Lawrence returns with Gassim. The music is soaring, the image-event is of Lawrence as a victor and a hero in both Arab and British terms. At the oasis it is from Ali's waterskin that Lawrence drinks after repeating "Nothing is written," and it is Ali's sleeping rug upon which he collapses. That night, when Lawrence wakens, Ali says, "El Aurens" (a term of honor) "truly, for some men, nothing is written unless *they* write it."

The landscapes chosen by Lean are again spectacular and extreme as Auda abu Tayi and the Howietats join forces with Lawrence and the Harifs. The red-gold cliffs of Wadi Lam dwarf the army as it rides out in formation and "barbaric" splendor to the eerie warbling cries of the Arab women. The openness, the ability to see vast distances, and the grand scale afford room once again for heroic thought and action. Tribal differences, however, almost destroy the expedition. In the midst of bleached, moon-white barren hills, the night before taking Akaba, a second event takes place for Lawrence through which the desert becomes a traumatic environment. Because he is English, with "no tribe," he volunteers to execute a Harif for killing a Howietat in order to prevent "a tribal bloodbath." It is Gassim, however, whom he must execute. After firing six bullets into him, Lawrence, with a horrified expression on his face, walks stiffly off and throws the gun as far from him as he can in an attempt to negate or disclaim his actions. In this image-event,

Lawrence has been drawn into the swift justice of the desert and the Arabs in order to meet *his* goal, taking Akaba. This is the first point where he is responsible for a death and is faced with the emotional consequences of his actions. He cannot rise above this event easily, as when Sherif Ali killed his first guide. The mood is set for further tragedy.

Akaba falls to Lawrence and the Arabs. The town is a white jewel where desert meets sea, and the gold of the water as Lawrence rides alone after the assault is reminiscent of the gold of the dunes in the first scenes of the desert. Lawrence looks wonderingly at the ocean, then, brought back to the present by the continuing sounds of looting in the town, he wipes his hands on his chest as if to cleanse them from that in which he has been involved. When Ali arrives and throws flowers into the surf, saying "The miracle is accomplished, garlands for the conqueror, tribute for the prince," Lawrence replies that he is none of those things. "What then?" asks Ali. "Don't know" is Lawrence's terse reply. Then he looks toward the desert and exclaims, "God, I love this country." He has defined himself by his relationship with the desert. He loves it for what it is, but also for what it has allowed him to accomplish and for what it has enabled him to become.

The major watershed in the change from positive to predominantly negative in Lawrence's experience of the desert occurs with his inability to save one of his servants while crossing the Sinai. This crossing requires more than enduring heat and hardship: Lawrence must choose directions. He must accept full responsibility as leader for his two young servants, Daud and Farraj. Lean's selected locations in the Sinai lack the simplicity and magnificence of the desert previously portrayed. Deformed pillars of salt and mud form a forest through which Lawrence and his servants travel. Washes and gullies carve the land and must be crossed. There is a "pillar of fire" that turns into a sand storm. In the roar of the storm, Lawrence becomes disoriented and loses both his compass and his way. He no longer has a modern technological advantage and lacks the Arabs' knowledge and experience with the land. When the storm partially clears, they head west seeking the Suez Canal. Once more there are magnificent golden dunes reminiscent of earlier scenes. Now, however, they become a trap as Lawrence leads Daud into quicksand. Daud perishes. Again there is no music, only the roar of wind and sand. In a scene of incredible futility, Lawrence, hair white from sand and dust, lies stretched out on the sand, holding Farraj to him, reaching toward the empty depression where Daud disappeared.

The following close-ups show that Lawrence has reached a breaking point both with his internal struggle and with his inability to deal with the desert. The exterior landscape is indicative of Lawrence's emotional condition. Upon reaching "civilization" they find a grimy, bombed-out, deserted outpost, worn by the elements. There is a torn screen, barbed wire, weather-blasted wood, and a warning sign. Lawrence crosses this threshold, through a screen door that swings and bangs, squeaking in the wind on broken hinges — and reaches the Suez Canal. On the other side a British soldier yells: "Who are you? Who are you?" Lawrence, silent, stares inward.

In the next desert sequence, Lawrence is seen setting off a charge of dynamite to derail a Turkish train. This is the first point in the film where the camera focuses on death. The destroyed train, the black smoke, and the blood of the slain stain the "clean" desert. The Arabs loot the train and the dead passengers. There is disorder. Lawrence walks the train roof, posturing as the Arabs shout his praise — viewing him as a kind of prophet and hero for leading them to victory. In this image-event Lean clearly indicates that Lawrence is becoming lost in the image of himself as hero and savior. Lawrence allows a journalist to take his picture, not believing, as the Arabs did, that a camera could steal *his* virtue. Lawrence is changing. He thinks his life is charmed, that *he* is the Arab revolt.

Later, a journalist asks, "What is it, Major Lawrence, that attracts you personally to the desert?" In this image-event, Lawrence, freshly washed, reclining on the fender of an automobile with a makeshift awning above

Figure 8–2. At a deserted outpost, vertical and diagonal lines, dust, and decay reflect both Lawrence's inner state and his changing relationship with the desert. Drawing by Tina Kennedy.

him responds, "It is clean." This is the last indication given in the movie that Lawrence regards the desert in a positive manner. He still sees the physical desert as something separate from, and in a sense, in contrast to, the political machinations in which he is involved. He does not understand that "place" is always encountered in specific situations. The desert, to him, is predictable and has its own internal logic. In contrast, he is worried about the unspoken agenda the British have for Arabia and how that meshes with what he has promised to the Arabs are the British intentions. He is troubled by the killing. He is deeply involved with the Arabs, but is not a part of them.

Lawrence's army shrinks with the approach of winter. The desert is portrayed as dark and cold. The strain of hiding out in a cave for an extended period of time, the pressure of his Arab companions, growing doubt about his motives, his own pride, and his promise to the British, lead to Lawrence's impulsive visit into the squalor of the town of Deraa. There, ironically, Lean has him symbolically walk on water again (a puddle in the road) just before he is captured. Lawrence is raped and tortured by the Turks, then discarded to lie face down in the muddy filth of the street. The cold of the winter landscape intensifies Lawrence's physical misery and the numbness of spirit that he experiences after the rape. He seems to finally recognize his limitations. In the dark shelter of the cave, when he is recovering from being tortured, Lawrence tells Ali that he has decided to return to the British in Jerusalem and request reassignment. He admits that he is "only a man . . . not the Arab revolt."

In Jerusalem, Lawrence requests release from service in Arabia because "The truth is, that I am an ordinary man . . . and I want an ordinary job, sir. That's my reason for resigning . . . it's personal. . . ." Colonel Allenby, representative of British mores, asks, "Are you mad?" "No. And I'd rather *not* go mad—that is my reason too" is Lawrence's reply. His request, a cry for help, is denied. Allenby ignores his passionate announcement: "I *have* no Arab friends, I don't *want* Arab friends . . . I just want my ration of common humanity." Allenby needs him for the "big push" to Damascus, so he unscrupulously plays on Lawrence's weaknesses, telling him that he is an "extraordinary" man and must not deny his destiny. When Lawrence finds he cannot yet quit the journey or get off the "whirlwind," he agrees to return to Arabia, but this time for Arab, not British, objectives. "All you want is someone holding down the Turkish Right. But I'm going to give [the Arabs] Damascus. We'll get there before you do, and when we've got it, we'll keep it."

Through dialogue, Lean makes clear that Lawrence is a changed man when he returns to Arabia. His interactions with Colonel Allenby were more destructive to his inner psyche than the rape by the Turkish Bey. Having separated himself psychologically from his old Arab friends, Lawrence surrounds himself with "assassins" and "outcasts" as body-guards—bought men with no honor and no loyalties except to him. The scene depicting the gathering of the Arabs for the push to Damascus reflects this loss of group cohesion as well as Lawrence's unharmonious relationship with the desert and its people. It is a scene of disorder, confusion, and dust. It is an image-event far different from the earlier ordered formation of the Arab army leaving Wadi Lam to take Akaba so gloriously.

On the march to Damascus, Lean portrays continuing extreme desert conditions, coupled with the horror of the remains of an Arab village after a Turkish massacre. Lawrence goes berserk and leads his own massacre of Turkish troops. His inner journey is further and further from acceptable British norms and societal expectations, deeper into madness. He is so trapped in himself and in the consequences of his actions that only his Arab friend Ali, the embodiment of the purity and cleanliness of the desert, can lead him out of the tangle of bodies and, to some degree, out of his own madness. After Lawrence's actions, the desert can never be "clean" for him again. Place and events are too integrally intertwined. The desert, like the bunch of grapes brought from Damascus by a scout, is sour.

After the failure of the Arab council to govern a Damascus replete with modern technology, Auda abu Tayi tries to convince Lawrence to return to the desert with him. Lawrence refuses and Auda asks, "Is it the blood? The desert has dried up more blood than you could think of." Lawrence answers, "I pray that I may never see the desert again. Hear me, God!" Auda persists: "There is only the desert for you"—believing, simply, that Lawrence belongs in the desert. He does not see that Lawrence's British background left him no mythical or religious framework within which to place a massacre or the dangerous things he discovered inside himself in the desert. Sherif Ali, on the other hand, understands. He tells Lawrence, "You tried very hard to give us Damascus." Lawrence answers, "It's what I came for." Outside in the courtyard when Auda points out that Ali loves Lawrence, Ali responds: "No, I fear him." "Then why do you weep?" "If I fear him—who love him—how he must fear himself who hates himself."

There was enough of Lawrence left to try to hold the Arab council together. When that failed, it was as though he had poured himself out and nothing was left. An image-event created at this point in the film is of a dry faucet in the Turkish hospital from which Lawrence tries to draw water for a silent, ghostlike patient. When the British medical officer slaps Lawrence and knocks him down, calling him a "filthy little wog," he lapses into hysterical laughter. The next image is of Lawrence's face reflected in the polished table that holds Allenby's hat—the symbol of British militarism. Lawrence's reflected image is of a lost, isolated man, a husk—a man emptied of his essential genius and idealism. Lawrence's strength was the strength of endurance and idealism. This strength is worn away during the movie through internal struggles, conflict with social norms, and his interactions with the extreme desert environment. Unlike Feisal, for whom the desert "has nothing," perhaps Lawrence found too much. Lawrence, who loved the desert initially, was transformed by the desert. But he was not of the desert; he was English. So, in *Seven Pillars of Wisdom* (1926, pp. 5–6) he writes:

> In my case, the effort for these years to live in the dress of Arabs, and to imitate their mental foundation, quitted me of my English self, and let me look at the West and its conventions with new eyes: they destroyed it all for me. At the same time I could not sincerely take on the Arab skin: it was an affectation only . . . Sometimes these selves would converse in the void; and then madness was very near, as I believe it would be near the man who could see things through the veils at once of two customs, two educations, and two environments.

The Socio-Political Context

World War I took place at the height of British imperial arrogance (Brauer 1990). In Lean's portrayal, British and Arab environments intertwine, their histories impinging upon each other. The Arabs are affected by British colonialism; the British in turn are affected by a long-standing fascination with Arabs and Islam—a tradition characterized by a mixture of romanticism and racial snobbery of which Lawrence was a descendant. Throughout the film the British look upon Arabs as "a nation of sheep stealers," "bloody savages," "wogs," or even "marvelous-looking beggars." The Arabs are considered illiterate (because most read no English), barbaric, undisciplined, and dirty. Furthermore, in Lean's portrayal, the Arabs are preindustrial, premodern, and have little previous experience fighting a "modern mechanized war." Their strengths lie in their understanding of the desert. For them, as with other premodern peoples, "the natural world was a fundamental base and crucial component of their everyday lives" (Katz and Kirby 1991, p. 261). Lean's Arabs are nomadic; the tribe the cohesive social unit. Warring upon each other is an honored pastime; looting the equivalent to a soldier's pay.

There is a portrayed reliance on individual power, strength, and endurance unlike the British dependence on strategy, regimentation, and machines—although in battle, individual acts of bravery are honored by both. The knife and the sword are the preferred weapons for the Arabs, fighting and argument is more personal. Modern technology and devices, with the exception of weapons, are seen either as useless or as toys. Weapons, however, fit within the Arabs' warring nature and within their myths. They recognize their need for artillery to match the firing power of the Turks. The British promised, but never gave the Arabs artillery for fear it would enable them to achieve and maintain independence.

In the film, Arabs are generally portrayed as a people who, compared with the organization and the technological level of the British, are incapable of self-government, at least in British terms. British terms would be a Western representative government, city-based with advanced technology. Technology as the powerful force in "modernism" plays an important role in the movie. Lawrence says in first meeting Sherif Ali, "So long as the Arabs fight tribe against tribe, so long will they be a little people, a silly people, greedy, barbarous, and cruel." The failure of the Arab council at the end of the film is predicated, however, on the Arabs' inability to understand and control technology, not on tribal hostilities. Lawrence's dream of helping the Arabs to gain their freedom is contingent upon changing a social order to conform to British standards.

At the end of the movie the Arabs, in order to attain an illusion of independence, are forced to accept British technical aid and influence, as Feisal had feared. In Dryden's words, "Well, it seems we are to have a British water works with an Arab flag on it. Do you think it was worth it?"

Conclusion

Lean's film is, in part, a reading of how Lawrence represents his own experiences in *Seven Pillars of Wisdom* (1926). Nonetheless, Lean's vision and purpose are vital aspects of the film. The locations he chose reflected his image of the environment as Lawrence experienced it. We have seen how the film's images of the desert change as Lawrence's perceptions of the desert change. Although a representation, *Lawrence* is yet a moving portrayal of changing person-place transactions. Lean achieves audience involvement through image-events of extraordinary behavior, in what is an extraordinary environment. Lawrence and the desert become "real" for us.

Lean portrays the evolution of Lawrence's character through significant events that occurred in Arabia. Although constrained by his British upbringing, Lawrence is portrayed as being deeply involved with the Arabic culture. As such, he is confronted not only with conflicting cultural values and mores, but also with conflicting elements within himself: for example, a desire for mercy and a pleasure in killing, a desire to be a hero/savior and a wish to be an ordinary man. Lean portrays these inner conflicts as integral parts of Lawrence's experience with the desert. These conflicts and the intensity and physical hardships associated with the extraordinary environment in which Lean's character is involved resulted in an ongoing transformation of the patterns of his transactions with the desert and in subsequent changes in himself. They contributed to Lawrence's descent into madness and to his final inability to cope with the desert.

Ultimately, Lean's film talks of the effect of the landscape on *one* man's actions and transactions. Lawrence did love the desert. His willingness to endure hardships and his fascination with the desert led him into the Arab revolt. The personal costs were great, including the loss of his love for the desert. While there is debate about the historic importance of the role of the actual man himself, from the myth perpetuated by the movie, there is little question that Lawrence left his shadow on the formation of a new place, the Arab state, on an altered people, and on millions who have seen the movie *Lawrence*. Certainly the film and the character of T. E. Lawrence are illusory in many respects, but they provide a myth that offers a model of heroic behavior that touches our awareness of the human condition.

Acknowledgments

I would like to thank Thomas Pagenhart and Rainer Bauer for their careful reading of the manuscript and for their suggestions and encouragement.

References

Aitken, S.C. 1991. A transactional geography of the image-event: The films of Scottish director Bill Forsyth. *Transactions, Institute of British Geographers* 16: 105–18.

Aitken, S.C. 1992. Theory development in contemporary behavioral and perceptual geography II: Behavior setting, territorial, learning, transactional and transformational theories. *Progress in Human Geography* 16 (4): 552–61.

Aitken, S.C., and Bjorklund, E.M. 1988. Transactional and transformational theories in behavioral geography. *The Professional Geographer* 40(1): 54–64.

Altman, I., and B. Rogoff. 1987. World Views in Psychology: Trait, Interactional Organismic, and Transactional Perspectives. In *Handbook of Environmental Psychology*, edited by D. Stokols and I. Altman, pp. 7–40. New York: Wiley.

Ausband, S. 1983. *Myth and Meaning, Myth and Order.* Macon, Ga.: Mercer University Press.

Barthes, R. 1957. *Mythologies.* London: Jonathan Cape (1972 translation by A. Lavers).

Brauer, K. 1990. Review of *Gordon of Khartoum: The Saga of a Victorian Hero. Victorian Studies* 34(1): 124–25.

Brown, M., and Cave, J. 1989. *A Touch of Genius: The Life of T.E. Lawrence.* New York: Paragon House.

Campbell, Joseph. 1949. *Hero with a Thousand Faces.* Cleveland: World Publishing.

Campbell, J., and Moyers, B. 1988. *The Power of Myth*, transcripts edited by Sue Flowers. New York: Doubleday.

Cavel, S. 1971. *The World Viewed: Reflections on the Ontology of Film.* New York: Viking Press.

Eliade, Mircea. 1963. *Myth and Reality.* New York: Harper and Row.

Glicksberg, C. 1968. The Tragic Hero. In *Heroes and Anti-Heroes: A Reader in Depth*, edited by Harold Lubin, pp. 356–66. San Francisco: Chandler.

Gray, P. 1989. The hero our century deserved. *Time* magazine, May 15: 80.

Ittelson, W. 1973. *Environment and Cognition.* New York: Seminar Press.

Ittelson, W., Proshansky, H., Rivlin, L., and Winkel, G. 1974. *An Introduction to Environmental Psychology.* New York: Holt, Rinehart and Winston.

Katz, C., and Kirby, A. 1991. In the nature of things: The environment and everyday life. *Transactions, Institute of British Geographers* 16(3): 59–71.

Kay, J. (1989). Human Dominion over Nature in the Hebrew Bible. *Annals of the Association of American Geographers* 79 (2): 214–32.

Lawrence, T. E. 1926, 1935. *Seven Pillars of Wisdom.* New York: Doubleday, Doran.

Little, B. 1987. Personality and the Environment. In *Handbook of Environmental Psychology*, edited by D. Stokols and I. Altman, pp. 205–44. New York: Wiley.

Lubin, H., editor. 1968. *Heroes and Anti-Heroes: A Reader in Depth.* San Francisco: Chandler.

Pfaff, W. 1989. The fallen hero (T.E. Lawrence). *The New Yorker,* May 8: 105–11.

Pratley, G. 1974. *The Cinema of David Lean.* London: Tantivy Press.

Russell, J., and Snodgrass, J. 1987. Emotion and Environment. In *Handbook of Environmental Psychology,* edited by D. Stokols and I. Altman, pp. 245–80. New York: Wiley.

Short, J.R. 1991. *Imagined Country: Society, Culture and Environment.* New York: Routledge.

Silverman, S. 1989. *David Lean.* New York: Harry Abrams.

Stokols, D. 1986. Transformational Perspectives on Environment and Behavior: An Agenda for Future Research. In *Cross Cultural Research in Environment and Behavior: Proceedings of the Second United States-Japan Seminar,* edited by W. Ittelson, A. Masaaki, and M. Kerr, pp. 243–60. Tucson: University of Arizona.

Sweeney, L. 1989. Lawrence in fine shape: Director David Lean and his refurbished film share an ovation. *The Christian Science Monitor,* February 13, p. 10, col. 2.

Wapner, S. 1987. A Holistic, Developmental, Systems-Oriented Environmental Psychology: Some Beginnings. In *Handbook of Environmental Psychology,* edited by D. Stokols and I. Altman, pp. 1433–65. New York: Wiley.

Yardley, M. 1985. *Back into the Limelight: a Biography of T.E. Lawrence.* London: Harrap.

Zonn, L. 1984. Landscape depiction and perception: A transactional approach. *Landscape Journal* 3(2):144–49.

Zube, E., and Kennedy, C. 1990. Changing Images of the Arizona Territory. In *Place Images in Media: Portrayal, Experience, and Meaning,* edited by L. Zonn, pp. 183–203. Savage, Md.: Rowman and Littlefield.

Filmography

Lawrence of Arabia. 1962, 1971, 1989. Columbia Studios. Director, Lean, D.

Part Three
Taking Time with Places

9

Filming Route 66: Documenting the Dust Bowl Highway

Arthur Krim

We are the first nation in the world to go to the
poorhouse in an automobile.

—Will Rogers

Few highways are more ingrained in American mythology than Route
66. This auto river of the American West that led Dust Bowl migrants of
the Depression era across mountains and desert to the promised land
of California should have left a great legacy on film, but the documentary camera recorded little of the social and physical realities of the great
exodus (Krim 1990a; Wallis 1990). In fact, maybe fifteen minutes of authentic stock footage of the Route 66 of the 1930s exists today. Perhaps
the sight of this select element of significant social change was so common for the times that only the most concerned saw need to capture its
essence. Further, had John Steinbeck not been so moved by the great
influx at his California doorstep to write *The Grapes of Wrath*, and thus to
help create the icon as the "mother road" of highways, and had John
Ford not made the novel into a movie, its role in American mythology
might have remained a relatively minor episode in American history and
a major episode only in folk memories of individual migrant experiences. It is safe to say, therefore, that despite the fact that these original
images were minuscule in volume, their role in creation of an icon was
considerable.

The few documented cinematic images of Highway 66 can be found
in John Ford's *The Grapes of Wrath* (1940), Pare Lorentz's recording of
the migrant trek on Dust Bowl highways in his documentary film *The
Plow That Broke the Plains* (1936), and early Pathé and Fox Movietone

newsreels made along the highways that led from Texas and Oklahoma. The fact that these various glimpses were made from vastly different motives, from commercial profit to social propaganda to pure sensationalism, does not matter; the gripping realities shown in these films of homeless families packed into overloaded vehicles hoping to reach California have formed a cornerstone of the highway's mythology. The pervasiveness of this national vision justifies a careful examination of the responsible cinematic images. The purpose of this chapter, therefore, is to examine the nature, character, and contexts of documented cinematic images of Route 66 as records of a significant moment in American history and to assess their roles in the formation of Route 66 as American mythology.

Those who made the few films of the Dust Bowl migration emerged from a spectrum of cinematic styles, each using dramatic effects to portray the visual character and motion of the highway exodus. The weekly newsreels recorded the event as a compelling graphic of the times, while government filmmakers, inspired by the Soviet montage style, attempted authenticity. Finally, the fictional drama of the Joad family exodus provided the location script for *The Grapes of Wrath*. This continuum between reality and fiction has clearly blurred the record and essence of actual footage. Thus, the documentary cinema of the Dust Bowl migration along Route 66 entwined with the needs and demands of cinematic style, which left the reality as a secondary element in the final and composite portrayal. The nature and the character of the iconography reflect these visions.

Newsreels, Pare Lorentz, and *The Plow That Broke the Plains*

In a strange irony, Route 66 was created in Oklahoma as a highway of hope during the prosperous years before the Depression. Conceived as a primary route linking the former Indian territory with Chicago and Los Angeles, it was promoted initially in 1925 by Tulsa Highway Commissioner Cyrus Avery as part of the new national numbering system (Scott and Kelly 1988). Its original signet of Number 60 was blocked by the governor of Kentucky and thus a second choice of Number 66 was made the following year (Krim 1990b). A Highway 66 Association was established to promote the route from Oklahoma to California as the "Main Street of America," which led in 1928 to a transcontinental footrace, the "Bunion Derby," between Los Angeles and New York (Thomas 1981). The front runner, Andy Payne, was captured by newsreels and photographs on the streets of Tulsa. These images became the earliest documents of U.S. 66 in its original period of Jazz Age boosterism (Scott and Kelly 1988).

If Highway 66 saw optimistic spirit in its conception, the calamity of the Stock Market crash in 1929 and the onset of drought on the Great Plains in 1930 soon turned the highway from a road of opportunity to a route of escape (Hurt 1981). Previous overproduction on ecologically fragile lands and a continuing cycle of drought had turned the Great Plains into the Great American Desert, complete with failed and abandoned farms and unusable land (Bowden 1976; Worster 1979). High surpluses from the productive years during and following World War I only added to the misery by dramatically deflating wheat prices. By 1933 the drought was overwhelming as great dust storms rolled across the devastated farmlands (Hurt 1981). During the storm of Black Sunday, April 14, 1935, in the panhandle town of Guymon, Oklahoma, *Washington Star* reporter Robert Geiger wrote that the whole region had become a "dust bowl," which quickly became the regional term adopted by the national press to describe the natural disaster (Worster 1979).

Documentary cameras from several sources were soon seen in the region with the intent of providing footage to American theaters. In September 1935, a Pathé News crew was sent to Oklahoma and Texas to film the mass outmigration of families destined for California (Stein 1973; Fielding 1978; Nightline 1992; Noren 1992). The resulting newsreel opened with the title "Dust Bowl Victims" as the narrator spoke of the "desperate people" fleeing their farms. A few moments of film showed old sedans, with faces pressed to the windows, passing before the camera in a steady stream along the dusty highway. Another ironic and poignant moment was the Pathé newsreel of official cars dedicating U.S. 66 as the Will Rogers Highway in January 1936, only months after the death of the humorist in a plane crash in Alaska (Associated Press 1936; Hopper 1992). Rogers was memoralized by the marking of the whole highway in his name from Chicago to Los Angeles (McSpadden 1979; Scott and Kelly 1988).

The March of Times newsreel featured a weekly segment on the "U.S. Dust Bowl" in June 1937 in the panhandle town of Dalhart, Texas (Dust Bowl 1937; Fielding 1978). The narrative described "hopeless and bewildered farmers set out on a tragic migration" as overloaded cars struggled across the dusty landscape. The camera panned to show a spare tire painted hopefully, "California or Bust—No More Dust Bowl." These images of the despair and migration functioned only as brief moments of distraction before the main feature, where the fantasies of a musical, western, or gangster film compelled the audiences' attention (Short 1991).

In 1935, the U.S. Resettlement Agency, later named the Farm Security Administration, sent a crew to the Texas panhandle to gather footage for a documentary (Meltzer 1978). The filmmaker Pare Lorentz had seen the beginnings of the drought when visiting his wife's family four years earlier (Snyder 1968; Lorentz 1992), and in 1934 he became agricultural reporter for *News-Week*, when he wrote on the plight of the farmers:

> Like Israel's seven sons they trekked somberly through the parched lands. They looked to Washington for some Joseph to load their sacks with grain and money against "seven years of famine when all the plenty shall be forgotten in the land of Egypt." (Lorentz 1934, p. 2)

Lorentz envisioned a film on the Great Plains drought and the plight of the American farmer. He had already experimented with a documentary format in his photo essay *The Roosevelt Year: 1933* in which running captions led the reader from page to page in cinematic style as stark photos of homeless families prefaced the account of the New Deal vision for democratic equality (Lorentz 1934; Lorentz 1992). Lorentz's social concerns in this work soon brought him to the attention of Rexford Tugwell, secretary of agriculture (MacCann 1973). The two met, whereupon Lorentz convinced Tugwell that a government film on the Dust Bowl disaster would be a worthy topic for the newly created Resettlement Agency, which catered to the problems of farm family dislocation (Snyder 1968). Lorentz gained approval for a Dust Bowl film in June 1935 and began filming in September (Snyder 1968). He hired three avant-garde filmmakers, Paul Strand, Leo Hurwitz, and Ralph Steiner, to assist in production. In 1934, the three had formed the Nykino film group, which was inspired by the Soviet experimental cinema, *Kino-Pravda* (Film Truth), which used the innovative technique of montage editing to create dramatic effects from silent footage (Campbell 1982; Zorkia 1989). Strand had already made the experimental film *Manhatta* in 1921, had won respect for his Mexican government documentary *The Wave*, and had been to Moscow to meet the Soviet director Sergei Eisenstein in early 1935 (Tomkins 1976).

Strand and his Nykino colleagues began filming in Montana, then worked south through Wyoming and Nebraska, and reached Dalhart, Texas, by October 1935. One particularly effective sequence was made of a lone sedan, piled high with belongings, headed west across a sand-blown highway (Lorentz 1992). The image was brief in the final film, but Strand's camera work clearly portrayed the car as a symbol of the mass migration from the Dust Bowl in which a solitary vehicle appeared overwhelmed by the forces of nature (Fig. 9–1).

Serious disagreements over cinematic style emerged between Lorentz and the Nykino group in late 1935. Strand and Hurwitz offered their vision of the filming:

> We wanted our films to possess at the same time a progression of emotion and a close and true relationship to the events and their causes, direct and submerged. (Campbell 1982, p. 127)

Lorentz disagreed, dismissed the group, and then moved on to California to find more footage before final editing (Snyder 1968). Here he met with Dorothea Lange, the San Francisco portrait photographer who had likewise been hired by the Resettlement Agency to document the Dust Bowl refugees in the Central Valley's migrant camps (Meltzer 1979;

Figure 9–1. Pare Lorentz. The Plow That Broke the Plains. *Migrant family headed west in Texas. October 1935. Movie still by Paul Strand. By permission of the University of Nevada Press from* FDR's Moviemaker, *by Pare Lorentz. Copyright © 1992. University of Nevada Press.*

Fig. 9–2). Lorentz visited the Shaster resettlement camp on Highway 99 in Bakersfield at the invitation of Lange, where she arranged a caravan of migrant cars for cameraman Paul Ivano. The sequence was used in the closing moments of the film (Snyder 1968; Lorentz 1992).

The final editing of Lorentz's film was completed in early 1936. He asked the Nebraska-born composer Virgil Thompson to write a musical score and Thomas Chalmers of the Metropolitan Opera to narrate the script with the title *The Plow That Broke the Plains* (Snyder 1968).

The film, which opened in New York in May 1936, concluded with scenes of Dust Bowl devastation by using the Nykino footage shot in Texas with the film from the California resettlement camps to create a

Figure 9–2. Dorothea Lange. Oklahoma drought refugees in the Central Valley, California. 1935. By permission of the Oakland Museum. Copyright © 1982.

montage of westward migration in the automobile (Lorentz 1936) as the narrator intoned:

> On to the West
> Once again they headed for the setting sun
> Last year in every summer month
> Thirty thousand people left the Great Plains
> And hit the highways for the Pacific Coast
> The last border
> Blown out—baked out—and broke!
> (Thompson and Lorentz 1942, p. 42)

The montage editing, Thompson's score of American folk themes, and the cadence of Lorentz's script combined to provide a powerful cinematic essay on the demise of the land and people of the Great Plains (MacCann 1973). Clearly, he had produced a successful government-funded documentary film for popular commercial release (Barnouw 1974).

John Steinbeck and *The Grapes of Wrath*

While Lorentz was filming *The Plow That Broke the Plains* in 1936, the impact of the migrant exodus to California had already generated considerable reactions by local artists and writers (Stein 1973). Among them was John Steinbeck, who had written *Tortilla Flat* in 1935 about migrant workers in his hometown of Salinas (Benson 1984). In the summer of 1936, Steinbeck was introduced by Dorothea Lange to Tom Collins, administrator for the Shaster camp in Bakersfield (Meltzer 1979; Benson 1984). Writing for *The Nation*, Steinbeck (1936, p. 305) described the graphic reality of the roadside camps in the vicinity:

> It is quite usual for a man, his wife, and from three to eight children to arrive in California with no possessions but the rattletrap car they travel in and the ragged clothes on their bodies.

With Collins as his source, Steinbeck learned that the migrants' route of exodus to California was U.S. Highway 66 from the Dust Bowl in Kansas, across the Texas panhandle, and over the mountains of New Mexico and Arizona to the Colorado River Bridge at Needles, California. Here the migrants followed Highway 66 at night through the Mojave Desert to the Tehachapi Pass, where the road turned north as U.S. 466 toward the opportunities in the harvest fields of the Central Valley (Stein 1973; Benson 1984). After a trip to the Soviet Union in the summer of 1937, Steinbeck and his wife, Carol, returned to the United States and in September followed the migrant route along U.S. 66 from Chicago to Oklahoma and west to California (Moore 1939; Krim 1991b). Arriving back at his home in Los Gatos in October, Steinbeck called Collins and together they followed Highway 66 east again across the Mojave Desert to the Colorado River Bridge at Needles (Benson 1984).

During the California floods of 1938, Steinbeck was drawn once again to the plight of the Dust Bowl refugees in the Central Valley. *Life* magazine commissioned him to write a story on the subject and assigned Horace Bristol to illustrate Steinbeck's material (Benson 1984; Bristol 1988). Steinbeck's initial commitment to develop a short picture article soon evolved into his broader image of portraying the exodus as a documentary drama. He began writing his "big book" during May 1938 (DeMott 1989). Soon afterward, he met Pare Lorentz through Dorothea Lange. Lorentz and Charlie Chaplin visited Steinbeck in August 1938 in Los Gatos, where they discussed a range of subjects, from film styles to the increasing political tensions in Europe (DeMott 1989).

Steinbeck was impressed with the cinematic technique of background montage he had seen in Lorentz's *The Plow That Broke the Plains* and the recent (1938) release of *The River* (Snyder 1968; Benson 1984). Thus, with the influence of Lorentz, and ultimately the Nykino group, he conceived his work as a sequence of general chapters in documentary montage style and narrative chapters of dramatic dialogue for the Joads, his fictitious migrant family (DeMott 1989). The migrant story would be written with the visual flow of a movie and the drama of a stage play.

Writing continuously through June, Steinbeck took a needed break over the Fourth of July and then began writing again, apparently using his road map from his 1937 surveys on Highway 66 for place names and town locations (DeMott 1989). He initially spelled out the highway number in his work, then quickly changed to "66" for clarity on the page (Krim 1991b):

Highway 66 is the main migrant road. 66—the long concrete path across the country, waving gently up and down on the map, from Missouri to Bakersfield—over the red lands and grey lands, twisting up into the mountains, crossing the Divide and down into the bright and terrible desert, and across the desert to the mountains again and into the rich California valleys. 66 is the path of people in flight, refugees from the dust and shrinking land, from the thunder of tractors and shrinking ownership, from the desert's slow northward invasion, from the twisting winds that howl up and out of Texas, from the floods that bring no richness to the land and steal what little richness is there. From all of this the people are in flight, and they come to 66 from tributary side roads, from the wagon tracks and from the country roads. 66 is the mother road, the road of flight. (Steinbeck 1939, p. 160)

In early September, Carol Steinbeck selected the title *The Grapes of Wrath* from a verse of "The Battle Hymn of the Republic" (Benson 1984). The final chapters were completed in October and a cover illustration of migrant cars was commissioned for the dust jacket by Elmer Hader, a California artist Steinbeck had used for his book *The Long Valley* (Krim 1991a). The muted colors of the cover served as a reference image for the novel and became a signet of the book when published by Viking Press in April 1939 (Benson 1984).

John Ford and *The Grapes of Wrath*

The publication of *The Grapes of Wrath* proved to be a popular success beyond the expectations of even Steinbeck (Benson 1984). The dramatic epic of the Dust Bowl migration drew immediate attention from Hollywood producers. In May 1939, Darryl Zanuck of Twentieth Century Fox offered Steinbeck $75,000 for the film rights, and a contract was signed in June (Gussow 1971; Owens 1989). Zanuck personally selected Nunnally Johnson, who had worked with author William Faulkner as scriptwriter (Stemple 1980). Johnson contacted Lorentz for insight into Steinbeck's style and eventually discussed the script directly with the novelist (Stemple 1980). The first draft and a working board were completed by July (French 1973; Stemple 1980).

Johnson found that the most difficult task was compacting the six-hundred-page novel into a two-hour film. He used the montage style of the background chapters for setting location shots, while Steinbeck's dialogue was left relatively intact with changes made only for narrative flow (French 1973; Millichop 1983). Thus, the filming of the "mother road" itself was scripted:

The scene dissolves to a MONTAGE: Almost filling the screen is a shield marker of the U.S. Highway 66. Superimposed on it is a montage of jalopies, steaming and rattling and piled high with goods and people. (Johnson 1943, p. 346)

Zanuck selected John Ford as film director. Ford had gained recognition in 1938 for his authentic landscape style in *Stagecoach*, the classic American western shot on location in Monument Valley, Arizona (Ford 1979; Trimble 1986; Short 1991; Buscombe 1992). Ford had just completed two other pictures for Fox studios in June 1939, *Young Mr. Lincoln* and *Drums Along the Mohawk*, both with Henry Fonda, the rising midwestern star (Ford 1979; Millichap 1983). Ford requested a summer break because of his hectic schedule, but Zanuck was pressing to begin filming before the expected war broke out in Europe (Gussow 1971; Ford 1979; Stempel 1980). The invasion of Poland on September 1 made the shooting schedule all the more imperative, and on September 15 filming began (French 1973; Stempel 1980).

To disguise the film from news coverage associated with the novel, a cover title of *Highway 66*, which described a light comedy of western travel, was given to the press (French 1973; Stempel 1980). Meanwhile, Ford's concern with achieving the documentary realism of Steinbeck's novel led him to assign Gregg Toland as studio cameraman in Hollywood and Otto Brower as second director for location footage (Ford 1979; Stempel 1980). Brower was an experienced cameraman familiar with U.S. 66 locations in southwest Missouri from his work with Nunnally Johnson on *Jessie James* in 1938 (Condon 1940; Stempel 1980; Academy Foundation 1992). He was on location in eastern Oklahoma by late September 1939, and then worked west along U.S. 66 through Texas, New Mexico, Arizona, and California by late October (Condon 1940; French 1973). Brower tried to film migrant cars directly along the highway in an effort at authenticity, but the families refused. He then purchased "twenty-four jalopies" for location shots between Oklahoma and California with the Joad family's Hudson as the key vehicle (Condon 1940).

The Brower location unit shot film at twenty specific sites along the Joad family route from Sallislaw, Oklahoma to Needles, California, including shots in Amarillo and Vega, Texas, Santa Rosa and Grants, New Mexico, and Flagstaff and Kingman, Arizona, and the Oatman Goldroad and Colorado River Bridge at Topok, Arizona (Scott and Kelly 1988). Several shots were made of U.S. 66 highway signs and line markers at Oklahoma City and Needles for the purposes of identification (Fig. 9–3A). The footage was shot at several speeds and using close-ups with matching angles from several directions (*The Grapes of Wrath* 1940).

The resulting three and a half hours of location footage was edited by Robert Simpson to three and a half minutes for the final Highway 66 sequences (Zinman 1970; Ford 1979). Eight montage highway segments were featured, including the Joad family truck on location (Fig. 9–3B).

Figure 9–3A and 9–3B. John Ford. The Grapes of Wrath. *U.S. 66 shield sign, Will Rogers Highway, Arizona. October 1935. Movie footage by Otto Brower. By permission of Twentieth Century Fox. Copyright © 1940.*

These were interspliced with dialogue scenes by cameraman Gregg Toland, who used key actors in Hollywood stage sets, and were enhanced with dramatic studio lighting effects similar to those he would use to striking advantage in Orson Welles's *Citizen Kane* (French 1973). However, when Lorentz reviewed the final cut, he confused the efforts of Toland and Brower when he noted that the brief landscape locations were overwhelmed by the studio scenes:

> But for all the beauty of his night effects and the difficult shots he made, Toland did not get the size of the Southwest, not the feeling of the sky and the land in his camera. (Lorentz 1940, p. 63)

On only one occasion, the swimming scene at the Colorado River when the Joad family first sees California, did the Brower location unit match with the studio crew on Highway 66. Henry Fonda, who played Tom Joad, recalled the filming location:

> The second unit went out and shot all the footage between Oklahoma and California. The river outside Needles, California, where we take our bath was the farthest away we went. The rest of the picture was shot in real "Okie" camps in the vicinity of Los Angeles. (Teichman 1981, p. 137)

The final editing of *The Grapes of Wrath* was made in November 1939 after forty-three days of shooting (Ford 1979; Stempel 1980). In December, Zanuck gave Steinbeck a private screening in Hollywood. The author heartily approved of the film. He was struck by its social realism in translating the "documentary" style of his novel to a popular movie:

> Zanuck has more than kept his word. He has a hard, straight picture in which the actors are submerged so completely that it looks and feels like a documentary film and certainly has a hard truthful ring. (Steinbeck and Wallsten 1975, p. 195)

The Grapes of Wrath opened in January 1940 to immediate popular and critical acclaim. It was to receive two Academy Awards, one for John Ford as director and the other for Jane Darwell as Ma Joad (Zinman 1970; Millichap 1983). The documentary style of the movie prompted *Life* magazine to compare images of the Dust Bowl migrants with those of the studio actors by publishing the original Horace Bristol photographs ("Speaking of Pictures" 1940; Bristol 1988). Oklahoma-born folksinger Woodie Guthrie was so taken by the realism of the movie that he composed a twelve-verse ballad of "Tom Joad" for his RCA record album

Dust Bowl Ballads (Klein 1980). In California, Dorothea Lange saw the irony of the documentary realism and carefully photographed *The Grapes of Wrath* billboards in Modesto (Lorentz 1941).

Despite the fact that the landscape of Highway 66 was limited to brief montage shots in early segments of the film, the exodus route of the Joad family trek was used on prominently displayed lobby posters for the movie during 1940 (Fig. 9–4). Movie stills with Henry Fonda and Jane Darwell were pasted along images of the heavy black line tracing the highway from Oklahoma to California, giving cartographic authenticity to the fictional drama of the film. The poster recalled a similar passage in the Steinbeck novel when the highway was traced from a road map with the route numbers providing direction through an unknown land:

> Ma said worriedly, "How you gonna find us?" "We'll be on the same road," said Tom. "66 right on through. Come to a place name' Bakesfiel'. Seen it on the map I got. You go straight on there." (Steinbeck 1939, p. 228)

Documenting the Dust Bowl Highway

Fifteen minutes of movie film document the Dust Bowl exodus on U.S. Highway 66. It has great value as American documentary cinema in preserving a visual record of a national drama played out along the western highways to California. Despite the poverty and despair of the migrants, it was the freedom to travel the open highway west to California that gave an element of hope to the Dust Bowl migration. Highway 66 symbolized a biblical exodus from the land of drought to the land of plenty. For the migrants, the double sixes were magic signs to follow and their numbers on the screen served to mark the trail to the audience as icons of the Dust Bowl route. Thus, a few brief shots of U.S. 66 shield signs in Pathé News film and *The Grapes of Wrath* are rare but important documents of American cinema in recording the actual highway location in authentic settings.

If actual U.S. 66 shield signs were rarely filmed, then the power of Highway 66 as a western route comes from the footage of moving cars in a moving picture film. It was the motion on the screen that brought the highway experience to life and ultimately gave drama to the footage; a motion of cars and people, faces peering out as the traffic moves by. To see a film of desperate people packed into old automobiles creeping slowly across the screen gave immediate pause to the great tide that flowed out of the Great Plains to California in the 1930s. It is this move-

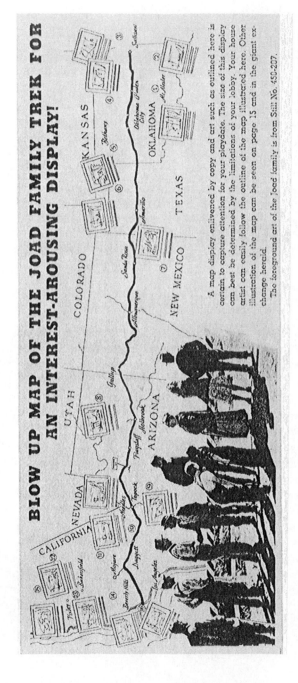

Figure 9-4. "Blow Up Map of the Joad Family Trek." The Grapes of Wrath *lobby poster. 1940. The map shows the route of the Joad family on U.S. Highway 66 from Oklahoma to California with still scenes from the movie. Reproduced with the permission of the Steinbeck Research Center, San Jose State University, California.*

ment that the first newsreels sought to capture and that was dramatized by Lorentz, Steinbeck, and Ford in their Dust Bowl documentaries.

The emotional power of the Dust Bowl films comes from the moving cars, and so the landscape of Highway 66 is nearly lost in the drama. Certainly, the early newsreels sought locations in the Dust Bowl states, where the flat prairie and drifting sand identified the region as the Great Plains, if not the Great American Desert. At the western horizon were the lush scenes of California, usually sobered by the roadside camps of the migrant, as in the case of *The Plow That Broke the Plains*. What was missing, and what Steinbeck's prose as descriptive geography provided for Otto Brower, was the scenic landscape of the Southwest, where the mountains and desert offer spectacular views along the "mother road." Even in the final film, however, the Brower location shots were limited to a few moments of authentic montage. Only at the Colorado River Bridge did the studio actors experience Highway 66 at its point of tangency with a real landscape of a specific place.

How truthful is the brief documentary cinema of Route 66 in the Dust Bowl years? Except for the news film, the migrant highway footage in *The Plow That Broke the Plains* and *The Grapes of Wrath* was contrived to fit the scenic need. Lange had the caravan of cars line up for Lorentz at the Shaster camp and Brower had to use hired vehicles to depict the migrant jalopies along U.S. 66. Such scenic direction was necessary, of course, for effective editing and these were authentic cars on actual location. Still, to say that these films are *Kino-Pravda*, true documentary cinema, seems generous to the contrived conditions of shooting location and prescribed arrangement.

What is left of the documentary truth is the intent of the cameramen to film the Dust Bowl migration as an act of realization of the human tide that was moving west along the highways. We know little of the newsreel crews that filmed for Pathé, but we know of Paul Strand and Ralph Steiner as advocates of *Kino-Pravda*, of Lorentz and his concern for the New Deal democracy, and of Brower and his concern for authenticity in presenting U.S. 66. At the least, all were trying to film the migrant plight with compassion and to record a motion picture of time and place.

Finally, there is the complex issue of documentary photography transformed to cinema, or rather moving pictures used as still frames. The fact that Dorothea Lange inspired Lorentz in her portrait work of migrant families, as Lorentz inspired Steinbeck in his montage writing, shows the fluid exchange from one medium to another. Indeed, the turn of Steinbeck from the Horace Bristol photo essay to the full novel and the irony of the Bristol photos used as models for the Joads demonstrates that movies and photographs fused their imagery to serve the subject. It was a dramatic epic of the Dust Bowl migration that attracted the graphic artists to the subject. However, if Steinbeck had not been compelled to write *The Grapes of Wrath*, the film record of the Dust Bowl exodus would have likely been limited to a few feet of neglected newsreels. Indeed, had not Zanuck insisted that the novel be filmed in authentic location, the cinema of U.S. 66 as the Dust Bowl highway might have been left to the Will Rogers memorial ceremony.

The collective cinematic portrayals of Dust Bowl migration created changes in the nature of what John Short (1991) has called a national environmental ideology, which is a kind of myth used in the evolution of a national identity. In this case, the ideology can be envisioned at two scales. First, and at a grander scale, the social attributes of the westward movement and settlement of the American frontier in the nineteenth century were reversed in the twentieth-century Dust Bowl migration. Elements of freedom, individuality, honor, self-knowledge, and the freedoms associated with a bucolic lifestyle disappeared as families of despair piled into cars to flee that same countryside. Further, the portrayals were primarily by and perhaps for citizens of the city who viewed the movement in a sympathetic, but somewhat paternalistic, context. Any envy of rural lifestyles was lost. Second, and at a much smaller scale but perhaps in a more enduring sense, the ideology of Route 66 was irrevocably established as a part of American mythology. The highway became a symbol that represented the Great Depression and thus reflected a significant flaw in American society.

In sum, what emerges from the fleeting images in the films of Highway 66 is the record of a road caught beyond its intention as a simple route between Chicago and Los Angeles. It was no longer a scenic trail through the vistas of New Mexico and Arizona, but instead, it was a river of refugees fleeing a deserted land, a steady stream of old cars crawling inexorably past spectacular landscapes hardly noticed. It was the strange irony that Will Rogers had seen that the great prosperity of the American economy had turned the seemingly wonderful automobile into a vehicle of poverty. A great migration was streaming and sputtering across the landscape, and the movie camera only briefly made record of the passing drama. It is in this frame that the few films of Route 66 should be appreciated as real documents of the real time of the Dust Bowl migration.

References

American Academy. 1992. Otto Brower file. Beverly Hills, Calif.: Academy of Motion Picture Arts and Sciences.

Associated Press. 1936. Names highway for Rogers. *New York Times,* January 6.

Barnouw, E. 1974. *Documentary, a History of the Non-fiction Film.* New York: Oxford University Press.

Benson, J. J. 1984. *True Adventures of John Steinbeck.* New York: Viking Press.

Bowden, M. 1976. The Great American Desert in the American Mind In *Geographies of the Mind,* edited by D. Lowenthal and M. J. Bowden. New York: Oxford University Press.

Bristol, H. 1988. Documenting "The Grapes of Wrath," *The Californians* 10: 40–47.

Buscombe, E. 1992. *Stagecoach* (BFI Film Classics). Bloomington: Indiana University Press.

Campbell, R. 1982. *Cinema Strikes Back: Radical Filmmakers in the United States.* Ann Arbor: University of Michigan Research Press.

Condon, F. 1940. The Grapes of Rap. *Colliers,* January 27: 23, 65–65.

DeMott, R., editor. 1989. *John Steinbeck, Working Days: The Journals of "The Grapes of Wrath."* New York: Viking Press.

Fielding, R. 1978. *The March of Time.* New York: Oxford University Press.

Ford, D. 1979. *Paddy: The Life of John Ford.* Englewood Cliffs, N.J.: Prentice-Hall.

French, W. 1973. *A Filmguide to "The Grapes of Wrath."* Bloomington: University of Indiana Press.

Gussow, M. 1971. *Don't Say Yes Until I Finish Talking* [Darryl Zanuck]. Garden City, N.Y.: Doubleday.

Hopper, P. 1992. Pat Kogen Enterprises. New York. July 7: telephone conversation.

Hurt, R. D. 1981. *The Dust Bowl.* Chicago: Nelson Press.

Johnson, N. 1943. "The Grapes Of Wrath" from the novel by J. Steinbeck. In *Twenty Best Film Plays,* edited by J. Gassner. New York: Crown.

Klein, J. 1980. *Woody Guthrie, a Life.* New York: Random House.

Krim, A. 1990a. Route 66, a Cultural Cartography. In *Roadside America,* edited by J. Jennings. Ames: Iowa State University Press.

———. 1990b. First numbering of Route 66 discovered in Missouri. *SCA News Journal* 11 (2):10.

———. 1991a. Elmer Hader and *The Grapes of Wrath"* bookjacket. *Steinbeck Newsletter* 4 (1):1–3.

————. 1991b. John Steinbeck and Highway 66. *Steinbeck Newsletter* 4 (2): 8–9.

Lorentz, P. 1934. *The Roosevelt Year: 1933.* New York: Funk and Wagnalls.

————. 1934. Agriculture. *News-Week,* June 9: 1–2.

————. 1940. The Grapes of Wrath. *McCall's,* April: 63.

————. 1941. Dorothea Lange, Camera with a purpose. *U.S. Camera,* January: 93–116.

————. 1992. *FDR's Moviemaker.* Reno: University of Nevada Press.

MacCann, R. 1973. *The People's Films: A Political History of the U.S.* Government Motion Pictures. New York: Hastings House.

McSpadden, P. 1979. *The Best of Will Rogers.* New York: Crown.

Meltzer, M. 1979. *Dorothea Lange, A Photographer's Life.* New York: Farrar, Straus and Giroux.

Millichap, J. R. 1983. *Steinbeck on Film.* New York: Frederick Ungar.

Moore, H. T. 1939. *The Novels of John Steinbeck, a First Critical Study.* New York: Normandie House.

Noren, A. 1992. Samuel Grinberg Film Libraries. New York. July 6: telephone conversation.

Owens, L. 1989. *"The Grapes of Wrath," Trouble in the Promised Land.* Boston: Wayne Publishing.

Scott, Q., and Kelly, S. C. 1988. *Route 66, the Highway and Its People.* Norman: University of Oklahoma Press.

Short, J. R. 1991. *Imagined Country: Society, Culture and Environment.* London: Routledge.

Snyder, R. L. 1968. *Pare Lorentz and the Documentary Film.* Norman: University of Oklahoma Press.

Speaking of Pictures. 1940. *Life,* February 19: 10–11 [Horace Bristol photographs 1938].

Stein, W. J. 1973. *California and the Dust Bowl Migration.* Westport, Conn.: Greenwood Press.

Steinbeck, E., and R. Wallsten. 1975. *Steinbeck, A Life in Letters.* New York: Viking Press.

Steinbeck, J. 1936. Dubious Battle in California. *The Nation,* September: 302–5.

————. 1939. *The Grapes of Wrath.* New York: Viking Press.

Stempel, T. 1980. *Screenwriter, the Life and Times of Nunnally Johnson.* San Diego: A. S. Barnes.

Teichman, H. 1981. *Fonda, My Life as Told to Howard Teichman.* New York: New American Library.

Thomas, J. H. 1981. *The Bunion Derby, Andy Payne and the Great Transcontinental Road Race.* Oklahoma City: Southwest Heritage Books.

Thompson, V., and Lorentz, P. 1942. *The Plow That Broke the Plains, Suite for Orchestra.* New York: Music Press.

Tomkins, C. 1976. *Paul Strand.* New York: Aperture Press.

Trimble, M. 1986. *Roadside History of Arizona.* Missoula, Mont.: Mountain Press.

Wallis, M. 1990. *Route 66, the Mother Road.* New York: St. Martin's Press.

Worster, D. 1979. *Dust Bowl.* New York: Oxford University Press.

Zinman, D. 1970. *50 Classic Motion Pictures.* New York: Crown.

Zorkia, N. 1989. *The Illustrated History of Soviet Cinema.* New York: Hippocrene Books.

Filmography

Citizen Kane. 1940. Mercury-RKO Pictures. Director, Welles, O.

Drums Along the Mohawk. 1939. Twentieth Century Fox. Director, Ford, J.

Dust Bowl. 1937 (11 June). March of Times.

Dust Bowl Victims. 1935 (September). Pathé News.

The Grapes of Wrath. 1940. Twentieth Century Fox. Director, Ford, J.

Jessie James. 1938. Twentieth Century Fox. Director, Ford, J.

Manhatta. 1921. Independent. Director, Strand, P.

The Plow That Broke the Plains. 1936. U.S. Resettlement Agency. Director, Lorentz, P.

The River. 1938. Farm Security Administration–Paramount. Director, Lorentz, P.

Stagecoach. 1939. United Artists. Director, Ford, J.

The Wave. 1935. Government of Mexico. Director, Strand, P.

Young Mr. Lincoln. 1939. Twentieth Century Fox. Director, Ford, J.

10

The City as Cinematic Space: Modernism and Place in *Berlin, Symphony of a City*

Wolfgang Natter

Warning: Those wishing to recognize place are urged to remember that violation of the 180-degree axis risks viewer disorientation.[1]

The effort to approach concepts of place or space made visible in the content of any particular film best begins with the recollection of that defining convention which orders meaning in most narrative film. Adherence to the 180-degree rule, referred to above, perpetuates the now familiar expectation of a common area from shot to shot, which sufficiently stabilizes space to orient the viewer within the scene. Crossing the axis of action, by contrast, disorients viewer continuity, leaving uncertain whether an ensuing shot is within the same spatial field or has shifted to a new locale. The convention of analytic editing is nothing other than the practice of spatial articulation in narrative and fiction films using master shots and cut-ins that respect the 180-degree axis of action. Continuity cutting refers to shot transitions marked by matches-on-movement and matches-on-action that likewise promote the illusion of a spatio-temporal continuum.

Several pertinent points ensue from these remarks. First, the reminder that film categorically depends on illusion in creating a representation of reality; second, that place and cinematic space, though in a relationship to each other, at the same time belong to different orders; third, that the general precondition for an assemblage of disparate images being viewed as having narrative meaning is the stabilization of any number of possibly imaginable symbolic spatialities into one that respects the 180-degree axis.

Having recollected these pertinent facts, I seek in this essay to animate a discussion of the submerged spatiality inherent to film and the filmic apparatus via questions that arise for me in teaching a form and content analysis of *Berlin, Symphony of a City* (Walter Ruttmann, 1927). *Berlin*, one of the most significant films of the modernist avant-garde, made the depiction of a highly contested urban place its central focus. It has entered film history as a pioneering effort defining the "cross-section," "street," or "slice of life" films of the 1920s.[2]

This analysis of *Berlin* as represented place begins by considering cinema most generally as a form of writing. Thought of as a form of writing—as the entire system sustaining film production and reception—cinema invites scrutiny of the process of recontextualization that occurs once images made of any given place enter the necessarily fragmented, symbolic space of filmic narration. With reference to *Berlin*, this issue invites many questions, including the character of documentary film as a particular representation of the social world, and the relations in operation in this genre among objects, subjects, and objectivity.

Second, drawing upon pertinent film theory (particularly work by Ruttmann's contemporary Walter Benjamin), the essay expands on familiar categories of film scholarship (which have tended to stress temporal categories governing filmic narration) in order to take seriously the inherently spatial aspects of the cinematic apparatus itself, as enacted by the dynamics of montage, framing, crosscutting, and juxtaposition, which also happen to be *Berlin*'s overarching compositional principles. I will argue that Benjamin's film essay offers a ready perspective from which to theorize the spatiality at work in film. While the continuity system of editing demands the stabilization of space in accord with the 180-degree law, Benjamin was alert to a filmic spatiality that countered its submersion as the inert and undialectical. Benjamin's sensitivity to the strangeness of the still young medium offers a "modernist" perspective on film that merits serious reflection again via a current of thought generally attributed to the "postmodern."[3]

In the last part of the essay, I will amplify my discussion of the relationship between place and cinematic space with an analysis of images from Ruttmann's film. This discussion takes its guidance from the contemporary reception accorded the film by Siegfried Kracauer and others. The reasons for Kracauer's denigration of *Berlin* will be critiqued on these grounds. Ruttmann's city will be viewed as a circulatory system, defined by accumulation and exchange, and as such, a materialization of the compression of space-time perception associated with modernism.

Film as Writing and Difference

In offering the appearance of a fullness of vision, film wants us to forget that it is always written. The sensual experience of film suggests an immediacy of full presence that would seem to elevate it above the mediation or artifice that permits the denigration of writing. Much film scholarship of the past few decades, however, has been—to borrow a formalist term—devoted to barring and denaturalizing the devices that conspire to give film the effect of an unmediated reality presentation. Thus, studies have analyzed the effects of censorship codes on content and form presentation, or considered the cinema as a system of representation, as an industry and institution, or as an ordering of experience that serves to create subject positions.[4]

Film can in fact never really be directly "spoken" or "heard." To begin with, all films are constructions and thus involve choices at every level, beginning with preproduction planning and ending with postproduction editing and distribution. Also, the mode in which a film's images and sounds is presented largely follows narrative and genre conventions that in turn define the parameters of reception or an audience's horizon of expectations. Finally, because both films and their viewers are "in history," contexts of reception matter in attempting to assign meaning to a particular image, unit, or entire film.

The desire to view film as an unmediated reality presentation (or to denigrate the "artifice" of writing), however, builds upon a ready arsenal provided by a tradition of metaphysics that has privileged speech over writing as the medium providing full presence and undistorted communication. Anchoring this privileging of the oral is a postulation of a face-to-face presence guaranteed by the identity and intentionality of the utterer. Film reception inherits this predisposition. But if it can be demonstrated, as Jacques Derrida has attempted in his critique of speech act theory, that the oral and the written are equally subject to the "distortions" (difference in both its spatial and temporal senses) that unsettle the presumed transparency of context, then the ontological difference between the two collapses, and with it the linchpin of logocentrism.

With the anchor of logocentrism unhinged, the challenge posed by difference for understanding communication—the former thought of as the repetition of the message that is not a repetition of the same, but rather one characterized by alterity — becomes that of coming to terms with the difficult question of context. Deconstruction has recently been characterized by Derrida as the "effort to take this limitless context into account, to pay the sharpest and broadest attention possible to context, and thus to an incessant movement of recontextualization."[5] Rather than set aside as anomalous or banish to the margins (as in the distinction between "serious" versus "nonserious" speech, for example[6]) conditions that would unhinge any particular system, deconstruction instead asks what such submerging of particulars can tell us about any particular universal mode of explanation. In this sense, too, one may say that deconstruction proceeds from the understanding that there is nothing outside of context.

Two particularly pertinent impulses from the above discussion guide the following analysis of documentary film: the concept of difference as distancing, and the related impulse to denaturalize the reality effect at work in film. Nowhere do the dangers, referred to earlier, of the appearance of unmediated presentation loom larger than in the documentary film. As films that explicitly take as their subject matter events that have occurred in the social world, documentaries acquire their force by suggesting not merely a representation of reality but a presentation of the thing (object, event) itself. What Hayden White suggests regarding narrative in general can, however, be applied equally to the filmic apparatus: As the frame permitting the representation of a particular content, the filmic apparatus already possesses a content prior to any actualization of it as a particular depiction and organization of objects and events.[7] The truth of the difference or affinity between documentary and fictional film reveals itself not in content but in the matter of form, and in its form, the documentary "does not form a simple opposition to the term narrative."[8] This is especially clear with documentaries in which social phenomena are organized around central characters and conflicts. One might say that documentary images are finally presentable only as organized by laws of narration, in contrast, perhaps, to completely abstract films.

Through an illusion, documentaries offer the promise of film simply capturing or mirroring what occurs in the world without the intrusion of "subjectivity" or other "artifices" that distance immediate presence. Fulfillment of the dictionary definition of objectivity is seemingly certified by the givenness of really existing objects, re-presented in film, whose independent status does not depend on, and indeed is separate from, any subjectivity.

Much could be stated against this view.[9] To begin with, such an understanding valorizes the conditions of immediate production (i.e., the shooting stage) at the expense of other production activities associated with the editing process. Further, even a hypothetical single camera recording a single place without temporal interruptions is, after all, a positioned camera, thus producing a particular frame, and not another, at a particular place and at a particular time. An uninterrupted shot at the beginning of *Blue Velvet*, a David Lynch fiction film (1986), provides a dramatic illustration of the importance of the precise placement of a camera. By tilting and lowering his camera from a perspective that framed what appear to be beautifully manicured lawns of an idyllic small town, the director allows the audience to discover at the micro scale of insects a world of savagery and terror, one that, it turns out, is fully part of the town's identity. The consequences which derive from the camera's positioning, as well as the processes of selection and omission that mediate fiction film, are equally at play in documentary film.

As all film is inherently and unavoidably tied to subjectivity, there arises a potential for the misuse of the concept of objectivity, particularly when that concept is taken to mean the finished (and hence fixed) presentation of an already given social reality, instead of social reality as a rendered process. In approaching documentary film, it is important not to confuse the standard of objectivity with that of truth. Objectivity, following the film scholar Noel Carroll, can be usefully understood as the adherence to the practices of reasoning and evidence gathered in a given field. A given work is objective "because it can be intersubjectively evaluated against standards of argument and evidence shared by practitioners of a specific arena of discourse."[10] This perspective, of course, refuses the primary meaning given the word in most dictionary definitions as the quality of being objective, or intentness to objects external to the mind, thus separating objectivity from the subjective, but is in accord with the definition's tertiary acknowledgment of ensuing contradictions, belying the separation of the two.

Objectivity conceived of as a task (or objective) is a laudable goal for documentary film (and other writing), but the predicate truth, at least in its everyday language meaning, risks the collapse of multilayered spatial and temporal horizons of meaning to the flattened univocity of "truth" and its opposite ("falsity"). In my view, an effort to place value on any given presentation of objects and their relations as assembled in a documentary film should therefore proceed from the assumption that the "reality effect" in documentary film belongs to a particular context, i.e., that this effect can be viewed as the outcome of a set of successfully performed narrative conventions, and not because of a univocal correspondence between the real and the reel. I turn now to consideration of what this might mean specifically in terms of cinematic space and place in film.

Walter Benjamin and the Provocation of Film

The German Kino-debate of the 1920s, largely perceived then as a debate regarding the legitimacy of film as an art form, has recently been reread as an effort by Weimar intellectuals to "define the common spaces between cinema and their modern urban society."[11] The arrival of the cinema and the return of flanerie, as in wandering around the city-spectacle, now suggest the confluence of "a privileged mode of specularity and its newest medium of recording," namely cinema. The development of new social space, and in particular, urban space in the late nineteenth century, offered new forms of activity and objects for perception, intensified forms of commodity exchange and fetishism, and most generally, signs of a reordering in apperception of temporal-spatial relations. As written about earlier by Baudelaire and then Ruttmann's contemporary, Walter Benjamin, the flaneur as social type paradigmatically enacts the sensual reorganization of sights and sounds in perception, as scenes of modernity pass by his observing eyes.[12]

Cinema, as an institution and apparatus, is likewise tied to a compression of space and time relations. As a historical materialist, Benjamin believed that over long periods of history, the mode of human sense perception changes with humanity's entire mode of existence. Such changes in perception are, for him, an expression of, and in turn contribute to, social transformations. For Benjamin, a contemporary phenomenon of greatest import was the increasing significance of the masses in social and political life. Benjamin saw in film both an expression of that import and certain consequences for traditional categories describing art as a model organization of the aesthetic for purposes of cognition.

Film had become the carrier of nonauratic art—art finally freed from its earlier religious or cultic function—precisely because film also relayed a reorganization of space and time for perception. The desire of the masses to "bring things 'closer' spatially and humanly," found expression in the urge to "get hold of an object at very close range by way of its likeness, its reproductions."[13] While artistic production in the service of the cult had depended on its hiddenness (the mystery that surrounds its not being on view) as well as "its unique existence at the place where it happens to be," photography, the phonograph record, and film "enable the original to meet the beholder halfway."[14] With respect to perception, technological reproduction enables the cathedral to leave its locale in the form of a photograph, a choral production performed in some symphony hall to resound in a private living room.

The processes of technological reproducibility already at work in these media constituitively define the production and reception of film. For Benjamin, the social-technical-aesthetic dimensions of film at least potentially provided cognitive grounds for the overcoming of an aesthetic whose value-markers remained concepts such as authenticity, eternal value, mystery, and genius.[15] For this earlier aesthetic, which had too easily been appropriated by fascism, the status of a work as "original" attained the attribute "authentic" by virtue of "its presence in time and space, its unique existence at the place where it happens to be."

Film and its enabling technology, by contrast—quintessential expressions of a modernist reorientation of perception and social relations—make the separation of the image from its referent the primordial "cut" in production and for reception.[16] "The reflected image has become separable, transportable."[17] Hitherto largely a matter for consideration within the avant-garde, film has inexorably made palpable and broadly manifest a "crisis of representation" regarding the relationship between the sign and "its" referent (object or event) in the social world.[18] The sign, as the materialized mediation between signifier and signified, cannot have its identity contained by reference to an initial context that generated it. A notion of context that makes it stable and repeatable—that is to say, transparent—by virtue of the presumption of a correspondence model linking image and thing has been unhinged by the *cut*, which gives filmic images an identity thoroughly permeated by technology. The unavoidable separation of an image from "its" immediate context (object or event) makes the transport of the filmic image a constitutive aspect of its condition. Where is the image transported, Benjamin asks? To the film public who, in contrast to theater-goers still captive to personal contact with the actor (her presence), are invited to discern the extinguishing of aura and thereby enabled the position of critics.

Finally, in terms of viewing and reception as a whole, it makes no sense with film to differentiate the "original" from a copy. An aesthetic system that had inscribed value (and reproduced existing social relations) based on a hierarchy of the original (its unique existence where it happens to be), thus permitting the denigration of mere reproduction and the valorization of genius and eternal value, had, with the advent of film as a mass experience and as an experience for the masses, been overturned as an arbitrator of value, because, to begin with, the exact same product could now be viewed in hundreds of places simultaneously.

Film pioneers of the past century, such as Georges Méliès and Edwin Stanton Porter, had encountered and experimented with exactly the reordering of perception Benjamin describes. They discovered that time could be compressed, expanded, or reversed. Eggs could unscramble themselves, people could leap out of water and onto diving boards, intervals of time could be literally cut out of a sequence, and temporal order could be modified at will.[19] Like the implementation of electric illumination, "which blurred the division of day and night, the cinema challenged traditional concepts of time, . . . by its willful re-ordering of temporal sequence."[20] In the production process, a jump from the window could be shot in the studio as a jump from a scaffold, and the ensuing flight, if need be, shot weeks later when outdoor scenes were taken.

Film, while of course subject to various (but also mutable) temporal and spatial requirements, could tear fragments taken in real time and place and reassemble them to suit the spatial and temporal demands of filmic narration. As Benjamin cogently noted, the pictures obtained by the cameraman "consist of multiple fragments which are assembled under a new law."[21] Time in film is, consequently, of a different order than that internationalized by the implementation of standard time at the turn of the century, because, to begin with, elliptical editing permits the shortening of plot duration by omitting intervals of story duration. Moreover, the ability to cut and reassemble events occurring in different places simultaneously permits the medium to reassemble spatial relations. In *Adventures of Dollie* (1908), D. W. Griffith reportedly shocked audiences by following a close-up of the face of a wife brooding about her long-lost husband with a cut to a scene of her husband alone on an island.[22] That quick cut across the ocean created a relationship of distance and proximity that has since become so naturalized as a technique that most viewers today have ceased to marvel at it. This early example of filmic crosscutting—editing that alternates shots of two or more lines of action occurring in different places, usually simultaneously—has since been so "naturalized" that it has dulled the recognition that an essential dimension of film is the medium's ability to relate any two points in space through similarity, difference, or development.

It seems to me, however, that we should not lose sight of the wonder such a technique invoked for then contemporary observers. Among other reasons, the wonder elicited by the medium's ability to reorganize space (and consequently time) via juxtaposition links film as an apparatus to the epochal transformation Foucault more recently has suggested occurred when he contrasted the nineteenth-century obsession with history to the present epoch's designation as "the epoch of space." In Foucault's words, "We are in the epoch of simultaneity: we are in the epoch of juxtaposition, the epoch of the near and far, of the side by side, of the dispersed."[23] His characterization of contemporary epistemic ways of thinking about social relations coincides with that aspect of filmic representation which so interested Benjamin.

In contrast to a shot—an uninterrupted segment of film time—the cut, as an instantaneous change from one shot to another, thoroughly defines film as spatial.[24] An example Benjamin cites illustrates the consequences for understanding social space:

> Our taverns and our metropolitan streets, our offices and furnished rooms, our railroad stations and our factories appeared to have us locked up hopelessly. Then came the film and burst this prison-world asunder by the dynamite of the tenth of a second, so that now, in the midst of its far-flung ruins and debris, we calmly and adventurously go traveling.[25]

The dynamite of the tenth of a second (today's technology would make that 124th of a second), which renders the world as represented object, corresponds rather well to the spatial dimension of difference (espacement) whose effect is to redefine identity as alterity, rather than a repetition of the same. The passage from place to cinematic space is marked not by repetition, but by alterity, whose visual emblem is the fragment.[26]

The close-up and the ability to connect them with medium and long shots make scale an essential element of this passage. Benjamin was again an acute observer. He saw in scale a remarkable opportunity for apperception. By focusing on hidden details of familiar objects and by exploring commonplace milieus under the relationary framework of scale, the close-up and the remaking of relationships through scale extend comprehension of the necessities that rule our lives. Everyday experience suggests a seamless web of naturalized social space. By working through reality "like a surgeon," however, the camera in principle at least could free us from the suggestion of "naturalized" social relations by becoming monumentalized and immutable in everyday experience. While everyday life presents the appearance of regulated coherence and order, the imposition of scale as a precondition of the object's representation permits viewers a recognition otherwise. The "dynamite" exploding the suggestion of a natural order is spatial: the expansion of space with the close-up, the shattering of unitary or fixed place by montage, the extension of movement by slow motion. This dynamite "reveals entirely new structural formations of the subject." Benjamin's considerations lead him to suggest that "a different nature" evidently "opens itself to the camera then opens to the naked eye."[27] Evidently, the camera doesn't simply "see" like the human eye, but instead organizes presentation according to its own optical laws, uncannily similar to, yet different from human sense perception.

Benjamin, as his Arcades project also suggests, is no less sensitive than Foucault became to the spatial ploys of discipline to assure the ordering of human multiplicities. In Foucault's words, discipline "fixes; it arrests or regulates movements; it clears up confusion; it dissipates compact groupings of individuals wandering about the country in unpredictable ways; it establishes calculated distributions."[28] For Benjamin, the film's ability to shatter existing spatial (and thus social) relations shocks us into recognizing that any given "calculated distribution" need not stand time immortal. Film teaches us that perspective—a social act—orders multiplicity. Moreover, the camera's "lowerings and liftings, its interruptions and isolations, its extensions and accelerations, its enlargements and reductions" introduce the viewer to an "unconscious optics" as had psychoanalysis to unconscious impulses. Benjamin's double reference to the unconscious may remind us that for Freud, it (id) knows neither time nor morality. The camera's refusal of such knowledge enables it to visualize a spatiality that may yet become in social life.

Let me conclude this discussion of Benjamin's theory of film by again stressing that space is the key to unlocking this "different nature," not least because an unconsciously experienced space is substituted in film for a space consciously explored by human beings. Many of the characteristics Benjamin describes have direct relevance to Ruttmann's *Berlin*. If nothing is more political than just the ways objects are distributed, then remembering the task Benjamin foresaw for the revolutionary camera of both sheering space of its opacity and freeing human subjects to "go wandering" remains a pertinent concern. As I have argued, this dynamic is already inherent to film at the level of its character as mechanical apparatus, prior to any actualization of it at the level of plot or story content.

Place and Space in *Berlin*

While Ruttmann's modernist, avant-garde depiction of Berlin is organized on one level by a temporal framework (a roughly twenty-hour period from a day in the city), I will argue that his depiction derives its authority from the spatial representation of the city both as the film's content and as its formal principle.

This focus on a form and content analysis of *Berlin, Symphony of a City* precludes an elaboration of the economy of film distribution, the conditions under which the finished film is supplied to the places where it will be shown, nor how this obviously spatial concept, akin to dissemination, in turn affects film production, except to note that Ruttman's film was a quota production of Fox Europe within the terms of a financial settlement imposed by Hollywood capital on a German film industry drastically affected by hyperinflation.[29] My discussion of the film instead dwells on three levels. The first involves the film's depiction of an actually existing place and its inhabitants at a specific time in the context of intense debate regarding the ethical value of urban life. The second is an analysis of the film as an avant-garde work, particularly notable in its efforts to depict a modernist sensibility toward time and space through its usage of the principles of montage, crosscutting, and framing. The third level considers the contemporary reception of the film in order to amplify more generally and from a contemporary perspective the inherent, though submerged, spatial characteristics of cinematic narration.

At stake with the first issue is not only the identity of Berlin at a particularly pregnant moment in time,[30] but the precise status of what in film criticism is called a documentary. As I argued above, Ruttmann's film invites analysis of the difficult question of context, beginning with the question of what was materially "present" to be filmed in 1927 and which means were available (given existing technology and filmic conventions, etc.), such that the film could be viewed and critiqued by contemporaries as a "re-presentation" of the city at that time. As will be discussed below, various contemporaries recognized enough of "their" Berlin in Ruttmann's film to decry the absence of those other parts that "should" have been included. Where are Berlin's department stores, the dwellings of workers, or the "real" lives of the city's inhabitants? As would be true for any documentary, Ruttmann's *Berlin* could not simply re-present the totality of relations present in the city, since the camera and the film cut, as Benjamin recognized, effect a displacement of place. Those contemporaries who yet found merit in the film despite "its" absences, did so by invoking the "aesthetic" or "musical" sensibility Ruttmann brought to the project. As I have argued above, given the subjectivity involved in all documentary production, any film depiction of place is open to criticisms regarding omission. A reading of the reviews that appeared following *Berlin*'s release points to the variety of Berlins that in 1927 might have entered cinematic space.[31]

As a depiction of a place that no longer exists as it did when the film was released, moreover, the film also invites questions for audiences today regarding the fusion of horizons unavoidably implicated by the incessant movement of recontextualization involved in viewing films that depict different places and times. Berlin, obviously, no longer exists as it did when Ruttmann filmed there. There exists no "original" with which to compare his representation (except equally partial historical sources). Like this one, films that survive their immediate context of dissemination preserve (in some incomplete form) places, which in time and on film become places of memory.[32] What is obviously true in this case because of the bombings and destruction of World War II (and somewhat because of the Nazis' only partially realized plans for the new Berlin, as well as postwar restructuring, which continues with a vengeance since 1989), is less obviously also true of *any* filming of places subject to transformation in time and space, as even re-viewings of films made ten years ago of any particular social space likewise may attest. In short, once a place is entered into cinematic space, it has, as a condition of its being-viewed, the capacity to become a place of memory, necessarily fragmented, with the myriad implications for understanding viewing practices that derive from this.

On one level, the film does function as a documentary, a "cross-section" depiction of images of the city of Berlin. As such, the film may be regarded as one progenitor (along with Alberto Cavalcanti's *Paris, Rien que les heures* and Dziga Vertov's *Man with the Movie Camera*) of a documentary style depicting urban life, which in Germany aligns it with the style called New Objectivity. Several contemporary film critics, most notably Siegfried Kracauer, interpreted the film on these grounds and consequently found it wanting. What Kracauer rightly presupposed in his critique was that any portrayal of Berlin had entered a highly contested ideological discussion on modernity, mechanization, and urbanization. As *the* metropolis of Weimar Germany, Berlin was the locus of both desire and anxiety in reaction to modernization much commented on by contemporaneous social theorists of the left and right.[33] One should not be so awestruck today by the cultural brilliance of the avant-garde, for whom the cosmopolitan atmosphere of Berlin represented the best impulses of Weimar Germany, to forget that for a broad spectrum of antimodernist and folkish Germans, Berlin and all that it stood for was the devil incarnate.[34] Berlin became a crystallization point of resentment against industrialization, capitalism, democracy, and the cultural influence of the West following Germany's defeat in the World War I. Antimodernists penned the term "asphalt culture" to refer to lack of genuine culture and social values promoted by urban life. The term connoted a loss of direct contact with the soil and the ethical life, an agrarianist ideology attributed to it, as well as the rootlessness (artificiality) of urban life. During the 1920s, this position was also explicitly tied to a critique directed against the democratic government of the Republic and its "soulless" culture, nowhere more materially manifest than in

Berlin. Wilhelm Stapel, a folkish writer and editor of *Deutsches Volkstum,* phrased the debate being waged in Weimar Germany as one between the German landscape and the city. "The spirit (*Geist*) of the German Folk rebels against the spirit of Berlin. Today's battle cry must be 'The resistance of the landscape against Berlin.' "[35]

Berlin assembles images that could marshall both affirmation and condemnation within the terms of this debate. Importantly, Ruttmann nowhere takes recourse to an agrarian celebration of landscape or uses that landscape as the other to stigmatize the city. At the same time, however, the sequence of images in Ruttmann's film offers endless illustrations of the acceleration of life patterns and deindividualization brought about by work mechanization, the emergence of a full-blown consumer society and its cult of distraction, and finally, the pure sensation of speed, at the workplace, in communication and transportation networks, and in the quest for pleasure. Viewers distressed by modernization would have found an ample catalogue of its symptoms depicted in the film.

Before making *Berlin,* Ruttmann had already garnered a significant reputation as a painter and then experimental filmmaker. He explained his reasons for turning to filmmaking in an essay whose title summarizes its impulse, "Painting with Time" (*Malerei mit Zeit*). Ruttmann declared speed and tempo to be the major characteristics of his age. As a consequence, a different way of experiencing and ordering events, places, and objects in the world had emerged:

The moment frozen in time has been replaced by movement, the dynamic event which occurs in time. The rigid side by side of individual points has been replaced by the image of a curve constantly in the process of becoming. This new sense of life [*Lebensgefühl*] calls for a new artistic form.[36]

The painted image remained subject to aesthetic laws that denied movement and temporal flux. Ruttmann's understanding of events, which he defined as being dynamic and not static, could not be accommodated to aesthetic conventions that served to wrench events outside of movement and into the timeless sphere of the immutable. His excitement regarding film lay in the medium's ability to take static places, events, and objects and put them in a relationship to others through movement. As a consequence, the constitution of an event "itself" was altered and no longer rigidly separable from others. Writing in the 1920s, Ruttmann used a vocabulary derived from music theory (and not geography) to describe the dynamicism now etched upon and between individual objects. For a reader today, however, the meaning ascribed to this relationary understanding is confluent with one now become familiar in spatial thinking.[37]

After World War I, Ruttmann also came to the conclusion that he could achieve his aims using concrete (*gegenständlich*) objects, that he must in fact use existing objects. During the years making abstract film, Ruttmann reports he could not free himself "from the desire to build a film out of living material, to create a film-symphony out of the millions of actually existing movement-energies of the metropolis."[38] In making this choice, Ruttmann had also chosen to broaden his audience. This decision meant that he no longer wished to address only those already initiated in the abstract formalism of absolute film.

Berlin self-reflectively opens with images that merge Ruttmann's earlier embrace of absolute film and his turn toward concreteness. The film begins by framing part of a lake, whose surface ripples and shimmers in reaction presumably to wind and sun. One might at this point expect a sequence that further develops a bucolic sense of place, perhaps in order to contrast it with the "artificiality" of urban space. Instead, an overlap reassembles these light and object relations presented through the naturalistic depiction of a lake into an abstract pattern of horizontal lines and shapes in movement. Nature will thus not be the extant ground that permits the denigration of a rootless urban lifestyle, for nature itself is shown to be composed of the same formal characteristics likewise in operation in the city. In a movement that establishes the analogy, this abstract sequence then makes way to the similar lines given by a railroad track and the cross bars lowering at an intersection, followed by a train that passes through a framing given by a static camera.

In his opening montage, Ruttmann has developed a similarity between abstract and concrete images that carries over into his subsequent montage of concrete images. While taken of actually existing objects, the images are framed and set in relationship to one another such that they express the formal principles depicted in the opening sequence. Underlying all natural objects depicted in the film is thus the possibility, particularly revealed by quick cutting, of relating them along formal lines in terms of euclidean space.

"Berlin" first appears as a signpost seen in passing from the perspective of a moving train marking the distance (15 kilometers) to the city itself.[39] The first images of the city are short clips shot from the train of industrial, Schreber-garden, and suburb landscapes that fill the distance separating the outskirts from the main train station. Upon the train's arrival (it never actually fully stops moving), the city is then depicted as a circulatory system. Before any human subject is shown, the city is rendered as a physical plant, multilayered horizons consisting of sewer systems, and facilities generating steam power, heat, and electricity. Once human subjects enter this world, their activities are likewise depicted in terms of circulation, with a cycle of movement regulated by work and leisure that frames the actions of those who inhabit it.

Ruttmann's film eschews psychology in depicting the experience of urban life. That is, while present and in great numbers, human subjects are not really the center from which meaning emanates. Objects such as trains, telephones, nylon stockings, elevators, typewriters, dishwashers, airplanes, store-window mannequins, and puppets are equally "actors" in the drama of modernization made cognizable by the film. Neither these nor human subjects, however, are psychologized.[40] In contrast to *Paris, Rien que les heures,* or *Man with the Movie Camera,* no sustained individual point of view perspective humanizes the city. Close-ups or medium shots of human subjects are rare. Close-ups are far more often framed on machinery or other objects. The most typical framing in the film is the medium-long shot. This framing strategy, along with the absence of an individual point of view perspective, contributes strongly to the distancing effect generated by Ruttmann's approach toward the city.

Further contributing to this distancing effect are brief sequences that present aspects of the city as a spectacle: The starting up and shutting down of work technology (pressing machines, typewriters, etc.), and the opening and closing of shop shutters and factory gates function analogously to the raising and closing of a stage curtain in a dramatic staging. The film's inclusion of actual dramatic stagings or of a fashion show is merely of a similar kind in generating the sense of city as spectacle. These movements, however, do not invite identification, and are disconnected to reactions of human subjects or "an audience" (consumers or producers) in the film. Thus, these sequences too remain unpsychologized.

In a modernist vein, the film has no plot or story with beginning, middle, and resolution, save the most basic one permitting the possibility of narrative order, namely events that occur between morning and night in the city. The film's narrative does not provide closure. The last frames of the film again foreground movement as the final impress.[41] The viewer leaves the film with the image of a modernist building being turned upside down by the camera, in a movement unique to cinematic space. Throughout the film, exterior reality no longer serves as a mere backdrop for the unfolding of a dynamic plot structure in *Berlin,* but setting itself has become dynamic, spatializing plot.

Berlin as a place proves in fact to be many places and as such is a permutatious vessel differentiated by all the divisions characteristic of Weimar Germany more generally, particularly divisions of class. All major activities that comprise a day in the life of a city's inhabitants are portrayed and organized (via crosscutting) in terms of class: how one gets to work (by bicycle, foot, tram, chauffeured car) and at what time (factory workers at dawn, managers after eight o'clock); where one eats (at the workplace or in elegant restaurants), what and how (harried, relaxed); finally, which form of entertainment, or available offerings chosen, bespeaking a general "cult of distraction" (spectator sports such as boxing, indoor bicycle races, window-shopping, broadway-style revues, a performance by Josephine Baker, the symphony). The same events comprising a day thus become spatially differentiated within the city itself. Where these events take place, from the elegant Kurfürsten-damm to the drab Scheunenviertel, is rendered all importantly as being a matter of class.

At the same time, Ruttmann's film stresses the interconnectedness of places within the city via networks of transportation, communication, circulation, and exchange. The street itself, instead of being a mere other to the privileged middle-class interiority localizable in the private spheres of dwellings, becomes one such site, connecting these places, events, and activities, providing a perspective on the city that insists upon the overcoming of any static or privatized understanding of place. The streets, while of course serving as a setting functioning to connect disparate places, are staged as sites of contestation in the film, where policemen, communists, soldiers, men searching out prostitutes, ven-dors, and various kinds of advertisements strive to assert competing or-derings of events and place. Depending on the interests of those "pass-ing through," the street as a setting may consist of many places simultaneously.[42] Thus, apart from its function in setting place, the street, as pure circulation and movement, defines the essence of the modernist city.

Although airplanes are depicted as objects (sometimes in flight, trans-porting other objects to other places), Ruttmann eschews use of a com-prehensive aerial view of the city. The flyer's gaze does not give clarity and the film leaves unvisualized a representation of Berlin as a totality. Instead, the city is something to be approached in parts or aspects as the opening sequences shot at dawn from or of trains (themselves ren-dered in partial, fragmentary form) approaching the city also establish. In place of city walls, the railroad station assumes the function of city gates, thus effecting a contrast between the definable inside/outside identity given a place by such walls with a framing of the city whose identity is permutatious and in motion. Fragmentation, paradoxically, is not overcome but instead accelerated by the seeming overcoming of space made possible by speed and technology. Benjamin's formal observation regarding the effect of the "dynamite of the tenth of a second" here finds its confirmation on the horizon of content as well.

Phrased differently, speed effects and incarnates the spatialization of place. A sensational shot taken from a train approaching the awakening city exemplifies this sense of speed by staging its effects. As the camera records it, the presence of the train does not leave landscape unchanged but dissects it. Speed sets even landscape in motion: the camera positioned at the train's window dissolves the stability of the landscape and nature, rendering its erstwhile fixedness a blur. Within the city itself (improperly speaking, because the director is at pains not to use an inside/outside economy of identity), there is no place of home, as in an interior family setting. As noted earlier, medium and medium-long shots predominate, while residences are shot only from the outside, adding to the sense of perpetual motion. The film's conclusion, an extremely long shot of a modernist structure, shown by the camera to turn on its head while fireworks explode on the bottom quarter of the frame, underscores movement again as the dynamite transforming a static perception of place.

The fragmentation enacted here on the level of content is reenacted at the formal level as well, by the director's rapid and sometimes discontinuous transitions between the framing of his portrayed objects on various scales (e.g., extreme close-ups, though rarely of human subjects, in which the scale renders the object shown very large, versus medium or long shots, and, tellingly, extremely long shots only rarely). The camera's tendency to make the presentation of any object a question of scale explicitly shatters, as does montage itself, any pregiven or "natural" order and serves to radically unmake and remake relationships, as noted in Benjamin's observations regarding the fragmentation performed by the camera.

For many contemporary reviewers, *Berlin's* dissection of the city offered little comfort. As suggested earlier, the metropolis as the incarnation of modernism's ills by itself provoked considerable anxiety for numerous contemporaries, and Ruttmann's distanced approach did nothing to humanize its reality. It is not surprising that no one on the right of the political spectrum presaged Benjamin's suggestion to celebrate the virtues of traveling in the wake of the dynamiting of "this prison world's" far-flung debris. Critics who praised (or continue to praise) the film for its "musical sensibility," however, take recourse to an idealist autonomous understanding of the aesthetic that divorces the aesthetic from the social.[43] More interesting today are the assumptions that underlie the attacks on the film made by leftist or centrist critics. Their import transcends the modernist context in which they were expressed, particularly with regard to a spatial understanding of film.

Like several other critics, Kracauer found aspects of Berlin's reality missing in the film. Insightfully, he (but as had Ruttmann) pointed to the "radius" of class-space intersections within the city, but wished that more of these had been presented (suburbs, Alexander square, etc.). Where, he asked, "is the Berlin of the worker, the white collar worker, the shopkeeper, the upper bourgeoisie, each of which according to professional and human categories occupies a definite radius, definite segments?"[44] Paul Friedlander offered the view that "one should have shown a day in the life of a proletarian or bourgeois from beginning to end," while Bernhard von Brentano derogatorily observed "the human being is absent in Ruttmann's film."[45] Kracauer sided with Carl Mayer (the film's original producer) against Ruttmann by praising the former's intent to "make a film about people."[46] All three criticisms bespeak the sense that Ruttmann should have made a film more in line with Cavalcanti's *Paris*, one in which human subjects provided the center for the depiction of social space.

Kracauer's important criticism of the film deserves fuller analysis. He is troubled by Ruttmann's seeming antihumanism: "Human beings are forced into the sphere of the inanimate. They seem molecules in a stream of matter . . . People in *Berlin* assume the character of material not even polished. Used up material is thrown away . . . The life of society is a harsh, mechanical process."[47] He takes Ruttmann's "surface" (I prefer the label approach) as evidence of a more general characteristic of New Objectivity and montage itself; namely an inherent neutrality in the presentation of an array of "facts," leading to its failure to assume a (political) position, and to the depiction of a "shapeless reality." For Kracauer, the filmmaker's voice is one of indifference, symptomatic of "a withdrawal from basic decisions into ambiguous neutrality."[48] Why, one might ask, does Kracauer make this assessment? His answer comes by way of a contrast made to Vertov's *Man with a Camera*, a film that he finds inspired by revolutionary convictions. Such convictions, curiously, are not a question of form versus content, but a question of which society the film portrays. For it seems that formalism can be excused in a revolutionary society, while the treatment of Weimar Republic's society demands content (story) and interpretation.

Vertov endeavors to live up to Lenin's early demand that "the production of new films, permeated with communist ideas, reflecting Soviet actuality, must begin with newsreels." He is the son of a victorious revolution, and the life his camera surprises is Soviet life—a reality quivering with revolutionary energies that penetrate its every element . . . Ruttmann, on his part, focuses upon a society which has managed to evade revolution and now, under the stabilized Republic, is nothing but an unsubstantial conglomeration of parties and ideals. It is a shapeless reality, one that seems to be abandoned by all vital energies.[49]

Had Ruttmann been prompted by Vertov's revolutionary convictions, Kracauer continues, "he would have been forced to emphasize content rather than rhythm. His penchant for rhythmic 'montage' reveals that he actually tends to avoid any critical comment on the reality with which he is faced."[50] Vertov implies content, Ruttmann shuns it. For Kracauer, Ruttmann manifests a formal attitude toward a reality that cried out for criticism, for interpretation. Consequently, *Berlin* "records thousands of details without connecting them, or at best connects them through fictitious transitions which are void of content," thus failing to penetrate his subject matter "with a true understanding of its social, economic and political structure." Ruttmann's dynamic juxtaposition of place becomes, for Kracauer, mere formal expediency, a structural function overshadowing whatever significance they may convey as content.[51] Not surprisingly, Kracauer concludes by stating that the film fails to point out anything "because it does not uncover a single significant context."

Read today, Kracauer's critique appears insufficient because of his implicit denigration of space as inert, undialectical, and immobile. Kracauer sees an empty formalism uniting images that, by staying on the surface, have failed to penetrate social reality. When, by contrast and following Ed Soja's understanding of Foucault and Henri Lefebvre, space is viewed as fecund and dialectical,[52] *Berlin, Symphony of a City* appears in light of the socio-spatial dialectic as more than a simple presentation of objects and facts; it is, instead, a film that exhibits through montage an ensemble of relations that stages them as simultaneous and synchronic juxtapositions. The "single most significant context" that Kracauer himself failed to discern is that of cinematic space. The film, in fact, goes further than any from the period in suggesting the spatialization of (hi)story, the making of history entwined with the social production of space. The means which invite such an understanding in the film are precisely the spatial characteristics of film manifested on a formal level, montage and then crosscutting, editing that alternates shots of two or more lines of action occurring in different places, usually simultaneously.

A contemporary reading of Kracauer's criticism suggests that his denigration of Ruttmann's "formalism" relied on assumptions that privilege "place" as the home of man and divide space and representation. Moreover, his argument that Ruttmann's film displays purely formal and not content-centered relationships implicitly separates the spatial from the social, or space from society. From a contemporary perspective, however, Ruttmann's modernist formalism may be thought of as adumbrating a sensibility that would lead later in the century to spatial science. It could be said of Ruttmann that he is intoxicated with geometry; that to speak with Benjamin, the unconscious optics of film for Ruttmann proves to be its disclosure of geometric space. The assumptions that inform Kracauer's critique, by contrast, attest to his subject-centered analysis and his suspicions regarding the presumed asocial context of geometric-spatial representation. These reservations, in a different context, remain important for contemporary geography, but they also attest to Kracauer's blindness (in an interesting way) to the insight of cinematic space. From a contemporary perspective, *Berlin, Symphony of a City* is as rich socially as it is spatially, if viewed, as we may today—fusing another horizon of significance—through the perspective of the sociospatial dialectic. This is not to suggest that Ruttmann "got it right" and Kracauer did not, but it is to recollect precursors and positions toward space and represention that should help us as we continue to grapple with the relationship.

Finally, although *Berlin* portrays real people and places (i.e., outside the confines of a studio and not in acting roles), it must, like other documentaries, be understood as a determinate selection of an imaginable totality of places and events coordinated by the editing technique of montage. Physical place is a "ground" only in a limited sense once it enters the fragmented space of film. Any given filmic image, while perhaps standing in correspondence to physical place (albeit in the manner of a nonunivocal relation between signifier and signified), is set in motion and recontextualized by virtue of, first, the illusion of movement given by 24 projected frames per second and, second, the reassemblage of these images as units through editing or montage. The authenticity of a place is not guaranteed by the fact that it was filmed there. Juxtaposition takes static place and sets it in a relationship. The marker of "place authenticity," which in today's poststudio films takes the form of the copyright credits and the acknowledgment of thanks to the "wonderful people of X and the State of X Commission of Film," should not be viewed differently. Instead, it should be critically examined as like-wise subject to the diffusion of aura thematized by Ruttmann's film and Benjamin's theory of the medium.

Acknowledgments

It is a pleasure to acknowledge the interest and editorial assistance of Stuart Aitken and Leo Zonn, helpful discussions with William Moritz, John Paul Jones, Ross and Dolores Whelan, and the dogged determina-tion of Sancho "Dusty" Howard. As always, Liz Natter inspires me to remember why critical theory matters to contemporary politics.

Notes

1. In their excellent book, D. Bordwell and K. Thompson make the follow-ing observation: "In the continuity editing system, [the 180-degree line is] the imaginary line that passes from side to side through the main actors, defining the spatial relations of all the elements of the scene as being to the right or left. The camera is not supposed to cross the axis at a cut and thus reverse those spatial relations." See *Film Art. An Introduction,* third edition, p. 408 (New York: McGraw-Hill, 1990).

2. See S. Kracauer, *From Caligari to Hitler,* pp. 181–90 (Princeton: Princeton University Press, 1947).

3. The suggestion of an epochal divide animating much of the discussion regarding postmodernism often rests upon a caricatured "modernism" that is little better than a straw man. In her study of Walter Benjamin's Arcades project, S. Buck-Morss offers a richer insight based on Benjaminian thought: "[It] makes no sense to divide the era of capitalism into formalist 'modernism' and histori-cally eclectic 'postmodernism,' as these tendencies have been there from the start of industrial culture ... Modernism and postmodernism are not chronolog-ical eras, but political positions in the century-long struggle between art and technology," *The Dialects of Seeing,* p. 359 (Cambridge: MIT Press, 1989). See too A. Huyssen, *After the Great Divide* (Bloomington: Indiana University Press, 1986), and J.P.Jones, Wolfgang Natter, and Ted Schatzki editors, *Postmodern Contentions: Epochs, Politics and Space* (New York: Guilford Press, 1993).

4. A good bibliography of scholarship working in this vein can be found in P. Brunette and D. Wills, *Screen/Play. Derrida and Film Theory,* pp. 199–205. (Princeton: Princeton University Press, 1989). The book itself is a helpful appli-cation of certain key Derridian concepts to thinking about film and cinema.

5. J. Derrida, *Limited Inc.,* p. 136 (Evanston: Northwestern University Press, 1988).

6. J. Derrida, Signature Event Context, in *Limited Inc*, p. 16.

7. See H. White, *The Content of the Form. Narrative Discourse and Historical Representation*, p. xi (Baltimore: Johns Hopkins University Press, 1987).

8. See B. Nichols, "Documentary Theory and Practice," *Screen* 17, no. 4 (1976/77): 36.

9. For further discussion of the "objectivity question" in the context of the reception accorded Michael Moore's recent documentary, see W. Natter and J.P. Jones, "Pets or Meat: Class, Ideology, and Space in *Roger & Me*," *Antipode*, Vol. 25, No. 2, 1993.

10. N. Carroll, "From Real to Reel: Entangled in the Nonfiction Film," *Philosophical Exchange* 14 (1983): 15.

11. See A. Gleber, Kino-Debatte: Preview to a Theory of Film and Weimar Modernity, in M. Jennings, editor, *Rethinking Weimar. Politics and Culture in the Weimar Republic* (Ithaca: Cornell University Press, 1993).

12. For a highly readable synthesis of Benjamin's corpus and in particular his Arcades project, see S. Buck-Morss, *The Dialects of Seeing* (Cambridge: MIT Press, 1989). Many similar questions are asked of the revolutionary space of the Paris commune in K. Ross, *The Emergence of Urban Space* (Minneapolis: University of Minnesota Press, 1988).

13. W. Benjamin, The Work of Art in the Age of Mechanical Reproduction, in H. Arendt, editor, *Illuminations*, p. 223 (New York: Schocken, 1969).

14. Benjamin, pp. 220–21.

15. Benjamin's critique of this earlier aesthetic is tied to his observation that the uncontrolled application of these concepts "would lead to a processing of data in the Fascist sense." See "The Work of Art in the Age of Mechanical Reproduction," p. 218.

16. In their film glossary, Bordwell and Thompson define "cut" as "1. The joining of two strips of film together with a splice. 2. In the finished film, an instantaneous change from one framing to another (or, in rare cases, an instantaneous change only of time; see jump cut)." I find an additional connotation useful, namely the reference to a violence barely contained by these two definitions; in contrast to a joining together and prior to the change between framings, "cut" indicates the fragmentation what is performed as the camera dissects the world.

17. Benjamin, p. 231.

18. Benjamin, p. 234: "Mechanical reproduction of art changes the reaction of the masses toward art. The reactionary attitude toward a Picasso painting changes into the progressive reaction toward a Chaplin movie. The progressive reaction is characterized by the direct intimate fusion of visual and emotional enjoyment with the orientation of the expert."

19. S. Kern, *The Culture of Time and Space, 1880–1918*, pp. 29–30 (Cambridge: Harvard University Press, 1983).

20. Kern, p. 29. Cinema is just one expression, for Kern, of a more general transformation wrought upon perceptions of time and space between 1880 and

World War I: "a series of sweeping changes in technology and culture created distinctive new modes of thinking about and experiencing time and space. Technological innovations including the telephone, wireless telegraph, x-ray, cinema, bicycle, automobile, and airplane established the material foundation for this reorientation; independent cultural developments such as the stream-of-consciousness novel, psychoanalysis, Cubism and the theory of relativity shaped consciousness directly," p. 1.

21. Benjamin, p. 234.

22. Kern, p. 218.

23. M Foucault, "Of Other Spaces," *Diacritics* 16: 22–27.

24. Bordwell and Thompson quote Dziga Vertov (*Man with a Movie Camera*) as an elated experimenter with filmic space: "I am Kino-eye. I am builder. I have placed you . . . in an extraordinary room which did not exist until just now when I also created it. In this room there are twelve walls, shot by me in various parts of the world. In bringing together shots of walls and details, I've managed to arrange them in an order that is pleasing." See *Film Art*, p. 215.

25. Benjamin, p. 236.

26. The German word Benjamin used for arcades is "Passagen." It refers both to the materialized architecture of the arcade, and to a sense which is spacial as in a place which one moves through. The flancur "passes through" the arcades, while at the same time the arcades, as not fossilized ruins, have themselves been "passed by" by newer organizations of consumer fetishism. See again S. Buck-Morss, *The Dialectis of Seeing*. The filmic image, as an object of reflection, participates in a similar passage.

27. Benjamin, p. 236.

28. M. Foucault, Panopticism, in P. Rabinow, editor, *The Foucault Reader*, p. 208 (New York: Pantheon Books, 1984).

29. Kracauer, p. 182. Some work currently underway has begun to pursue the question of the "Americanization" of Weimar cinema and its consequences for style, plot, and genre. The production of Ruttmann's film demonstrates, however, that one should not too quickly assume a wholesale adaptation of American forms of filmic narration in Germany, but instead recognize the differential market and aesthetic conditions thereby engendered.

30. A slew of recent works have "rediscovered" Berlin during the Weimar Republic. Some of the best include *Berlin, Culture & Metropolis*, Charles Haxthausen and Heidrun Suhr, eds., (Minneapolis: University of Minnesota Press, 1990), which should also be of interest to cultural geographers, Walter Lacquer, *Weimar: A Cultural History, 1918–1933* (New York: 1974), Peter Gay, *Weimar Culture: the Outsider as Insider* (New York: 1970), John Willitt, *Art and Politics in the Weimar Period. The New Sobriety 1917–1933* (New York: 1978) and Keith Bullivant, *Culture and Society in the Weimar Republic* (Manchester: 1977). Interested readers are also directed to works by Tom Childers, *The Nazi Voter: The Social Foundations of Fascism in Germany, 1919–1933* (Chapel Hill: 1983), Jeffrey Herf, *Reactionary Modernism. Technology, Culture and Politics in Weimar and the Third Reich* (Cam-

bridge: 1984), and Renata Bridenthal, *When Biology Became Destiny. Women in Weimar and Nazi Germany* (New York: 1984) which have significantly added to our understanding of the social processes which are entwined with the production of cultural texts. Readers of German are directed to the classic works by Jost Hermand/Frank Trommler, *Die Kultur der Weimarer Republik* (Munich: 1978) and Anton Kaes (ed.), *Weimarer Republik. Manifeste und Dokumente zer deutschen Literatur 1918–1933* (Stuttgart: 1983) and Detlev Peukert, *Die Weimarer Republik* (Frankfurt: 1987).

31. A compilation of them appears in *Walter Ruttmann. Eine Dokumentation,* Jeanpaul Goergen (ed.), pp. 27–31.

32. Virtually no trace remains of the vast majority of the films actually produced before 1945. This situation by itself should alert us to the fallacy of drawing hasty conclusions about an era or dominant style based upon "representative" films, since their continued presentation depends upon what turn out to be the haphazard circumstances through which films have been preserved. Any writing of film history must acknowledge such gaps as one enabling limit.

33. See the essays assembled in the collection *Berlin—Provinz. Literarische Kontroversen um 1930* (Marbach: Marbacher Heften, 1985).

34. It is simply not the case that any given citizen of Weimar saw a Brecht play, for example, and exclaimed "Yes, that describes my world and my sensibility." Most would have exclaimed quite the opposite. To forget the general climate of antipathy toward such avant-garde experimentation is to do an injustice to the achievements of these figures who now "represent" the Weimar Republic.

35. See *Berlin—Provinz*, p. 11. WN translator.

36. See Jeanpaul Goergen, editor, *Walter Ruttmann. Eine Dokumentation,* p. 21 (Berlin: Freunde der Deutschen Kinomatek, 1989).

37. As Matthew Bernstein notes, *Berlin* is conventionally discussed in terms of its "rhythms." [Yet] the imprecision of the blanket description "rhythmical" accounts for only the most general characteristics of the film. Attention to patterns of shot articulation and spatial constructions reveals that the film's exposition follows the general principles of analytical editing. See "Visual Style and Spatial Articulations in Berlin, Symphony of a City" (1927), *Journal of Film and Video* Fall 1984, 36: 6–7. Second, my reading of German geography as practiced before 1945 points to the overridingly conservative character of academic geography's social theory during the 1920s making any engagement with its version of place/space useless.

38. Quoted in *Walter Ruttmann*, p. 26.

39. The fact that a train should be the first concrete object shown in movement in the film is not mere coincidence. The association between the railroad, speed, and the ideology of progress is well developed in European literature of the nineteenth and early twentieth centuries. See, for example, W. Schivelbusch, *The Railway Journal. The Industrialization of Time and Space in the 19th Century* (Berkeley: University of California Press, 1977). Amplifying Benjamin's analysis of the relationship, S. Buck-Morss observes: "Railroads were the referent, and

progress the sign, as spatial movement became so wedded to the concept of historical movement that these could no longer be distinguished." Spatial movement becomes cognizable as speed; speed, in turn, equals progress. See *The Dialectics of Seeing*, p. 89.

40. On this tenancy in silent film more generally, see A. Kaes, editor, *Kino-Debatte. Texte zum Verhaltnis von Literatur und Film 1909–1929*, p. 25 (Munich: Deutscher Taschenbuch Verlag, 1978): "The revaluation of matter corresponds to the abolition of psychology in silent cinema."

41. See Ruttmann's contemporary, Yvan Goll, who likewise believed that the actual "Urstoff of the filmic element" is "movement," the very movement "which also characterizes modern everyday life." Quoted from Kaes, *Kino-Debatte*, p. 138. See too A. Gleber, "Kino-Debatte: Preview to a theory of Film and Weimar Modernity," for an illuminating discussion on film, movement, and the flaneur sensibility.

42. The German word *Verkehr* connotes in equal measure traffic, transport, communication, commerce, and sexual intercourse. All five meanings of the word are set in motion in these street scenes.

43. See *Walter Ruttmann*, p. 28.

44. S. Kracauer, "Wir schaffens," *Frankfurter Zeitung*, November 13, 1927, quoted in *Walter Ruttmann*, p. 30.

45. Quoted in *Walter Ruttmann* p. 28.

46. Quoted in *Walter Ruttmann* p. 26.

47. Kracauer, *From Caligari to Hitler*, p. 186.

48. Kracauer, p. 187.

49. Kracauer, pp. 185–86.

50. Kracauer, p. 187.

51. Kracauer, p. 187.

52. See E. Soja, *Postmodern Geographies. The Reassertion of Space in Critical Social Theory* (London: Verso, 1989).

Filmography

Adventures of Dollie. 1908. American Mutoscope & Biography Company. Director, Griffith, D.

Berlin, Symphony of a City (Berlin, die Symphonie einer Grosstadt). 1927. Fox Europe. Director, Ruttman, W.

Blue Velvet. 1986. De Laurentis Entertainment Group. Director, Lynch, D.

Man with a Movie Camera. 1929. Vufku (Ukraine). Director, Verov, D.

11

We're Going To Do It Right This Time: Cinematic Representations of Urban Planning and the British New Towns, 1939 to 1951

John R. Gold and Stephen V. Ward

In the film *Town and Country Planning* (1946), two characters debate the future. One is gloomy about the magnitude of the task of rebuilding Britain, the other is convinced that great opportunities lay ahead. Against a quick-fire montage of images of workmen laying bricks and machines feverishly engaged in building programs, the latter excitedly proclaims:

> Remember how we cleared those airfields and built those airports. Well, we have got the same machines and we know the new methods so we can do it again for the new housing sites, the roads, and the towns. Yes, and *we are going to do it right this time.*

Another equally breathless barrage of scenes follows—new flats and houses, hospitals, swimming pools, tennis courts, and people contentedly at work and leisure. The accompanying commentary makes it clear that "doing it right" means not just building houses, but

> whole neighbourhoods . . . We'll need schools that are handy for the houses and away from main roads. We will want the shops where we can reach them. We will need health centres, clinics, libraries, nurseries, parks, cinemas and theatres; the whole bag of tricks located and designed according to a proper plan.

This was not the first time that such ideas had been expressed. Concern about the congestion, squalid inner-city housing, and suburban

sprawl of the major British cities had been voiced for many years,[1] but
was now given far greater urgency by the scale of the problems facing
Britain in the mid-1940s (Addison 1985; Gold 1989). Industry, commerce, and the infrastructure had sustained severe damage and had become run-down through diversion of resources to the war effort. Housing posed particularly severe problems. Aerial bombardment had
destroyed or rendered uninhabitable half a million houses and seriously
damaged a quarter million more. Three million had suffered lesser
damage. These difficulties were compounded by the effects of population increase (a rise of one million between 1939 and 1945), a decrease
in household size, and the fact that investment in slum clearance and
other housing programs had been halted for the duration of the war.
The case for tackling these problems by comprehensive rather than
piecemeal approaches was never more persuasive, and served as a stimu-
lus for intense activity by groups committed to the notion of a planned
society in general and town planning in particular. Associations were
formed, tracts and pamphlets were circulated, exhibitions were held,
and films were made and shown.

In this essay, we focus specifically on the use made of film in promoting the case for town planning in the period between the outbreak of
war in 1939 and the fall of the Labour government in 1951. The first
section locates the films discussed here within the documentary tradition, but recognizes that promotional elements increasingly encroached
in the late 1940s. The second section explores the contents of three
films that propagandized for comprehensive town planning, namely,
The City (1939), *When We Build Again* (1943), and *Proud City* (1945). The
third section recognizes that once the case for comprehensive town
planning had been effectively met with the passage of the 1947 Town
and Country Planning Act, film became a vehicle for the promotion of
the concept of the new town as a specific prototype for future urban life.
Three films are examined in this context: *New Town* (1948), *Planned
Town* (1948), and *Home of Your Own* (1951). The conclusion summarizes
and reviews the evidence on cinematic representations of the city and
of the emerging planning profession.

Documentaries and Boosterism

The development of films promoting the case for town planning needs
to be placed in the broader history of the British documentary tradition.
Documentary films are defined broadly as films with high factual and

sociological content that charted the lives of people in their normal living and working environments. In Britain, their development was prompted primarily by recognition that the commercial cinema was ignoring the severe social and economic problems of the times (Gold 1985). The production and distribution policies of the feature studios effectively presented cinema audiences with a diet of escapism and fantasy. Film censorship also played its part. In their efforts to shut out overtly political themes, the censors implicitly encouraged people to regard their economic and social condition as a personal and not a political problem—something that was achieved not through overt propaganda but by the exclusion of alternative viewpoints (Pronay 1981, p. 125).

Little, however, could be done to challenge matters while technical and economic considerations confined filmmaking to the large feature studios. This situation changed in the late 1920s. The introduction of nonflammable safety films, smaller film formats, and cheaper and more portable equipment made it possible for independent companies and even amateurs to participate in making films up to professional standards. The result was a rapid increase in film production for commercial, educational, and especially, documentary purposes.

The resulting documentary movement produced perhaps its finest work in the 1930s (*inter alia*, see Rotha 1973; Sussex 1975; Low 1979; Barnouw 1983; Macfarlane 1987; Swann 1989; Aitken 1990). Drawing inspiration and initial direction from the work of the Scottish filmmaker John Grierson, the documentary movement produced more than one thousand films between 1929 and 1952.[2] Conventional wisdom typifies these films as low-budget undertakings made by small production companies with funds from state agencies or industrial sponsors (notably the Post Office and the gas industry), for screening in drafty halls to small committed audiences (Aldgate 1981; Sinyard 1989). While these assertions are substantially true, certain qualifications must be made. For example, a significant minority of the films were made by larger companies such as Pathé and Rank, with their full complements of creative and production staff. In addition, some documentaries were shown to much wider audiences than is commonly supposed. Industrial sponsors, such as the gas industry, arranged their own showings of documentaries at their showrooms and other places. Moreover, film distributors had to ensure that a certain amount of material screened in British commercial cinemas emanated from domestic sources, and they often found that documentaries provided useful short "fillers" for their programs.

From the outset, documentary filmmakers did not see themselves as passively mirroring reality, as did those of their colleagues who embraced *cinéma-vérité* techniques.[3] As Grierson (quoted in Aitken 1990, p. 7) noted:

> You don't get truth by turning on a camera, you have to work with it . . . you don't get it simply by peep hole camera work . . . There is no such thing as truth until you have made it into a form. Truth is an interpretation, a perception.

Instead, documentarists constructed their films in line with a distinctive ideology that gave weight to both aesthetics and social purposiveness. Aesthetically, documentarists sought to go beyond mere compilation of information and reports on social problems in order to construct a visual art, which can convey a sense of beauty about the ordinary world, the world on your doorstep (ibid., p. 11). Indeed, some critics regard the aesthetic element as the movement's prime cinematic legacy. Barsam (1989, p. 15), for instance, argues that

> it is the editing of sound images in relation to the visual images—in the contrapuntal collision that is the legacy of Joris Ivens, Helen van Dongen and Alberto Cavalcanti, among others—that one finds the greatest contribution to film from the British documentary of the 1930s and early 1940s.

Sociologically, documentary filmmakers worked hard to produce films that enlarged the film industry's purview of Britain and British society in the 1930s and 1940s, seeking to confront their audiences with the realities of life in the countryside, in the workplace, and in the cities. In doing so, they took up a position that was less politically radical than that of their American counterparts (Campbell 1982) or of left-wing film groups in 1930s Britain, such as the Workers Film Association or the Progressive Film Institute (Macpherson 1980). This was perhaps inevitable. The British documentary movement relied on sponsorship and commissions from commercial and state agencies to make its films in the first place. Overt politicizing was set aside in favor of the "middle way" of social-democratic reformism (Aitken 1990, pp. 8–9).[4]

Town planning was an ideal subject for such treatment, since those who campaigned for it invariably sought reform within existing norms and the broad social consensus. During the late 1930s and especially during the war years, a wide spectrum of opinion upheld the need, first, for programs to clear urban slums and rehouse the population and, later, for planned action to rebuild and reshape British cities (Esher 1981, pp. 15–71). In turn, the content of documentary films closely mirrored the course of this emerging consensus. The issue of housing provided the documentary movement's entrée into concern with cities and city life. Films such as *Housing Problems* (1935), *The Great Crusade* (1936), *The Smoke Menace* (1937), *Kensal House* (1937), and *New Worlds for Old* (1938) charted the decrepit and verminous state of slum housing and chronicled the progress of clearance schemes. Significantly, perhaps, none of them make any firm statement on who was responsible for causing the slums, which, at best, are presented as the result of history and unenlightened practices. That strategy remained when the focus switched from the specific issue of housing to the more general question of town planning. As we will see later, planning, like housing, was advocated as a logical, scientific, and technical response to a particular set of human needs. The underlying political issues of resource redistribution, responsibility, and blame were largely omitted from the analysis.

Before we leave this discussion, it is important to recognize that the goals of the documentary movement changed over time. Committed, at least initially, to public education and mass democracy (Sinyard 1989), the war years saw such films acquiring a marked promotional edge. Film was now viewed as a medium to *sell* planning and reconstruction proposals to the wider public, especially to potential users. Thus, while retaining the interwar documentary movement's endeavor to portray real social issues, the propaganda element was much more significant and overt; audiences were increasingly presented with a very specific vision of the future rather than a picture of present possibilities. Moreover, the means employed to convey the message also diverged from the prewar documentary ideal. Films now relied increasingly on the use of acted scenes to overcome the stilted contributions of ordinary people and to improve the general palatability of the message to mass audiences.

It becomes possible at this stage, therefore, to identify an element of aggressive and self-conscious place promotion to attract business and mobile investment. This type of purely growth-oriented "boosterism" had many precedents in urban North America (Morris 1989; Holcombe 1990; Ward 1991) but was not previously significant in the British scene, aside from seaside resorts, suburbs, and the special case of the two privately funded Garden Cities at Letchworth and Welwyn (Ward 1988a, 1992; Yates 1988; Miller 1989; Gold and Gold 1990). The passage of the New Towns Act (1946) by Clement Attlee's Labour government, however, imposed the task of developing important new towns and cities in a relatively short space of time. This, in turn, imposed new needs for promotional work, a task made more urgent by the public relations disaster that marked the opening of the new towns program.

To elaborate, Stevenage, the first of these towns, was designated before the 1946 New Towns Act became law in a bold attempt to get the program under way without delay. The means for doing so was the "garden city" clause of the 1932 Town and Country Planning Act and the general power of the Minister to act when a local authority was in default (Orlans 1952). While perfectly legal, there was little attempt to explain the plans or this somewhat unorthodox course of action to the area's existing inhabitants. Hence when Lewis Silkin, the Minister of Town and Country Planning, arrived at the town's railway station for a local meeting, he found its name-board replaced with the word SILKINGRAD and a vigorous local campaign of opposition under way involving, among others, the novelist E. M. Forster (Forster 1946, pp. 66–68; Orlans 1952, p. 69). The legitimacy of Silkin's actions was eventually supported by the House of Lords, highest legal arena in Britain, but a legacy of mistrust remained.

This experience, not surprisingly, sparked considerable discussion about the need for well-presented information to influence local public opinion in the early days. As one official of the Ministry of Town and Country Planning pointed out in July 1946:

> The process of discussion among a community such as Stevenage or Crawley only unfolds itself slowly, and if no-one is available to keep pace with it and supply the right information at the right time, a great deal of harm will be done.[5]

Some practice ideals were defined, including the need to set up a well-equipped information bureau with a full-time and well-qualified public relations officer and to prepare models and plans of the projected town for public display. In addition, there was a specific commitment to use film, the most potent visual medium of communication available in this period before mass ownership of television receivers.[6] Suitable films were to be shown at local cinemas for the purpose of selling proposals for a specific new town to an area's existing local inhabitants. They were also shown to prospective residents or industrial migrants, or more generally to help secure approval for a potentially controversial new idea. We will see later the way that films were used to meet these objectives.

The Case for Planning

We noted above that much of the initial impetus for both the planning movement itself and the filmmakers' interest in planning had stemmed from concern about the state of British housing. Not surprisingly, therefore, two contrasting views of urban housing provided the *de rigueur* opening shots for many films, being generally accepted as symbolizing the problems that occur without adequate planning. The first was the image of the crowded and decrepit inner-city slum (e.g., Fig. 11-1). The dilapidated state of the urban fabric symbolized the historic legacy of unplanned development, with the obligatory shots of children playing in the gutter emphasizing the waste of human potential. The second image was that of low-density, suburban ribbon development along arterial roads (e.g., Fig. 11-2), symbolizing the costs of allowing the tentacles of the town to creep outward to engulf villages and farmland close to the city—a view overlain with the general distaste for suburbia felt by many professional commentators at the time (Gold and Gold 1989).

These images set the scene. The story line that followed was usually that the solution of the housing crisis lies in looking beyond housing per se. What was needed instead were comprehensive approaches that saw rehousing the population as involving other key functions of the city—including transport, workplace and employment patterns, recreation, neighborhood planning, and postwar reconstruction. The relative weight laid upon these elements, however, would vary over time and from film to film. This point is amply illustrated by three films: *The City* (1939), *When We Build Again* (1943), and *Proud City* (1945).

The City (1939)

The City was commissioned by the General Post Office in 1938, but was not released until after the outbreak of war. One of the first full-scale treatments of the need for town planning, it comprises an analysis of the condition of contemporary London and possible solutions for the metropolis's problems, emphasizing the question of transport. The core of the film is an illustrated talk by Sir Charles Bressey, an architect-planner who was coauthor of a report that emphasized the need for radical engineering improvements to improve the functioning of London's transport system (Bressey and Lutyens 1937). Bressey's talk is punctuated by scenes from a day in the life of the capital. Continuity is supplied by a narrative from Herbert Hodge, a London taxi driver whose whimsical turn of phrase well suited the "satirical and surreal attitude to documentary" (Sinyard 1989, p. 252) of the film's Brazilian-born producer, Alberto Cavalcanti.

The opening sequences introduce the scale of the problem. London

Figure 11–1. Outmoded and overcrowded inner-city housing provides the moral imperative for action. Source: Homes for All (1945). Photograph courtesy BFI Stills, Posters and Designs.

Figure 11–2. Low-density ribbon development along an arterial road. Source: Homes for All (1945). Photograph courtesy BFI Stills, Posters and Designs.

is described as a city of 800 square miles in which more than nine million people live in a "higgledy-piggledy mass of bricks and concrete." Bressey opens an atlas to show that, a century previously, the city had only been one-twentieth its present size, a point illustrated by a map of the extent of London in 1840. The progressive transformation to the present size is shown, with extent of the city growth (shown in black) seemingly oozing out into the (white) countryside until by 1940 the black mass virtually fills the screen.

The question of the morning's journey-to-work is used as a means to introduce the socio-spatial composition of London. Residential London is divided into three zones. The commentary begins with the suburbs, with tranquil scenes of children playing, the wife cooking in her spacious kitchen, and the pipe-smoking husband pottering in the garden. The mood soon changes as the scene cuts to people hurrying for their morning train into London, traveling "packed like sardines in a tin." The commentator notes: "We arrive at our work tired before we begin and sometimes we wonder whether our home in the suburbs is worth it." The second zone comprises the slums, where rents are high and wages low. Against pictures of dilapidated houses and extreme deprivation, he states: "Our bit of England is a rented room . . . We live here huddled up in London's dirt . . . buried in the smoke and grime: close to our work in the slums." The third zone is the City of Westminster in London's West End, which contains the homes of the rich. Scenes of elegant dwellings with numerous liveried servants, chauffeur-driven cars, and nannies with perambulators provide a quick portrait of an area that alone carries the advantages of both proximity to the workplace and being spacious and light.

Two additional areas of London are identified. One is the industrial London of smokestack industry and the bustling port, which is depicted as supplying the lifeblood of the nation and empire, but also struggling to survive in light of the strangling effects of severe traffic congestion. The other area is The City, London's historic core. After panning the skyline, the camera focuses on the spire of one of Sir Christopher Wren's churches and the narrator makes a key point:

> In Wren's time, London had what might have been a very lucky accident for us. The Great Fire of London swept away masses of wooden houses that had stood for centuries.

The camera then cuts to a portrait of Wren and pans back to show that it is hung on the wall of Bressey's office. Bressey takes up the narrative:

Sir Christopher Wren alone was wise enough to see the great opportunity. He planned a new London that looked like this . . . (unrolls plan) . . . a plan so enlightened, so far seeing that it would even have met the needs of modern traffic. Broad sunlit avenues, well-placed monuments and public buildings. Wren's London would have been a noble city: well-adapted to be the centre of the world's industry and commerce. But it was not to be. *The forces of conservatism were too strong.*

At this point, Bressey rolls up the plan and drops it into a rack with a sigh.

The impression conveyed here, of the man of vision frustrated by forces of conservatism, is the key to the film's message. After a lengthy discourse on London's traffic problems and a focus on the General Post Office's privately built underground railway, which expedites mail across London, the narrator returns to the subject of Wren: "Just as Wren made a plan for seventeenth-century Londoners, so Sir Charles Bressey has worked out a plan for us." The plan is then explained. To prevent traffic congestion in the center—"the quart pot of the arterial road [discharging] into the pint mug of the city"—a system of inner and outer orbital roads is proposed. Elevated cross-city roads would be constructed, tunnels built, and road junctions handled by multilevel traffic circles and clover-leaf intersections. However, Bressey clearly considers himself thwarted like Wren before him. Looking out of his office window at the evening traffic, he notes: "In a London replanned like that, I might be home in fifteen minutes. Tonight it will take an hour."

Considered overall, *The City* contains two vital aspects that are representative of wider arguments given by advocates of town planning. First, it supplies a damning analysis of the city, which is seen as being in need of drastic surgery to fit it for present-day needs. Second, it argues powerfully for the planners, the visionaries who champion large-scale planning exercises, to be given their chance to tackle urban malaise. This would become a familiar ideological standpoint for the emerging planning profession in the postwar period.

When We Build Again (1943)

When We Build Again was also conceived before World War II. In 1936–38, the Bournville Village Trust[7] had carried out a regional survey that identified three residential zones in the city of Birmingham. These were the Central Wards (the oldest parts of the city); a middle ring of housing areas built before 1914 and consisting of straight streets of tunnel-backed "by-law" housing; and an outer ring of lower density suburbs, which included the large municipal estates built after the war. Employing this framework, the Trust arranged interviews with more than 7,000 people to find out what they thought about their present homes and where, if anywhere, they would move if they could. Among other things recorded were the length of the respondents' journeys-to-work, the time they took, and how much they cost. The results were presented in the monograph "When We Build Again" (Bournville Village Trust 1941).

A film of the same name was commissioned by Cadbury Brothers to convey the survey's results to a wider audience and to promote the case for better urban planning. Released in 1943 and made by Strand Films, *When We Build Again* brings together some celebrated talents—a narrative partly written and spoken by Dylan Thomas, architectural plans and models by architect Thomas Sharp—but it suffered from trying to accommodate the changing external environment. While taking the survey as their text, the filmmakers also attempted to address the question of postwar reconstruction, which seems to have created tensions and abrupt leaps in the film's story line. Nowhere is this shown better than in the opening scenes in which a standard analysis of the urban fabric is unduly complicated by new story lines to reflect wartime concerns.

To elaborate: the film opens with a brief sketch of the different character of the three zones. The central wards are visually summarized by pictures of decrepit housing and blackened factories jammed together and of children playing in "their inherited nursery—the gutter." The inhabitants of this zone may live close to their work, but they endure the appalling living conditions of the slums. Middle ring housing is depicted as better quality than the slums, but still consisting of gray, airless, and poorly planned rows of terraces, where children have insufficient room to play. The outer ring has the advantages of more air and space and better quality dwellings, but these too are poorly planned with haphazard layouts and their residents enduring long journeys-to-work. Thus far, all seems straightforward, but this is overlain by a theatrical device intended to give the film greater topicality. The film tracks the path of three soldiers, played by actors, returning home on leave. Each lives in a different zone: the first in the central area, the next in the middle ring, and the last in the outer suburbs. We are shown their dwellings in turn, finally following the third soldier on his weary trek to the outer suburbs. Once we see him arrive home and close the front door, this particular story line is dropped and little more is seen of the soldiers during the film. Instead, the film reverts to a standard documentary treatment of planning issues. A series of face-to-camera interviews follow, with residents articulating their liking or discontent with their current homes. This is followed by a summary of the survey's key findings, for example, that one-third of all those surveyed want to move into new houses, that 90 percent want houses with gardens, but that only 5 percent want to live in flats.

The rest of the film is spent showing what can be done with better planning. In a notable scene an architect (believed to be played by Thomas Sharp himself) sets to work with an eraser on a map of part of Birmingham. Overlays show how it could be redesigned by introducing zoning principles and modern ideas about neighborhood planning. Unexpectedly, given the film's Garden City pedigree, flats are seen as part of the matrix "for those that want them"—and seemingly for rather more of the population than the 5 percent mentioned above. (This detail may well reflect the influence of Thomas Sharp who was not as antithetic to flats as those more closely associated with the Garden City movement.) The film carries shots of the Emily Street flats in Birmingham and later there are glimpses of Quarry Hill (Leeds), a scheme widely regarded as the most progressive flatted estate to be constructed in interwar England.

This theme is developed further by means of a three-dimensional model, which shows how a new town might be put together. The model shows the full mixture of dwelling types—houses with gardens, terraced housing, flats in low-rise blocks arranged in a Zeilenbau pattern,[8] and even the suggestion from the narrator that "a tall block would be very nice too." Factories are placed in special zones, away from residential areas but easily accessible to them. A functionally designed road system keeps through traffic out of residential areas and moving swiftly on its way. Schools are placed on the edge, their playing fields merging into the open countryside that surrounds the town.

Toward the end of the film, perhaps predictably given the close links between Bournville and the Garden City movement, the thrust of the proposals turns squarely toward Garden City ideas. It is suggested that what is required are numerous garden cities "planned together to make a unity . . . a new city outside the city replacing the slums and inner circle." The film ends with a stirring affirmation of what can be achieved by planning, finishing with the words: "Nothing is too good for people; the future will belong to them."

Proud City (1945)

Whereas *When We Build Again*'s analysis focuses on tackling urban problems through construction of new, freestanding settlements, *Proud*

City places the spotlight on reconstructing the existing city. As such it is a direct product of wartime thought about bombing and urban reconstruction. Commissioned by the Ministry of Information and directed by Ralph Keene, *Proud City* is devoted to explaining the principles behind the County of London Plan (1943), an influential document that embraced many ideas that would become part of the orthodoxy of postwar planning. These included the containment of cities by limiting their physical size, principles of neighborhood planning, land-use zoning, and the creation of satellite towns to receive overspill. The film is also notable for the fact that the plan's proposals are expounded by those chiefly responsible for them. These include Lord Latham, head of the London County Council (LCC) that commissioned the plan, J. H. Forshaw, the LCC's chief architect, and his staff, and, most notably, Sir Patrick Abercrombie, who was responsible for many city plans during the 1940s.

In structural terms, the film follows the familiar pattern and contains an urban imagery which, by now, many contemporaries regarded as stereotypical (see the discussion of *New Town* below). The splendors of historic London are reviewed, but it is made clear that the city has problems. Many of them are due to its rapid incremental growth. Given Abercrombie's strong feelings on the subjects of ribbon development and unplanned suburban sprawl, it is not surprising that the commentary views the matter with some disdain:

> London used to be a collection of scattered village communities. Only 200 years ago, the central core was quite small. Round it were the villages each living in its own community life, and each surrounded by open country. But as London grew, the villages grew also, and spread closer and closer together until they joined up in one huge and untidy sprawl, which is London as we know it today.

Against sweeping panoramas of urban encroachment into the countryside, the point is made that housing estates and factories have sprung up all along the main roads and railways radiating out from the main city, "reaching far into what should have remained open fields and woodlands." The case for better planning, therefore, was readily apparent before the war. With the addition of wartime damage the case was held to be overwhelming.

Images are provided of experts working to improve matters—surveyors busy on bomb sites with theodolites and poles (Fig. 11–3) and architects and planners discussing ideas and meticulously carrying out

Figure 11–3. Surveyors at work on a London bomb site. Source: Proud City *(1945). Photograph courtesy BFI Stills, Posters, and Designs.*

drawings. Each of the major parties involved (Latham, Forshaw, and Abercrombie) make statements to the camera, with Abercrombie in particular being introduced as "the world-famous British authority on town planning." The strategy behind the plan is explained. The plan rejects either reconstructing London with no preconditions or total dispersal in favor of retaining the old structure and reconditioning it to work under present-day circumstances. Maps are used to explain the plan, with Arthur Ling, then a member of the LCC's Architect's Department, explaining the sociological principles behind the plans for the creation of a new social fabric for London, particularly in relation to the East End (Fig.11–4). Scale models are shown of how the new London might look, a varied landscape of new planned residential neighborhoods that would retain, or so it is asserted, the essential character of London life.

Proud City was not the last film to campaign for full-scale planning systems. *Land of Promise* (1946), made in the last days of the war, argued for a fully planned system of housing provision. *Town and Country Planning* (1946) propounded the Labour government's commitment to comprehensive planning within the framework of a mixed economy, emphasizing the need for a national plan for housing with close cooperation between central and local authorities. *The Way We Live* (1946) energetically supported the notions behind the replanning of the bombed-out center of Plymouth, another of Abercrombie's schemes. Yet the battle for planning, as such, was nearly won. The creation of a comprehensive town and country planning system occurred in 1947 with the passage of the Town and Country Planning Act. Thinking turned much more to propagandizing for the various different models available for new urban development. It is to this issue, in the shape of promotion of the New Town idea, that we now turn.

Selling the New Towns

Planned Town (1948)

The first film dealing with the New Town idea, *Planned Town*, is catalogued as dating from 1948 but appears to have been made and possibly released earlier.[9] The film reviewed both the planning principles and development record of Welwyn, founded in 1919 as the second Garden City. Much use is made of plans to outline the major planning ideas, with the main architect-planner Louis de Soissons directly involved in making the film. In true documentary style, however, *Planned Town* uses

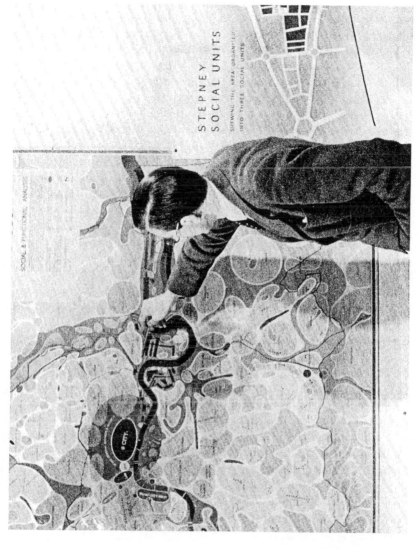

Figure 11–4. Arthur Ling explains ideas behind the County of London Plan. Source: Proud City (1945). Photograph courtesy BFI Stills, Posters and Designs.

real people and families to highlight the main advantages of the town, emphasizing the quality of home and community life. As such, it represents a straightforward presentation of the Garden City ideal. Existing cities are seen as simply too large and saddled with the familiar problems of congestion, obsolescence, slums, and lack of community.

By contrast, Welwyn's experience of development by a private Garden City company is presented as a model approach for the planning of new (and the replanning of old) towns. Clean, orderly developments of houses, factories, shops, and community facilities are shown. We see workers cycling home to enjoy their lunch al fresco in their spacious gardens. Many of these ideas were being taken up in New Town planning, but it is important to realize that the film was made at an important turning point. The New Towns Act (1946) had created a new model whereby growth was handled by an appointed development corporation. The lack of any direct references to this act means that the film effectively records Welwyn's development on a pattern that would soon be superseded. (Despite their protests that previous success had entitled them to be left in charge of the development process, the Garden City Company was replaced by a development corporation shared with neighboring Hatfield in 1948; see Filler 1986, pp. 153–57, and de Soissons 1988, pp. 112–21).

This is not the only aspect of the film that appears out of touch with the realities of early postwar Britain. Throughout, the film retains a self-satisfied, middle-class tone. This is conveyed by the kinds of people and activities depicted, the way they are described in the narrative, and not least, in the accent of the narrator. Despite its overt intention to provide a model for elsewhere, the lasting impression is of an oasis of middle-class stability and order in a generally troubled and disorderly world.

Little is known about public and other reactions to *Planned Town*. However, a Welwyn film, almost certainly this one, was shown as part of early New Town promotional activity, despite its obvious contrasts with the prevailing social values of late-1940s Britain. There was little choice: Welwyn was the nearest approximation to both the ideal and the reality of New Town building, even if it diverged significantly from the outcome that Silkin and his officials sought. There is certainly evidence of a general distaste for Welwyn within the Ministry and a desire to drop it as soon as possible as an exemplar of the New Town idea.[10] It was also strongly rumored that Silkin, a wartime resident of Welwyn, had taken a specific dislike to its middle-class character and that this had been an important factor in his decision to supersede the Garden City Company.

Seen against this background it is clear that, while it may have helped promote the New Town idea to the public at large, the film would have done nothing to dispel the prejudices of Labour politicians and civil servants about Welwyn. Indeed, it seems to have strengthened their resolve to prepare a promotional film much more in keeping with the spirit of the new towns that they were trying to create.

New Town (1948)

In May 1946, discussions began within the Ministry of Town and Country Planning (MTCP) and the Central Office of Information (COI) about possible New Town publicity films. The prime mover was Sir Stephen Tallents, once closely associated with John Grierson in promoting the work of the early documentary movement, who was currently working with the Ministry.[11]

The most difficult issue for the MTCP and COI officials was how to present the new towns to be built under the 1946 Act on film given that none had yet been started. Forman of the COI warned Tallents that their efforts would inevitably meet the same problems that had been experienced with some of the later wartime reconstruction films, specifically mentioning *Proud City*, *The Way We Live*, and *Land of Promise*. He continued:

> The visuals will depend on largely the same resources, maps, models, and shots of such towns as Welwyn Garden City. We are dealing with a type of film which is becoming dangerously threadbare. . . .[12]

These issues were circumvented in a novel manner, by making the film as a color cartoon. The well-known British cartoon filmmakers John Halas and Joy Batchelor were hired to make a one-reel short for free theatrical release available to some 3,500 cinemas for showing as an insert in normal programs. This was intended to be the first of a series of such releases that would provide a showcase for the government's program of social and economic legislation. The reasons for adopting the cartoon form were made abundantly clear in the press release that accompanied *New Town*'s release in March 1948:

> War and all that it entails is the very stuff of film. White Papers are not. Social and economic legislation even if packed with latent drama are not easy film subjects. There is nothing to shoot until the buildings go up.

The cartoon form provided something "that will entertain an audience nurtured on Mickey Mouse and Donald Duck."[13]

Much high-level political and official interest was taken in the film. Silkin and Evelyn Sharp, his deputy permanent secretary, made detailed suggestions about the film's length and its content.[14] In some respects they were unsuccessful: Silkin, for example, wanted it to be longer and both wanted to omit any references to pubs. In other respects, they did secure alterations, for example, ensuring that tower blocks and heavy industry were not categorically ruled out.

The film was based around the central character of Charley, who tells how he and his friends (Fig. 11–5) decided to correct the problems of the older towns and cities in their New Town plan. The cartoon format allows the building of the town to be treated in a surreal and humorous manner with socially balanced housing, factories, and so on being provided by Charley and his friends literally pushing the different building types into position rather like moving furniture (Fig. 11–6). A plan is shown of the new town, which careful scrutiny shows to be the plan for Stevenage inverted (partly to avoid identifying the film with a specific town, but also because the legal controversy over Stevenage was still raging). Landscaping and play areas are provided in the manner of unrolling a tablecloth or mat. In effect, the "dangerously threadbare" character of earlier planning films was being replaced by something far more unreal, which grossly simplified the problems of implementing the New Town plans.

In part, the MTCP and COI got away with this presentation because the format itself was novel and a refreshing contrast with earlier efforts, but additional factors were also at work. Although the film's initiators were not, as we have noted, short of notions as to how the new-towners ought to live, the middle-class and overtly paternalistic tone that was apparent in films like *Planned Town* had gone. Charley himself was deliberately constructed as an ordinary working figure, clad in a coverall to signify manual working-class origins, but also wearing a shirt and plain dark tie to balance this with white-collar worker associations. His accent was representative of the affluent Home Counties of southeast England, but had no class pretensions. Overall he was a new model citizen of postwar austerity Britain and the vision he magically converted into cartoon reality was altogether more plausible to a mass audience than earlier efforts.

If anything it was too plausible, which made the actual reality of severe housing shortage even harder to bear. The film ended with the words "just you try it," advice that was not easy to take given the slow progress of the early New Town building program. The COI was perturbed when it received a letter from a Mr. K. Ross of Sidcup a few days after the film's release, asking for the chance to try.

Figure 11–5. Charley and his friends tend the garden. Source: New Town (1948). Photography courtesy BFI Stills, Posters and Designs.

*Figure 11–6. The New
Town appears. Source:
New Town (1948).
Source: BFI Stills, Posters,
and Designs.*

I could be a good citizen in one of your New Towns. Send me more details—if you can—and I will endeavour to try it sometime! If you cannot, please omit these words from your next similar production, and save the people who are leg weary and mind weary (from looking for a house); from groaning aloud in the cinemas.[15]

This complaint touched a raw nerve in official circles and there was a distinct slackening in central government efforts to promote the new towns. Something of these changing attitudes can be sensed in the reactions to Silkin's ideas for developing a joint New Town exhibition for the 1951 Festival of Britain. The Ministry's chief planner, Samuel Beaufoy, spoke for many other officials when he said: "In my view, the public would rather see a few bricks laid rather than another exhibition."[16]

Home of Your Own (1951)

While the general need to publicize the New Town idea and the specific need to promote the creation of particular New Towns was much diminished by 1950, a new phase of boosterism was emerging. Individual development corporations were increasingly trying to assert their individual identities to attract residents and, to a lesser extent, private investment. Whatever Silkin's predilections for cooperation, a more competitive mood had developed as the Festival of Britain approached:

> Harlow, however, have gone all out to make the world Harlow-conscious. They are having their own exhibit at Harlow, have produced a pamphlet and have the strong backing of the Festival as a "supporting activity." We know that Hemel Hempstead have their film.[17]

This film was the first attempt by an individual development corporation to promote its own town. Hemel Hempstead had been designated in 1947 and incorporated an old-established town that was already larger than almost all the other New Towns begun in the 1946–50 period. Its development corporation, headed by Lord Reith, quickly established a reputation for itself as the most vigorous house-builder among the New Towns. The film is fully representative of the contemporary concern to ensure that Hemel was the first New Town to be finished, and indeed it casts specific light on some of the methods used to accelerate progress.

Home of Your Own (1951) attempts an authentic portrayal of an ordinary working-class man, George Wilson, his wife, Jenny, and their aspirations for a better way of life. They are played, fairly convincingly, by actors and we hear them tell their own story and enter their thoughts and hopes in voice-overs. From the outset the dominant tone is carefully moderated to appeal to working-class sensibilities. The film opens with a party of men out on a bus trip, singing together, before chancing upon the old town of Hemel Hempstead where a pageant is in progress. As the bus stops, we see a group of working-class women dancing in the street, clearly having a good time. Shortly afterwards we are treated to a bathing beauty contest. The mayor awards the first prize with a kiss amid a good deal of good-natured shouting and cheering. The social tone is completely different from that of *Planned Town.*

The film then follows the bricklayer hero back to his two-roomed home in Willesden, a district of northwest London. Here we meet Jenny and the Wilsons' two daughters. We see something of the tensions between them, and Jenny's weariness and skepticism about his grand ideas of moving to the New Town. At this point the film takes an abrupt change, reminiscent of the sudden switch in direction of *When We Build Again.* The film cuts to the different world of the development corporation planners, with Lord Reith presiding, on whom our family's dreams depend. This part of the film is more traditional in style and the accents change accordingly, implicitly admitting that this is less interesting to the ordinary citizen. The window on this separate world of planning is soon closed and we return to the family.

George's application to be considered for the New Town has meanwhile yielded an interview at the local housing department. This provokes mixed feelings and his wife is reluctant to allow herself to become too hopeful. Eventually though she gives him her support and we learn something of her thoughts, feelings, and fears of disappointment, partly on his account. After a brief scene showing the mayor of Hemel Hempstead speaking about the New Town, George is seen at work building New Town houses and then himself being allocated a house. The remainder of the film portrays husband and wife making their own plans, and Jenny reflecting on the "little things that mean a lot to a woman, like a good husband." The scene fades to her waking up in the new home and undertaking domestic tasks in a mood of apparent serenity. They then go out on their first social event as new-towners. The final scenes show them returning home, while George reflects on the nature of house and home and his own role in enabling others to achieve this.

Overall, therefore, the New Town is portrayed less as a creation of the planners rather than of ordinary workers as both builders and citizens. Indeed, while the two previous films effectively suggested a sense of unity between planner and society, *Home of Your Own* seems to emphasize their separateness and to underline the class nature of the divide.

Hence, there is no attempt to make the bricklayer articulate the overall principles and planning ideals of the New Town, as Charley is made to do. He and his family discover and make their own life. The key to this is housing. Planning is seen as a rather technical and remote means to that end, "best left to the experts" rather than being any central part of the end itself, at least as the family wants to experience it. In that sense the film mirrored perfectly the larger political shift away from planning and toward housing as a primary goal of government policy in the 1950s.

Conclusion

The implications of that policy shift for filmmaking necessarily lie outside the scope of this paper, as do other issues arising from the return of a Conservative government in 1951 and a changing agenda of political priorities. Nevertheless, it is worth reflecting on the extent and varying ways in which filmmakers had already attempted to adapt to new circumstances and issues in the period under consideration here.

At the outbreak of war in 1939, the fight for a planned urban future had still to be won. Housing supplied the routine starting point for the films campaigning for that cause. Scenes of the dramatic squalor of the slums and seemingly formless, low-density suburbia symbolized the difficulties that arise in the absence of planning and provided the moral imperative on which the case for intervention rested. Thereafter, filmmakers presented whatever examples of good practice they could find to confront their audiences with the choices available. This was a relatively difficult task. Scale models, plans, and drawings were pressed into service but, understandably, these lacked animation or, to judge from contemporary critical review, visual excitement. Well-known examples of "progressive" estates of flats, planned neighborhoods, and high-speed transport systems were similarly paraded before the viewer, but these conveyed only fragmentary glimpses of the shining new future. The task of indicating how one would move toward that future proved to be even more difficult. At best, filmmakers relied on an image of planning as a rational, scientific, and apparently apolitical activity to make the connection. The problem of injecting that element of "science" into the film—especially when using face-to-camera lectures from distinguished planners (Bressey, Sharp, Abercrombie, Ling)—often led to uncomfortable breaks and discontinuities in the story line.

With acceptance of the general case for planning in the late 1940s, the task confronting filmmakers became somewhat easier. Those promoting the New Towns had available a well-rehearsed imagery under-pinned by Garden City ideology. The scenario, at least initially, became stereotyped. Audiences were presented with glowing images of good housing, easily accessible and well-planned employment, impressive community facilities, plenty of open space, and easy access to the coun-tryside juxtaposed against an imagery relentlessly hostile to the diseased metropolitan city. More pervasively there was the promotion of an or-dered and sociable community life, but one in which the nuclear family was portrayed as the central social unit. All films stop well short of pro-moting a collectivist new society.

Yet while these films continued to confirm the central importance of the planning objectives of community and environment, the filmmaker still struggled to find ways of communicating the complex ideas that underpinned town planning to a lay audience. The characters and de-vices of the planner were seen increasingly as remote from ordinary ex-periences—"dangerously threadbare" to repeat the phrase used earlier. We therefore saw filmmakers turning to invented characters to help bridge the gap. Charley, the cartoon character from *New Town*, was made to carry the full burden of the New Town message. It is perhaps signifi-cant that he was a fantasy figure. George Wilson, from *Home of Your Own*, has greater plausibility *precisely* because he represents a significant re-treat from the wider idea of planning into a more individualistic, home-based conception of the urban future. However, the implication of doing so was to suggest that even at this juncture—the high water-mark of postwar British Labourism—there was a profound gap between plan-ner and society. In view of the events that were to follow during the wholesale, *planned* reconstruction of British cities in the 1950s and 1960s, this is a finding with considerable significance.

Notes

1. For more on this debate, see Esher (1981), Saint (1987), Cherry (1988), Hall (1988) and Ward (1988b).

2. A note on chronology: 1929 is usually taken as the start of the British documentary movement since it was the year in which Grierson's film *Drifters* was made, although "documentary" is a slightly older term (John Grierson first used it in 1926 in connection with Robert Flaherty's film *Moana*). The abolition of the Crown Film Unit by the Conservative government in January 1952 is usu-ally taken to mark the end of the documentary movement.

3. There is no space here for a detailed discussion of either *cinéma-vérité* or

realism in the documentary. For more on these subjects, see Levin (1971), Williams (1980) and Silk (1992).

4. Indeed, given their close relationship with state and commercial agencies for sponsorship and funding, some have questioned whether the movement embraced a radical ideology at all or whether its work represented an apology for the status quo (Evans 1974, pp. 43–50; Swann, 1989).

5. Public Records Office, London (henceforth PRO) HLG 90/38, Note of Jenkins-Dobbie July 23, 1946.

6. The British Broadcasting Corporation began television broadcasting in 1936, but mass ownership of television sets was not achieved until the late 1950s.

7. The Trust administers the model industrial settlement of Bournville, which was originally established by George Cadbury in 1879. Bournville is widely recognized as one of the hearths of British town planning and a precursor of certain aspects of Garden Cities.

8. A system in which rows of flatted housing were laid out at right angles to an east-west road rather than the traditional pattern of being constructed around an interior court. The resulting north-south alignment of the buildings meant that rooms would face either east or west and receive the maximum benefits of sun and light.

9. A Welwyn Garden City film, presumably *Planned Town*, is referred to in 1947 (PRO HLG 90/38, Note of Meeting, July 29, 1947). This suggests that the cataloguing date in the Hertfordshire County Record Office is wrong.

10. PRO HLG 90/38, Note of June 14–15, 1949.

11. He had extensive prewar experience of modern film promotional methods as secretary of the Empire Marketing Board (Constantine 1986, p. 4) and Public Relations Officer of the General Post Office (Richards 1984, p. 248).

12. PRO HLG 90/36, Forman-Tallents, May 31, 1946.

13. PRO INF 6/1349, Press Release, March 15, 1948.

14. PRO HLG 90/34, Memos, February 6, 1947; March 8, 1947.

15. PRO HLG 90/34, Ross-COI, March 22, 1948.

16. PRO HLG 90/37, Note, May 22, 1949.

17. PRO HLG 90/37, Minute, February 19, 1951.

References

Addison, P. 1985. *Now the War Is Over: A Social History of Britain, 1945–51*. London: British Broadcasting Corporation.

Aitken, I. 1990. *Film and Reform: John Grierson and the Documentary Film Movement.* London: Routledge.

Aldgate, T. 1981. Ideological Consensus in British Feature Films, 1935–47. In *Feature Films as History*, edited by K.R.M. Short, pp. 94–112. London: Croom Helm.

Barnouw, E. 1983. *Documentary: A History of the Non-Fiction film.* Oxford: Oxford University Press.

Barsam, R. 1989. John Grierson: His significance today. In *Image, Reality, Spectator: Essays on Documentary Film and Television,* edited by W. de Greef and W. Hesling, pp. 8–16. Leuven: Acco.

Bournville Village Trust. 1941. *When We Build Again.* London: George Allen and Unwin.

Bressey, C., and Lutyens, E. 1937. *Highway Development Survey (Greater London).* London: HMSO.

Campbell, R. 1982. *Cinema Strikes Back: Radical Film-making in the United States, 1930–1942.* Ann Arbor: University of Michigan Research Press.

Cherry, G.E. 1988. *Cities and Plans: The Shaping of Urban Britain in the Nineteenth and Twentieth Century.* London: Edward Arnold.

Constantine, S. 1986. *Buy and Build: The Advertising Posters of the Empire Marketing Board.* London: Public Record Office.

de Soissons, M. 1988. *Welwyn Garden City: A Town Designed for Healthy Living.* Cambridge: Publications for Business.

Esher, L. 1981. *A Broken Wave: The Rebuilding of England, 1940–1980.* London: Allen Lane.

Evans, G. 1984. *John Grierson and the National Film Board: The Politics of Wartime Propaganda.* Toronto: University of Toronto Press.

Filler, R. 1986. *A History of Welwyn Garden City.* Chichester: Phillimore.

Forster, E. M. 1946. The Challenge of Our Time. Reprinted (1965) in E.M. Forster, *Two Cheers for Democracy,* pp. 66–68. Harmondsworth: Penguin.

Gold, J.R. 1985. From "Metropolis" to "The City": Film Visions of the Future City, 1919–39. In *Geography, the Media and Popular Culture,* edited by J.A. Burgess and J.R. Gold, pp. 123–43. London: Croom Helm.

Gold, J.R. 1989. The urban imagination of the Attlee years. *Urban Design Quarterly* 31:22–25.

Gold, J.R., and Gold, M.M. 1989. "Outrage" and Righteous Indignation: Ideology and the Imagery of Suburbia. In *The Behavioural Environment: Essays in Reflection, Application and Criticism,* edited by F.W. Boal and D.N. Livingstone, pp. 163–181. London: Croom Helm.

Gold, J.R., and Gold, M.M. 1990. "A Place of Delightful Prospects": Promotional Imagery and the Selling of Suburbia. In *Place Images in Media: Portrayal, Experience, and Meaning,* edited by L. Zonn, pp. 159–82. Savage, Md.: Rowman and Littlefield.

Hall, P. 1988. *Cities of Tomorrow: An Intellectual History of Planning and Design in the Twentieth Century.* Oxford: Basil Blackwell.

Holcombe, B. 1990. *Purveying Places: Past and Present.* Piscataway, N.J.: Working Paper No. 17, Center for Urban Policy Studies, Rutgers University.

Levin, G.R. *Documentary Explorations: Fifteen Interviews with Film-makers.* Garden City, N.Y.: Doubleday.

Low, R. 1979. *Films of Comment and Persuasion of the 1930s.* London: Allen and Unwin.

Macfarlane, J. 1987. *Catalogue of Films and Television Programmes on Architecture, Town Planning and the Environment.* London: the author.

Macpherson, D., ed. 1980. *British Cinema: Traditions of Independence.* London: British Film Institute.

Miller, M. 1989. *Letchworth: The First Garden City.* Chichester: Phillimore.

Morris, R.J. 1989. The reproduction of labour and capital: British and Canadian cities during industrialisation. *Urban History Review* 18:48–63.

Orlans, H. 1952. *Stevenage: A Sociological Study of a New Town.* London: Routledge and Kegan Paul.

Pronay, N. 1981. The First Reality: Film Censorship in Liberal England. In *Feature Films as History*, edited by K.R.M. Short, pp. 113–37. London: Croom Helm.

Richards, J. 1984. *The Age of the Dream Palace. Cinema and Society in Britain, 1930–1939.* London: Routledge and Kegan Paul.

Rotha, P. 1973. *Documentary Diary.* London: Secker and Warburg.

Saint, A. 1987. *Towards a Social Architecture: The Role of School Building in Post war England.* New Haven: Yale University Press. Silk, J. 1992. *A Rationale for Film Research in Geography.* Discussion Paper 11. Reading: Department of Geography, University of Reading.

Sinyard, N. 1989. Grierson and the Documentary Film. In *The Cambridge Guide to the Arts in Britain*, volume 2: "The Edwardian Age and the Inter-War Years," edited by B. Ford, pp. 246–53. Cambridge: Cambridge University Press.

Sussex, E. 1975. *The Rise and Fall of the British Documentary: The Story of the Movement Founded by John Grierson.* Berkeley: University of California Press.

Swann, P. 1989. *The British Documentary Film Movement, 1926–1946.* Cambridge: Cambridge University Press.

Ward, S.V. 1988a. Promoting holiday resorts: A review of early history to 1921. *Planning History* 10(2):7–11.

Ward, S.V. 1988b. *The Geography of Interwar Britain: The State and Uneven Development.* London: Croom Helm.

Ward, S.V. 1991. The local role in promoting economic growth 1870–1939: A transatlantic comparison. Paper delivered to AESOP/ACSP Conference, July 8–12, Oxford, UK.

Ward, S.V., ed. 1992. *The Garden City: Past, Present and Future.* London: Spon.

Williams, C. 1980. *Realism and the Cinema.* London: Routledge and Kegan Paul.

Yates, N. 1988. Selling the seaside. *History Today* 38:20–27.

Filmography

The City. 1939. GPO Film Unit for Anglo-American.

The Great Crusade. 1937. Pathé Films for the Ministry of Health.

Home of Your Own. 1951. Data Film Unit for Hemel Hempstead Development Corporation.

Housing Problems. 1935. British Commercial Gas Association.

Kensal House. 1937. Gas, Light and Coke Company.

Land of Promise. 1946. Films of Fact.

New Town. 1948. Halas and Batchelor Cartoon Film Production for Central Office of Information.

New Worlds for Old. 1938. Realist Film Unit for the Gas Industry/Paul Rotha Films.

Planned Town. 1948. Welwyn Garden City Company.

Proud City. 1945. Greenpark Productions for Ministry of Information.

The Smoke Menace. 1937. Realist Film Unit, for British Commercial Gas Association.

This Modern Age: No. 1 Homes for All. 1945. Rank.

Town and Country Planning. 1946. Army Bureau of Current Affairs Magazine Series, Army Kinematograph Services for War Office.

The Way We Live. 1946. Two Cities for Rank.

When We Build Again. 1943. Strand Films for Cadbury Brothers.

Subject Index

aborigine, 143, 145, 151–53
aesthetics, ix, 232
allegory, ix, 123, 124
American culture, 37–39, 107, 111,
   121, 123, 133, 184, 195
American dream, the, 3–4, 185, 190,
   195, 198
American West, 3–4, 120, 183, 185,
   188–90, 192, 195, 197–98
anti-hero, 85
Arabia, 16, 161–62, 164–70, 173–77
aristocracy, 78, 83
art, 32, 34, 36, 113, 121, 123, 119, 131,
   139, 150, 207–8
Australia, 10, 11, 137–44, 156
Australian Film Commission, 11, 137,
   141–44
auterism, 41

beach, 79–80, 92
Berlin, 213–14, 216–18
body, the, 105–6, 112, 115
bourgeois, 36, 114
Britain, 70, 76–77, 162, 165–70, 173–
   77, 230, 246–48

camera technique: and camera angles,
   55, 101–3, 166, 203, 207, 211; and
   close-up shots, 77, 101–3, 105, 168,
   171, 192, 210, 212, 216; and color,
   16, 101–3, 120, 126–29, 119, 129,
   131–33, 168, 170–71; and lighting,
   16, 105, 119, 120, 122–26, 128–31,
   169, 194; and scale, 166, 168, 206–
   7, 210–11, 219; and speed, 55–56,
   215, 219
capitalism, 29–30, 36, 72, 95
cartoon, 53–54, 247, 254
censorship, 36, 231
children, 33–34, 103–5, 107, 111
China, 12, 137, 145–49, 153–56

Christianity, 75–76, 79, 91–94
cinematic style, 183–84, 187, 190
city, 16, 53–54, 70–71, 95, 97, 107–8,
   119–33, 204, 216–18, 235–37
class, 111–13, 122, 108, 218, 246, 248;
   upper, 69, 74, 78, 82–83; working,
   72–75, 82, 85, 122, 251
cognitive mapping, ix, 20
colonialism, 35, 39, 175
color, 16, 101–3, 120, 126–29, 131–33,
   168, 170–71, 191
Columbia, 33–34, 126
comics, 132–33
commodification, 29–31
communicative process, 48, 110, 153,
   205, 254
communism, 125
community, 8, 101, 105, 106–7, 109–13,
   153–54; planned, 230, 241, 244,
   246, 251–52, 254
conservation, 137, 150, 155
Coorang, 144–45, 150–51
cosmology, 71, 89
crisis of representation, 14
critical theory, 9
crosscutting, 203–4, 211, 213, 218, 220
culture, 138, 154, 165–66, 168, 177

deconstruction, 205–6
desert, 3–4, 16–17, 161–62, 164–77,
   183, 185, 190, 197
discourse, 14–15, 20, 27–28, 30, 35, 58,
   207
documentary, 12–14, 53–54, 55, 112,
   124–25, 183–86, 189–90, 192, 194–
   95, 197, 206–7, 213, 222, 230–31,
   240–41
domination, 58
dramaturgy, 7
dualisms, 162

259

Author Index

Film Index

265

About the Contributors

Stuart Aitken is Professor of Geography at San Diego State University.

Martyn Bowden is Professor of Geography at Clark University.

Larry Ford is Professor of Geography at San Diego State University.

John Gold is Professor of Geography at Oxford Brookes University (U.K.).

Jeffrey Hopkins is Assistant Professor of Geography at the University of Western Ontario.

Christina Kennedy is Assistant Professor of Geography at California State University.

Arthur Krim is Lecturer at the Boston Architectural Center.

Gerald Macdonald is Assistant Professor of Geography at Villanova University.

Wolfgang Natter is Associate Professor of German at the University of Kentucky.

Stephen Ward is Principle Lecturer of Planning at Oxford Brookes University (U.K.).

Denis Wood is Professor of Design at North Carolina State University.

Leo Zonn is Professor of Geography at East Carolina University.